CW01369547

SPANISH FIGHTERS

Spanish Fighters
An Oral History of Civil War and Exile

Neil MacMaster
Lecturer in History
University of East Anglia

MACMILLAN

© Neil MacMaster 1990

All rights reserved. No reproduction, copy or transmission
of this publication may be made without written permission.

No paragraph of this publication may be reproduced, copied or
transmitted save with written permission or in accordance with
the provisions of the Copyright, Designs and Patents Act 1988,
or under the terms of any licence permitting limited copying
issued by the Copyright Licensing Agency, 33–4 Alfred Place,
London WC1E 7DP.

Any person who does any unauthorised act in relation to
this publication may be liable to criminal prosecution and
civil claims for damages.

First published 1990

Published by
MACMILLAN PRESS LTD
Houndmills, Basingstoke, Hampshire RG21 2XS
and London
Companies and representatives
throughout the world

Filmset by
Wearside Tradespools
Fulwell, Sunderland

Printed in Great Britain by
WBC Print Ltd., Bridgend, Mid Glam.

British Library Cataloguing in Publication Data
MacMaster, Neil
Spanish fighters: an oral history of civil war and exile.
1. Spanish Civil War
I. Title
946.081
ISBN 0–333–51021–6

To the memory of
Consuelo Granda
1922–90

Contents

List of Plates		ix
Maps		
Asturias		7
The Itineraries of David and Consuelo Granda		117
Introduction		1
1	Village Life Before the Civil War – David	27
2	Stormclouds gather, 1930–1936 – David	44
3	The War in Asturias – David	57
4	The Civil War in Asturias – Consuelo	77
5	The Fall of Asturias – David	89
6	Escape from Asturias – Consuelo	94
7	Catalonia in War – David	99
8	Exodus across the Pyrenees – Consuelo	106
9	Across the Pyrenees – David	112
10	Refugee Labour – Consuelo	116
11	The Concentration Camp of Septfonds – David	126
12	Aspres Concentration Camp – Consuelo	141
13	The Camps of the Holocaust – David	147
14	The Coming of the Liberation – Consuelo	161
15	The Coming of the Liberation – David	169

16	Life in Exile – Consuelo	180
17	Life in Exile – David	185
18	Homecoming – Consuelo	192
19	Homecoming – David	201
20	Uprooted – Consuelo	211
21	Uprooted – David	213
Notes		229
Index		244

List of Plates

1 The village school at Paladin, c.1925.

2 Republican militiamen laying siege to the Nationalist forces inside Oviedo during the early months of the Civil War.

3 David Granda in Gijón, Christmas 1936, on a two-day leave from the 31st Anti-Fascist Regiment, the 'Maxim Gorky'.

4 Consuelo Granda, aged thirteen, just prior to the outbreak of the Civil War.

5 Consuelo's mother, Maria Contreras-Gutierrez, c.1935–36.

6 Spanish refugees, flanked by French mobile guards, crossing the border at Le Perthus, January 1939.

7 The rearguard of the Spanish Republican army crossing the frontier at Bourg Madame, February 1939.

8 Wounded soldiers and civilian refugees in a compound prior to their dispersal to the concentration camps.

9 David Granda in the concentration camp of Septfonds 1939.

10 Consuelo Granda with a group of Spanish refugee workers on a farm at Lus-la-Croix-Haute in the spring of 1939.

11 Consuelo Granda in Marseille, December 1945, shortly after the Liberation.

12 David Granda outside his parent's house at Paladin on his first return to Spain, August 1957.

Introduction

Until the 1970s, in spite of the many thousands of books and articles written about the Spanish Civil War, very little was directly known about the experience of the rank and file, the millions of common people who were caught up in one of the most bloody internecine conflicts of modern history. There are a number of explanations for this 'silence of the masses'. Within Spain during the long, bleak period of the Franco dictatorship it was extremely dangerous for any individual, especially of the left, to make any public statement about the events of 1936–9 or to 'tell the truth'. Nor, if they had been brave or foolhardy enough to have attempted this would they have found a publisher or escaped the rigours of state censorship and police repression. Official Francoist versions of the war, portrayed as a holy crusade against barbarous and bloodstained communist hordes, was too important to overall political control and systematic indoctrination via classrooms, newspapers, radio and television to tolerate any accounts that undermined the myths.[1]

For the working class within Spain during the thirty-six years of dictatorship silence was reinforced by other factors. They, more than any other class or group, were the victims of a terrible post-war 'white terror' during which some 200 000 people were summarily executed or murdered while at least twice that number were imprisoned.[2] This, combined with a whole apparatus of surveillance and control by police and Falangists at local level, meant that the ability to find work and literally to survive in a period of appalling misery and hardship depended on toeing the line. Even the smallest villages had been torn asunder by the war and in the claustrophobic universe of the post-war *pueblo* the only way in which victims and perpetrators of the most savage brutality, murders, seizure of property and land, denunciations and reprisals could continue to live alongside each other was by drawing a total veil of silence over the past. Even a whisper threatened to pull the mask off events that were too terrible to contemplate, to revive passions that were too raw and dangerous: life must go on.

Down to the 1970s there had been a literature of first-hand experience of the Civil War, most of it published abroad by Spanish Republicans in exile or by foreign journalists and members of the International Brigades.[3] However, this was in most respects the history or testimony of a political or literary élite, of Republican generals, ministers, professors and party leaders or of foreign poets, novelists and intellectuals, not of the Spanish 'under-mass'. Many of these writers had an axe to grind, personal and partisan positions to defend, and imposed strongly ideological interpretations on the events.

During the seventies a number of developments enabled a new oral history to emerge. The death of Franco in November 1975 and the dramatic shift to an open, democratic society created the political conditions under which ordinary people could, for the first time, talk openly about their experience of the Civil War. The long passage of time appears to have healed some of the scars, and participants, both of the right and left, appeared to be able to face up to the most searing personal tragedies with a degree of equanimity and objectivity. At the same time these years saw the growth and increasing acceptance of oral history as a discipline in the United States and Britain and significantly it was Anglo-Saxon historians who first began to apply this new approach to recover the hitherto unrecorded experience of the Spanish working class.[4] The leader in this field, Ronald Fraser, had already produced two oral histories in the declining years of Franco, *In Hiding, The Life of Manuel Cortes* (1972) and *The Pueblo, A Mountain Village on the Costa del Sol* (1973), but his major work was to be published in 1979, *Blood of Spain, The Experience of Civil War 1936–1939*.[5]

When this latter book appeared I had already begun the series of interviews of David and Consuelo Granda which form the substance of this volume, although the approach is rather different.[6] Fraser, in his marvellous study, has limited his inquiry to the period of the Civil War itself as viewed through the eyes of some three hundred participants. This provides a rich, multiform picture but has the disadvantage of leaving out the 'before and after' and reinforces one of the distorting effects of the historiography which tends to segment and compartmentalise the Civil War, so that we have numerous books on either the causes of the war prior to 1936, or on the war itself, or on the post-war Franco dictatorship. One advantage of the biographical approach adopted here is that by taking a long time span, from the 1920s to the 1970s, the continuities and interrelationships between these three phases are illustrated. Thus the Grandas' account begins with their upbringing and youth in the backward peasant society of Asturias, northern Spain, during the inter-war depression and the Second Republic and reveals the increasing divisions at village level that were to culminate eventually in civil war; it continues through the dramatic events of the Civil War itself (July 1936 to February 1939) and on into the years of exile and imprisonment in the concentration camps of Vichy France; the Resistance and Liberation of 1944–5, life in an expatriate community of Republicans and the clandestine anti-Francoist activities of the Spanish Communist Party cells. Finally the Grandas relate, in a moving and extraordinary passage, their return to their home villages after an absence of two decades only to discover the ravages of twenty years of Francoist repression and dictatorship on a Spanish society in which they no longer felt 'at home'. Eventually they resigned themselves to a life of permanent exile in France.

If there is a unifying element in all this it is the way in which the life histories of two individuals, who would not regard themselves as in any way heroic or significant, were fundamentally shaped and determined by the fight against fascism. A conventional perception of most British and American people is that the great war against fascism was largely confined to the period 1939–45. This view reflects the experience of the millions of soldiers who were conscripted in 1939 or later and who returned home in 1945 after the defeat of Germany, Italy and Japan. Fascism was taken on and defeated in a neatly demarcated five-year war. However, for millions of people in continental Europe the struggle against fascism was a much longer and more bitter process and for no group of people was this more true than for the Spanish Republicans. For many Spaniards, the Grandas included, the conflict had clearly begun with the anti-fascist Asturian insurrection of October 1934, continued through the Civil War, with Italians and Germans already in direct combat, and then on, with barely a break, into the Second World War in which tens of thousands of Republicans died fighting with the Allies from Narvik to North Africa or in the French Resistance. Nor did it end there since the betrayal of the Allies in refusing to topple Franco, the remaining fascist dictator in 1945, meant that the Spanish left was doomed to continue its dangerous and clandestine struggle on into the 1950s and beyond. What emerges so strongly from the Grandas' account is the outstanding courage, humanity and modesty of this couple throughout this long period of hardship, war and exile and a realisation of the extent to which the battle against the evil of fascism was largely borne by those who have been until quite recently largely invisible in history.

And it is here that oral history can play an important part in restoring a sense of the significance of the role of the great mass of ordinary people not only to a general public but also to the participants themselves. The hitherto dominant and hegemonic view of history that only leaders or élites have played an important and deciding role in the events of the past has been damaging to the self-perception of working-class actors. This message has been powerfully transmitted through the way in which history is taught in schools or promulgated by the media and the thousands of published diaries, biographies and histories by and about 'important' figures, a message that has robbed the working class of a consciousness of their own historic role. It is significant that the Grandas should have been initially surprised and sceptical of the request to record their life histories; they were, they said, just ordinary people who had seen no important battles, assumed no special responsibilities; they were like so many others. But gradually, through the process of recording and discussion, came the realisation that history is not something created and possessed by the powerful, bearing their unique imprint, and that generals without troops are reduced to absurdity. What follows is *their* history.

The remaining part of this introduction provides a general historical background to the period and places the Grandas' individual experience within a broader framework of reference. This is mainly intended for those readers who may have little previous knowledge of the Civil War or its aftermath and it can be passed over by those who wish to move straight into the Granda's account which starts in Chapter 1.

THE ORIGINS OF THE CIVIL WAR

David Granda was born on 29 December 1914 in Paladin, a hamlet situated in the valley of the River Nalón some fifteen miles to the west of Oviedo, the capital of the province of Asturias. Most of the people of the village were extremely poor peasants who barely scraped a living from the tiny parcels of land which they farmed. His father was a cartwright and carpenter who also made a living by working a small water-mill which he rented. Consuelo Granda was born in Tampico, Mexico, on 21 April 1922. Her mother, like so many thousands of Asturians, had emigrated to Latin America to escape the dire poverty of northern Spain. However, shortly after the birth of Consuelo Granda, her Mexican father died unexpectedly from a heart attack and her mother returned to her home village of Valle near Infiesto in central Asturias and it was here that the young girl was brought up.

In recent years historians have emphasised the immense regional and local diversity in the origins, nature and experience of the Civil War, itself a reflection of the great variation in the geographical, cultural, economic and political map of Spain.[7] The early experience of the Grandas in the 1920s and 30s needs to be placed within the unique context of the region of Asturias as well as of the nation as a whole.

During the first three decades of the twentieth century the development of the Spanish economy remained quite uneven and stagnant: there was a degree of modernisation and industrialisation in the Basque, Asturian and Catalan regions, but overall the economy remained predominantly agrarian and backward. The most glaring feature of this society was the immense disparity between the wealth and power of the landowners and industrialists and the terrible hardship of the rural and urban working class. In the south the owners of the big estates, the *latifundios*, through the agency of ruthless managers, armed thugs and brutal local policemen, repressed and exploited one of the most poverty-stricken groups of labourers in Europe. Elsewhere a conservative and God-fearing peasantry barely survived on the resources of their tiny farms. In the urban and industrial regions the contrasts were equally pronounced between a turbulent proletariat, working for low wages, in unhealthy and dangerous environments and lacking in basic social security and welfare rights, and a singularly egotistic and exploitative class of industrialists. It was this stark contrast between the dominant ruling class and the huge mass of poor workers which provided the main pressure for reform and eventually revolution.

Nowhere were these pressures to build up more strongly than in the famous coalmining and metalworking areas of Asturias. The coal basins are located in the upper reaches of the Nalón and Caudal Rivers and surrounded by the spectacular jagged peaks of the Cantabrian Mountains. Here the towns of Mieres, Turón, Sama de Langreo, Trubia and La Felguera became important centres of anarchism and socialism from the late nineteenth century onwards. The Asturian miners were, as we shall see, the shocktroops of the 1934 Revolution and among the most courageous fighters of the Spanish Civil War, renowned for their expertise with dynamite. David Granda's native village of Paladin was situated on the western borders of the industrial region; although this was a predominantly peasant community it was sufficiently close for men of the area to walk daily to work in the metal and engineering factories of Trubia. It was through this contact with the world of industry, with trade unionism and socialism, that the villagers were to undergo a process of political radicalisation during the 1930s; however, David Granda's account of poverty and hardship is set within a predominantly rural context. Here one of the profound roots of the Civil War can be located in the stark material conditions of daily life. The peasant families of Paladin were large – David was himself one of eight children – and the dense population pressed hard on the resources of tiny plots of land owned or rented by each household. The widespread nature of the poverty is shown in his account of the villagers' inadequate diet, the damp and unhealthy housing, the deadly ravages of tuberculosis and by the high levels of emigration to South America. The harsh conditions of existence were bitterly resented by the poor because of the contrast with the wealth of the village 'bosses', the *caciques*, who exploited them through their control of land and rents or through the notorious *comuña* system by which the poor tended their livestock. David Granda's father and mother laboured day and night in the water-mill for a small return, yet a large part of the flour which they received in payment went in the form of rent to a wealthy local tax collector who in turn used it to feed his hunting dogs.

David Granda grew up under the monarchy of Alfonso XIII and the dictatorship of General Primo de Rivera (1923–30). During this period the ruling class of landowners and industrialists did not seek to ameliorate the living standards of the great mass of poor rural and urban workers through a programme of liberal reforms but, on the contrary, used every means, including the heavy-handed violence and repression of the civil guard and the army, to maintain a system of naked exploitation. An extremely conservative Catholic Church lent its full ideological weight to the maintenance of the status quo, denouncing even the mildest reforms as the work of dangerous atheists and communists. The ruling classes, in spite of the introduction of universal male suffrage in the Constitution of 1869, blocked any possibility of democratic political change through a system of electoral manipulation, corruption and intimidation known as '*caciquismo*'.[8] David Granda provides evidence of such interference by the *caciques* in the elections at Paladin; the poor would be bought off with bribes of food, clothing or mattresses while right-wing

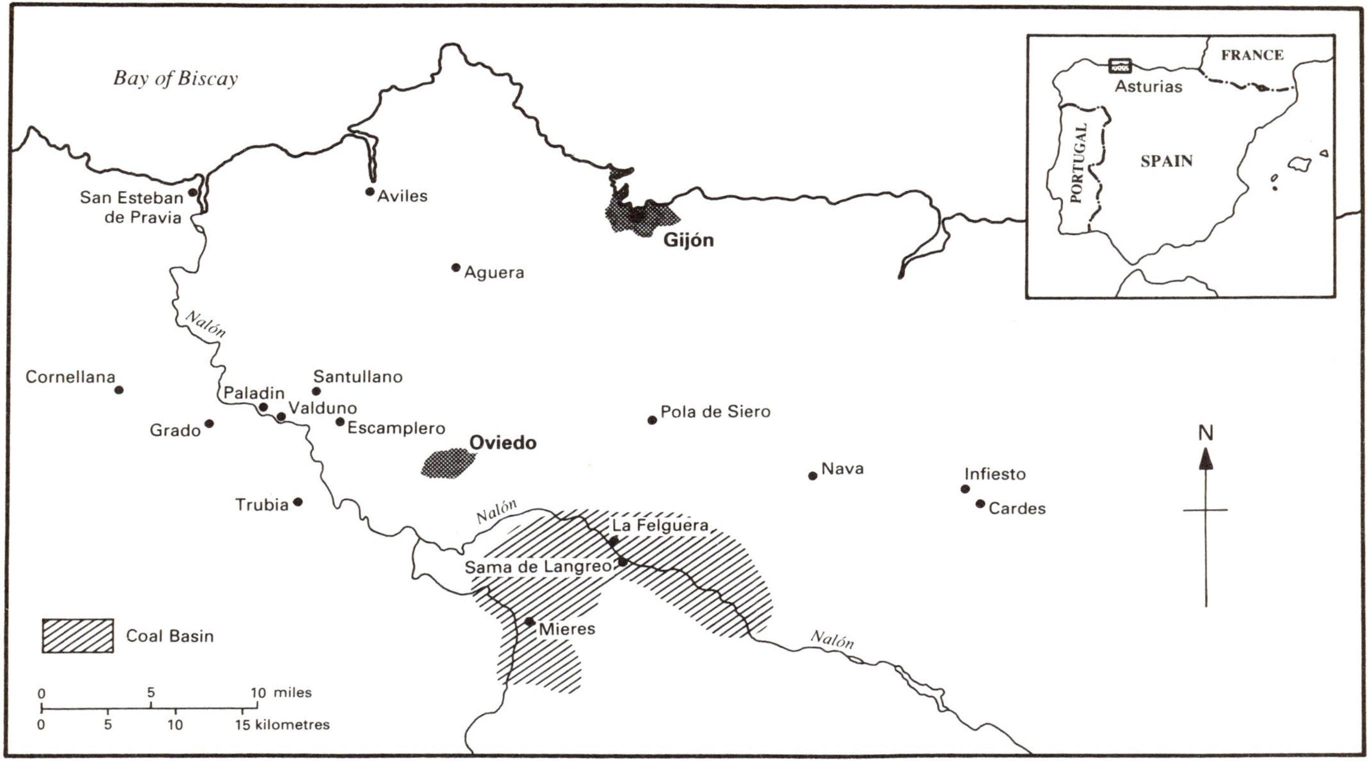

MAP 1 *Asturias*

henchmen intimidated voters going into the polling station. Consuelo Granda's mother was threatened by her employer with the sack if she voted for the left in the election of February 1936.

The pressures for change building up from below, faced with the rigid and unbending structures of a conservative and repressive order, like steam within a rusty and antiquated boiler, seemed likely to blow Spanish society to pieces sooner or later. However, the mould of monarchist politics was cracked with the coming of the Second Republic in April 1931 and appeared to open the way to peaceful reform and modernisation. The dictatorship of Primo de Rivera from 1923 to 1930 had only succeeded in temporarily buttressing the traditional economic, social and political system; indeed, by postponing democratic processes of change, it ensured that the eventual clash of interest between the privileged élites and the great undermass of the deprived would be even more pronounced. By 1930 a loose alliance of middle-class liberals and working-class leaders, after the departure of General Primo de Rivera into exile, reached agreement on the need to remove King Alfonso XIII who had been discredited by his support for the dictatorship. Their goal was achieved with surprising ease and speed; the Republicans won a landslide victory in the municipal elections of 12 April 1931 and Alfonso XIII simply packed his bags and left the country. To contemporaries the declaration of the Republic on 14 April had all the appearances of a bloodless revolution. The rural poor and the urban working class were gripped by an almost millenarian fervour, a great expectation that the whole repressive and exploitative system under which they had suffered for so long would rapidly crumble away and be replaced by a new age of social justice and plenty. David Granda remembers the excitement of the moment and the firing of rockets, and Consuelo Granda, although only nine years old at the time, has sharply etched in her memory the image of a proud young woman walking along the highway waving the flag of the new Republic.

However, the Second Republic, which began so auspiciously, was to culminate only five years later in bloody civil war. It is possible that Spain could have moved through a peaceful transition towards political, economic and social modernity but such a process of reform was to be frustrated for a number of reasons. The coming of the Republic had all the appearances, but none of the substance of a revolution; Socialist and Radical deputies controlled the Cortes, but the old élites were unchanged and still kept a firm grip on economic, religious and military power. The speed with which the Republican government was able to introduce reforms to improve the conditions of the working class was severely restricted. For example, agrarian reforms which were intended to ease the desperate plight of the landless labourers in the south were obstructed in the Cortes by right-wing deputies employing a battery of amendments and technical questions. At the same time the impact of the general economic recession was felt in a rising level of unemployment and employers went onto the offensive, laying off workers, cutting wages while increasing work loads. The frustration and anger of the workers spilled out in a wave of strikes, many of them led by the powerful anarcho-syndicalist trade union, the Confederación Nacional del Trabajo (CNT). The heavy handed and sometimes bloody repression of such movements by the notorious civil guard, as at the massacre in the village of Casas Viejas in January 1933, severely damaged the reforming image of the Republic.[9] For most workers conditions appeared to be as bad, if not worse, than under the monarchy.

By late 1933 the Republican Government had largely failed, therefore, to answer the needs of the working class which as a consequence became increasingly radical and politicised. Following the elections of 19 November 1933 a right-wing government came to power and began to dismantle the few reforms that had been achieved over the previous two years. During this period of reaction (November 1933 to February 1936), known as the '*Bieno Negro*', the political atmosphere became extremely tense and ominous. The Socialists were acutely aware of the rapid spread of fascism in Europe and of its offensive against democratic institutions, trade unions and parties of the left. Mussolini had already been in power since 1922; in 1933 Hitler consolidated his hold after the Reichstag fire while in February 1934 Dollfuss crushed the left in Austria. In Spain the right, including industrialists, monarchists, middle-class property owners and Catholic traditionalists, regrouped under the umbrella of Gil Robles' extreme right party, the CEDA (Confederación Española de Derechos Autónomos). Gil Robles made threatening and provocative speeches in which he praised the fascist model and more than hinted at his wish to destroy the Republic and the working-class movement. The Socialists, fearing the worst, began to lay plans for a defensive, anti-fascist uprising and this was eventually launched when three CEDA members entered the cabinet on 4 October 1934. Although the October revolt was easily crushed, except in Asturias, in many ways it marked a point of no return and the opening act of the Civil War. The road to peaceful change had been blocked and the forces of the right began to prepare for an ultimate showdown.

In no region was the pressure leading towards civil war more apparent than in Asturias. During the First World War the coalfields had enjoyed an unprecedented prosperity; more competitive British coal was excluded and Asturian coal held a monopoly in the domestic market. The huge demand for coal and a corresponding increase in prices explains why it became profitable during this period for David Granda's father and other villagers to salvage coal which had been washed downstream from the pits and deposited in the bed of the River Nalón. However, after the war the Asturian coalfields entered a period of profound crisis; prices collapsed and mine owners responded by laying off workers and cutting wage rates while increasing productivity and the intensity of labour. The crisis was further deepened during the early 1930s by the impact of the general recession. David Granda reached working age during the depression and his brothers experienced the unemployment and hardship faced by thousands of young Asturians.

During the period 1930–34 the Asturian miners, led by their powerful union the SMA (Sindicato de Obreros Mineros Asturianos), entered a period of dramatic radicalisation. The disillusionment with the Second Republic, which failed to remedy their situation, led to an early recognition that social change would have to be fought for, if need be by revolutionary means. Faced with the mounting threat from fascism, the anarcho-syndicalist CNT and the Socialists, who were split by bitter rivalry in the rest of Spain, joined together in March 1934 in a Workers' Alliance, the Alianza Obrera. The Alliance provided the basis for a powerful and united workers' movement that was unparalleled in the rest of Spain and the remarkable solidarity and strength of the Asturian left was to carry over into the period of the Civil War itself.

When news of the appointment of three CEDA deputies to the Cabinet on 4 October 1934 reached the leadership of the Socialist Party they sent out a secret order to launch the anti-fascist uprising. This quickly fizzled out in Madrid and Barcelona, but Asturias witnessed one of the most astonishing revolutionary movements of modern times and a direct frontal assault on the power of the state. Miners stormed the garrisons of the civil guard and army and revolutionary committees took over the organisation of everything from transport, water and gas supplies, military recruitment and hospitals to provisioning; even money was abolished and replaced by a voucher system.[10] An army of 26 000 professional soldiers had some difficulty in regaining control of the region and there followed a brutal repression during which 30 000 men were imprisoned and many tortured. Despite its failure the October Revolution marked an important stage in the events leading towards Civil War: negotiation and compromise between the forces of the right and left no longer seemed possible. The upper classes, and particularly the military élite, shocked by the realisation that an Asturias writ large would mark the end of the old order, began to prepare the counter-revolution.

The radicalisation of Spanish and Asturian society during the period 1931 to 1934 is clearly reflected at the local, village level in David Granda's account. Men from Valduno, the parish in which Paladin is located, and the surrounding area worked in the big state cannon factory at Trubia, a centre of socialist activity, and carried radical ideas from there into the scattered hamlets where they lived. Others lived and worked in the more distant coalfields, but retained close links with their home villages which they helped to politicise. Among them was Ramón Gonzalez Peña, born at Valduno in 1888 and one of Spain's leading Socialists. A son of a poor peasant, he went to work in the mines at Mieres from an early age, was a founder member of the miners' union, the SMA, in 1910 and helped organise the October Revolution. Another major influence on David Granda and other villagers was the SMA newspaper *Avance*. In July 1933 Javier Bueno became the editor and quickly transformed the rather dull paper into a highly militant journal which carried an enormous influence with the working class. Bueno established a network of local correspondents, including one at Trubia and another in Grado near Paladin, while an efficient distribution system ensured that the daily run of 23 000 copies reached all parts of the mining region and the surrounding countryside.[11]

On the whole those peasants of Paladin who had no links with the world of industry or mining tended to be much more conservative, religious and potentially reactionary. However, even for them things were changing. By 1931 the Socialist Party at a national level had come to realise that the agrarian problem in Spain was as important as the industrial sector in which it had, until then, centred most of its activity. It launched a widespread propaganda campaign in the countryside which drew a phenomenal response: within one year the membership of the landworkers union, the FNTT (Federación Nacional de Trabajadores de la Tierra), shot up from 100 000 to

445 000 members. In Paladin David Granda's father played an active role in this process by helping to found a local FNTT branch for which he acted as secretary. The Asturian section of the FNTT campaigned not only for economic aims, the introduction of co-operatives and the modernisation of agricultural techniques, but also for wider political goals including the end of electoral fraud by *caciques*, direct intervention in municipal and national elections, and widespread educational provision to end ignorance and poverty. The failure of agrarian legislation under the Second Republic to make any noticeable impact on the terrible hardship of the countryside was a major factor in the radicalisation of the peasantry.

David Granda provides a penetrating insight into the build-up of the tensions that were finally to erupt in the October Revolution and, soon after, in the Civil War itself. These tensions were rooted in the widespread misery and hunger of the peasantry, high levels of unemployment, disillusionment with the reforming intentions of the Second Republic, a new and radical political awareness and the fear of a fascist takeover. Although Paladin was not directly involved in the fighting and the revolutionary organisations of October 1934, which were located to the east in the mining region and Oviedo, it still played a major role in the events of the Revolution. The main arms cache of the Revolution was secretly landed on the Asturian coast by the *Turquesa* and then concealed in the parish church at Valduno. Millions of pesetas seized by the Socialists from the Bank of Spain in Oviedo were also hidden underground in the parish after the uprising had been crushed and David Granda was arrested during the search by the civil guard for arms and money. Many miles to the east, in the small town of Infiesto, Consuelo Granda's mother was being secretly smuggled into the prison at night to dress the wounds of prisoners who had been brutally beaten and tortured.

From the time of the October Revolution the alignment of the forces of the left and right in two irreconcilable and opposing blocks was almost complete; some people spoke openly of a coming civil war. In May 1935 Gil Robles became Minister of War and did all that he could to enable a group of generals, which included Franco, to organise a conspirational network, the Unión Militar Española, the aim of which was to overthrow the Republic. After the victory of the left in the elections of February 1936 it was simply a matter of time before the military launched their coup d'état. During this period David Granda was doing his military service in Burgos which, unknown to him at the time, was one of the major centres of the conspiracy. However, there were clear signs that something was afoot; conspirational juntas of the Unión Militar were spreading into the army corps and he noted the increasing nervousness of pro-Republican officers, some of whom were to be murdered in the opening days of the rebellion. David Granda took part in large scale military manoeuvres which simulated the defence of Burgos, in preparation for the uprising. Similar manoeuvres were taking place in Asturias and outside Madrid.[12] The die was cast.

THE CIVIL WAR JULY 1936–FEBRUARY 1939

On 12 July 1936 General Mola, the key director of the military rising, sent a secret message from Pamplona to officers with the élite Army of Africa in Spanish Morocco to launch the rebellion on 17 July. On 19 July General Franco flew from the Canaries, where he had been posted by a suspicious government, to Morocco and organised the airlift of the crack units, experienced by years of colonial warfare, across to the Spanish mainland. Simultaneously rebel officers seized control in the garrisons of Pamplona, Burgos, Segovia, Avila, Salamanca and other towns. The conspirators had hoped that everything would be over in a matter of days, but the failure of the uprising in Madrid and Barcelona and in the industrial heartlands of Spain meant that a bloody and protracted civil war was inevitable. The Republican government, after a moment of confusion and weakness, began to arm the workers. In a matter of weeks the insurgents controlled about one third of the country in a single block which covered western Spain, from Gibraltar in the south to Galicia in the north, and in a wide band across the northern region from Galicia to Saragossa. At this early stage the balance of human, economic and military resources lay if anything with the Republicans; their control of the coal, iron and steel and chemical industries gave them a manufacturing base that could have provided a crucial advantage in the production of armaments. However, this was to be outweighed by the speed with which Germany and Italy provided soldiers, airmen, aeroplanes and advanced equipment to the rebels.

In the far north the Atlantic seaboard provinces of Asturias, Vizcaya and the Basque country remained under Republican control, but with the fall of Irun on 5 September this long east-west coastal strip was completely cut off from the rest of Republican Spain. Supplies and personnel could only be brought in by air or by ships running the blockade of Nationalist warships. Asturias, with its powerful left-wing and trade union movements, was solidly Republican, except for the capital Oviedo which was captured by a rebel force under Colonel Aranda. At a meeting of Socialist and mineworkers' leaders in Oviedo on 19 July to discuss what action to take in the light of the uprising, Aranda, the military commander of Asturias, suggested that a large contingent of workers be sent south to cut off a rebel advance towards Madrid. The ruse worked and while 2000 armed militants moved south by train and lorry Aranda transferred some 900 civil guard from rural barracks into Oviedo. Joined up with soldiers from the garrison and fascist volunteers well equipped from the armaments factory they turned the city into a rebel fortress. The trick was to do incalculable damage to the Republicans by tying down a huge force of some 10 000 militiamen in a long and ultimately fruitless siege.

In June 1936 David Granda had managed, by a strange stroke of fortune, to make special arrangements to take an early summer leave from the army. When the military revolt took place on 18 July he was in Paladin and immediately joined the militias on the Oviedo front. If he had been in Burgos, one of the centres of the uprising, he would have been trapped in the Nationalist zone and might have ended up fighting, as did many of his regimental friends, on the other side. This illustrates one of the crucial features of the Civil War: so rapid was the division of Spain into 'Red' and 'White' zones that untold numbers found themselves caught on the 'wrong' side and under the control of political and military forces which they secretly opposed. Some escaped in time across the front, others constituted a potential fifth column.[13] Consuelo Granda was to witness the sinister implications of this as a nurse in the Gijón hospitals where it was suspected that crypto-fascist doctors carried out unnecessary amputations on Republican wounded.

David Granda spent nearly two weeks at the seige of Oviedo before volunteering to join guerrilla bands that were moving westwards to confront a much more serious and dangerous threat, a regular army of Nationalists advancing from Galicia. The first months of the Civil War throughout Republican Spain witnessed an extraordinary and spontaneous mobilisation of workers and peasants. This assumed various forms but the key features were the creation of thousands of local revolutionary committees at village and town level and the formation of independent popular militias to combat the fascists. David Granda gives a dramatic picture of the chaos and excitement as workers in boilersuits, the famous '*mono*', elected their own leaders and armed with a weird assortment of hunting guns and ancient rifles went up into the mountains to block the advance of a professional army. In the rear the revolutionary committees took over municipal power; requisitioned cars, lorries, foodstocks, arms and buildings; arrested suspects and counter-revolutionaries; imposed 'popular justice' and distributed food, clothing and other supplies. David Granda, sent home with a slight bullet wound, was asked to requisition potatoes from his wealthy and reactionary uncle, a fact that the latter was never to forget. At Infiesto Consuelo Granda's mother was asked to set up and equip a hospital for the wounded in a former villa and she went with militiamen to requisition beds, furniture and linen from the houses of the wealthy inhabitants. This aroused extreme anger and resentment on the right and for this act alone she would have been killed by local Falangists if she had ever decided to return from exile in France after the war. In some areas of Spain these first months of the Civil War did see a 'Red Terror'; small and uncontrolled goups of men killed priests, fascists and unpopular employers and burned down churches. In Asturias there appears to have been little of this, a fact that can be ascribed to the maturity and self-discipline of the working class and to the unity of Anarchists, Socialists and Communists since the Alianza Obrero of 1934. Significantly David Granda was sent with other militiamen to prevent the church of Trasmonte from being destroyed by a rogue group of Anarchists.

For many Republicans these first months were remembered as the 'heroic' phase of the Civil War, a time when the ordinary people threw aside the repressive constraints of the old society and demonstrated an astonishing inventiveness and organisational skill that had never been allowed to flower. Consuelo Granda has an abiding memory of the warm comradeship and unstinting self-sacrifice of the nurses and ambulance drivers with whom she worked. However, the Republicans were soon to be internally divided by profound and bitter disagreements over the ultimate purpose and management of the war effort, a fact that was to contribute to their final defeat. At the heart of the fragmentation of Republican unity lay a central dilemma. On the one hand it was argued by Communists, moderate Socialists and middle-class professionals that the immediate goal was not social revolution but the military defeat of fascism. To achieve this aim it would be necessary to subordinate the anarchic proliferation of people's militias and autonomous industrial or agricultural collectives to a centralised and orderly structure of command. There was no point in a collectivised factory converted to arms production turning out munition if it did not match the calibre requirements of the army units. An effective war effort also needed to be built upon a broad popular front which would include bourgeois elements; mass collectivisation of private property would alienate both them and capitalist foreign powers, especially Britain, France and the USA, from whom the Republicans hoped to obtain arms and materials. Opposed to this were Anarchists and far-left groups who argued that the Civil War constituted a true social revolution and that the way to defeat fascism was to mobilise the enormous energy of the masses through the common ownership of wealth and the destruction of capitalist relations. It ran counter to the deepest political instincts and traditions of Spanish Anarchism to see the reimposition of hierarchical power structures, whether in the Republican army or the state. So profound were these differences that they eventually led to a civil war within the Civil War in Catalonia in May 1937. David Granda relates how in Asturias the process of militarisation, or the absorption of independent militias into regular army formations with commanding officers, led to a certain degree of resistance. However, the government's attempt to cut off units from their dependence on political parties was only partially successful and David Granda himself was integrated into the Maxim Gorky battalion which was dominated by Communists. Consuelo Granda notes how during this same period women, including her mother and herself, who had been up near the front line as stretcher bearers and even soldiers, were ordered to the rear and relegated to the traditional female roles as cooks and nurses. However, Asturias, in contrast to other regions of Republican Spain, was remarkable for the degree of political unity between Anarchists, Socialists and Communists; a unity that had deep roots in the pre-war era. It was this solidarity and high morale which enabled the Asturians to put up a tremendous resistance to the Nationalist onslaught in 1937.

In November 1936 Franco's forces were unable to take Madrid and became bogged down; in March 1937 they decided to switch their efforts to the rich steel and coal regions of Asturias and the Basque country. From the very beginning the odds were heavily stacked against the Republicans in the north. The British and French heads of state, terrified that any involvement on their part in supporting the legitimate Republican government would unleash a general European war, clung with a mixture of wilful blindness and hypocrisy to the fiction of Non-Intervention. In practice this meant that the Republican government was unable to purchase arms abroad while Italy and Germany supplied immense quantities of arms and men to the Nationalists. The Asturian and Basque armies had some Soviet equipment and advisers, but the key to the battle in the mountainous terrain of the north lay with the vastly superior airpower of the fascists. The full weight of this was to be demonstrated on 26 April 1937 when the Condor Legion of the German air force carried out a saturation bombardment of the small market town of Guernica; high explosive and incendiary bombs almost completely destroyed the town in the first anti-civilian blitzkreig in history.[14]

In February David Granda was seriously wounded during a major offensive outside Oviedo and after contracting gangrene had to have his leg amputated. It was while he was convalescing in the hospital at Infiesto, suffering from a deep depression, that he met the young nurse Consuelo Contreras and they fell in love. However the couple were soon to be separated in the chaotic events surrounding the final collapse of the northern front. The Republican army was fighting a hopeless battle against the Nationalists and the Council of Asturias decided on 20 October 1937 to save as much of the army as possible by evacuation using every possible ship, fishing boat and vessel available. Surrender was unthinkable; thousands of the soldiers had experienced imprisonment and torture in the October Revolution of 1934 and they had no illusions as to the kind of mercy they could expect from the fascists. Many hundreds of those who failed to get out by sea took to the mountains where they continued to survive in guerrilla bands as late as the 1950s. During the chaotic retreat both David and Consuelo managed to escape in separate ships both of which got through the Nationalist blockade and after a perilous voyage far out into the Atlantic reached Bordeaux.

However, this was not the end of the war for them since the French authorities transported the thousands of Asturians who had escaped, in sealed trains across southern France and the Pyrenees into Republican Catalonia. In the winter of 1937–8 the Republicans were still holding out in the Madrid redoubt and controlled all of eastern Spain, but during the spring of 1938 well-equipped and motorised divisions of the Nationalist army broke through the Republican front south of the River Ebro and reached the Mediterranean coast on 15 April. The Republican zone was now cut in two and the only escape route from Barcelona and Catalonia was across the frontier into France.

During all of 1938 and until the fall of Catalonia in February 1939 Consuelo Granda lived with her mother in the small northern town of Compradón, situated in the foothills of the Pyrenees. What came as a shock to her, as it did to David Granda, was the contrast between the unity and high morale that prevailed in Asturias and the deep divisions, egoism and corruption that prevailed in Catalonia. Here again is interesting evidence of the tremendous regional diversities of the Civil War. Consuelo Granda's overriding impression from this time, apart from unrelenting hunger, was of being like a refugee in an enemy territory; the morose and conservative local peasants showed hostility towards the 'outsiders' who required food and shelter. Like so many in the Civil War they seem to have been caught by geography on the opposing side and were biding their time to welcome the victorious soldiers of the Nationalist army as they marched north. David Granda living in Barcelona noticed the bitter political divisions between the Anarchists of the CNT and the Soviet-backed Communists, divisions that were to cripple the war effort severely. The prominent role on the Catalan front of the International Brigades, volunteer fighters from France, Germany, Wales, Scotland and elsewhere, gave a considerable boost to Republican morale but after the defeat at the great battle of the Ebro in August even they were sent home by the government. In March David Granda witnessed the carnage produced by Italian bomber raids on Barcelona: the use of high explosives, penetrating bombs, incendiaries and anti-personnel bombs led to the highest number of civilian deaths yet recorded in this newly invented form of 'total' war. The rest of Europe looked on shocked and fascinated by the new art of blitzkreig and wondered if this was something that they too would soon be experiencing in a general war that seemed ever imminent.

Overall the Grandas provide a penetrating insight into the low state of morale during the last year of the war and proof of the extent to which battles are won or lost as much in the rear, in the unity and purpose of the civilian population, as at the front itself. However, nothing which they had experienced so far was to match the horror of the final rout. By mid January 1939 Barcelona was without food or electricity; tens of thousands of hungry civilians began to flee in panic towards the French border. On 23 January Prime Minister Negrín and his government left the city; archives that could not be moved were hastily destroyed. Two days later the forces of General Yague moved virtually unopposed into Barcelona and by evening fascist sympathisers were on the street, welcoming their liberation. On the roads to the northern border there was chaos. The Grandas once again lost contact with each other in the confusion of the retreat and were not able to make contact until the end of the Second World War. They provide a painful but deeply moving account of the final débâcle, of how they passed, in the depth of winter with some half-a-million Spaniards, children, women, aged and wounded soldiers, through the snow and ice of the Pyrenean mountain passes. For many Republicans this was the most terrible experience of the Civil War, a moment of nightmare horror and defeat.

FRANCE UNDER THE GERMAN OCCUPATION

After the defeat of the Republicans a savage white terror was unleashed inside Spain; tens of thousands were rounded up by fascist gangs, shot, imprisoned or put in labour camps. The Grandas only discovered the extent of the repression in their own villages on their first return many years later. However, for the hundreds of thousands of Republicans who crossed the Pyrenees in early 1939 there was, despite the hardship, some optimism that they had escaped to the security of a sympathetic sister Republic. The Popular Front government of 1936; France's reputation as a state which had traditionally provided a safe haven for political exiles; and, as David Granda shows, the image that the Spanish left had of France as *the* country of Revolutionary fame, of *liberté, égalité, fraternité*, all seemed to provide a guarantee of a friendly reception for the weary refugees. However, these illusions are quickly shattered.

The French authorities were hopelessly ill-prepared to cope with the huge numbers involved and lacked the accommodation, food, clothing, medical aid and technical staff necessary for an emergency relief operation on the scale that was required. This explains in part the appalling conditions under which the Republican exiles were forced to live, but far more crucial was the political climate of hostility and xenophobia which prevailed at the time. The considerable influx of foreign labour during the inter-war period, combined with the unemployment of the world depression, had resulted in widespread racism. The right-wing and gutter press deliberately whipped up the already widespread anti-foreigner sentiment by portraying the Republicans as dangerous 'Red' terrorists who would swarm in armed bands through southern France, spreading lawlessness and disease. The Minister of the Interior, Albert Sarraut, obsessed by a threat to 'national security' issued instructions to the prefects that the Spaniards were to be treated with the greatest strictness and the policemen and soldiers who controlled the refugees certainly treated them with considerable harshness and brutality. The inhumanity of the treatment of the Spanish refugees was one of the least glorious episodes in French history, and one which has been significantly neglected by national historians.[15] During February 1939 tens of thousands of refugees were herded into barbed wire compounds on the beaches of St Cyprien, Barcerès and Argelès where they dug holes in the sand for shelter from the winter rain and wind and died in their hundreds from disease and exposure.

David and Consuelo Granda provide a detailed and harrowing picture of the appalling conditions suffered by the Spanish Republicans, both before and during the Vichy regime and under the German occupation. During the nine months prior to the declaration of war with Germany thousands of Spaniards were exploited as a cheap source of labour, as was Consuelo Granda who was drafted into an Alpine village, or herded into enormous concentration camps. David Granda recounts how in the camp of Septfonds the military command carried out a calculated policy of propaganda and humiliation to force the Republicans to return to Franco's Spain. Many did so only to face imprisonment and execution. Consuelo Granda's younger sister Angelina who was separated in the Pyrenean crossing was eventually located in the department of the Gard but the French authorities not only refused to allow her to rejoin her mother but sent her back to Spain as an 'orphan'. Mother and child were never to see each other again.

In September 1939 France declared war on Hitler's Germany and after some months of inactivity during the so-called *drôle de guerre* ('phoney war') France was very rapidly invaded and defeated in May–June 1940. France was divided into a northern occupied zone, effectively under German military control, and a southern non-occupied zone administered by the Vichy government of Marshal Pétain. Most of the Spanish Republicans, including the Grandas, were in the non-occupied territory. With the declaration of war the French found themselves in conflict with the same enemy that the Spanish exiles had been fighting since 1936. This led to a momentary change of attitude towards the Republicans: as David Granda recounts the military commander of Septfonds made a remarkable about turn. One week the Spanish soldiers were humiliated, treated as parasites on the French economy and pressurised to return to

Franco's Spain; the next week they were treated as anti-fascist veterans who should now join the French in a war against the common enemy. In spite of the bad treatment which they had received, thousands of Spanish Republicans welcomed the opportunity to leave the camps and to take up arms against Hitler. Battle-hardened and experienced, these men played a major combat role during the Second World War, a fact that has been deliberately ignored by many French historians. Indeed, that great moment of symbolic and national pride, the Liberation of Paris, witnessed the arrival in the centre of the city of a vanguard of Spanish soldiers in armoured vehicles flying the Spanish Republican flag.[16]

From June 1940 until the Liberation in the summer of 1944, the Grandas lived in territory directly governed by fascist authorities. Conditions in the concentration camps became even more harsh and repressive. The camp authorities began to weed out the Communist or Anarchist leaders whom, it was feared, might form the nucleus of underground political organisation and resistance and sent them to the punishment centres of Collioure or Vernet. Prisoners who had also experienced the German concentration camps reported that conditions in the former were worse. Later on some 10 000 Spanish Republicans were dispatched, along with Jews, to the Polish extermination camps. However, the most widespread threat facing the majority of Spaniards was hunger and disease. As the war progressed the French civilian population faced increasing problems of food shortage, but in the concentration camps the Republicans faced starvation. During 1941 French doctors and relief organisations were shocked by the signs of severe malnutrition in the camps; rations were down to 500 calories per day and physical weakness, combined with squalid sanitary conditions, led to outbreaks of dysentery that killed hundreds of internees. The Grandas give a vivid picture of the daily life of the camps, especially of the overwhelming preoccupation with food and the desperate search for the additional scraps which could make a difference between life and death. At one stage David Granda, slowly going blind from malnutrition, resorted to eating grass while an unfortunate cat provided a feast for a whole barrack.

In spite of the terrible conditions, what comes through most clearly in the Granda's account is the indomitable courage and even humour of the Spanish exiles. In part this high morale can be attributed to the tough political will and the fierce pride which inspired the Republicans. In spite of the repression and deportation of their leaders, the Republicans still managed to establish a clandestine political organisation in which discussion and analysis of the current European situation, of the anti-fascist war and the role of the Republicans played a prominent part. This inspired a sense of direction and purpose. David Granda gives a fascinating account of the rich cultural life of the camps: among the thousands of refugees were artists, craftsmen, actors, musicians, intellectuals and opera singers. Artistic performances and creation helped maintain morale and a sense of worth in the midst of degradation, but also constituted a 'culture of resistance', as in the wonderful celebration of 14 July 1939 which fêted a great revolutionary moment and put the French to shame. In the camp of Aspres where Consuelo Granda was interned after a police round up in April 1942, the Spanish women annoyed and defied the fascist guards by singing and dancing flamenco and other regional music.

As the war progressed, and especially after the German invasion of the non-occupied Vichy zone in November 1942, the Spanish Republicans began to take a leading role in the resistance movement itself. About 1 800 000 French soldiers were held as prisoners of war while after early 1943 another 630 000 men were forced to do compulsory service in Germany. This lead to a chronic labour shortage in the French economy which was partly resolved by transferring thousands of Spanish men from camps into foreign worker brigades, the GTEs (*Groupements de travailleurs étrangers*). The GTEs were frequently located in mountainous regions like the Alps, the Pyrenees and the Massif Central where they worked in forestry, mining and agriculture – precisely the zones best suited to the organisation of the Maquis. Because of their experience in warfare and their ideological commitment the Republicans came to play a formidable part in the Resistance movement, out of all proportion to their numbers. Again this was a contribution to the liberation struggle which many French commentators have chosen to ignore. In 1943 David Granda was transferred from the camp of Gurs to a GTE in the mountains of the Puy-de-Dôme where in time he was to work as interpreter with a Spanish Resistance group. Consuelo Granda on one occasion carried gun parts concealed in a suitcase of potatoes from the Alps to Resistance contacts in Marseille. By the time of the Liberation in the summer of 1944 few groups anywhere in Europe had had such a long record of anti-fascist struggle as the Spanish Republicans in France.

IN EXILE AND THE FRANCO DICTATORSHIP

For millions of Europeans the defeat of the Axis powers in 1944–5 was a time of euphoria and of promise; at long last people could look forward to rebuilding their lives. The Spanish Republicans in exile were also full of hope; tens of thousands of them had fought with the Allies in what they perceived to be a continuation of the Civil War and there was a widespread expectation that once Hitler had been defeated the victors would turn their armed might to dislodge Franco. They were to be bitterly disappointed. During the Second World War Franco had maintained Spanish neutrality; the country needed a breathing space to recover from the terrible human and material losses of the Civil War and at the same time Franco played an opportunistic waiting game, ready to join the Axis side when their victory was assured and most of the fighting over. After the defeat of the Germans at Stalingrad in late 1942 Franco began to make overtures to the Allies and with peace the USA and Britain were reluctant to switch weary soldiers into a new campaign.[17]

When the occupying German forces pulled out from Clermont-Ferrand on 27 August 1944 David Granda moved, along with other Spanish and French Resistance fighters, down from the mountains of the Auvergne into the towns of the plain. He had only just arrived in the small provincial town of Riom when many of his Republican comrades in great haste and excitement piled into lorries and drove south to join up with a partisan army. A quite considerable force of 2000 men, still armed from the Resistance, penetrated through the Pyrenees into Spain by the Aran Valley. The planning of this operation still remains shrouded in some mystery but the intention appears to have been either to open a front which would force the Allies into a major intervention or to trigger an internal popular rebellion. In the event the invasion was a catastrophe; a large Nationalist army had no difficulty in containing the ill-equipped forces in the mountains and the partisans were forced to retreat back into France, with a loss of 1400 men taken prisoner.[18] Some weeks later a few dejected men found their way back to Riom.

On 15 August 1944 American forces began to land on the Mediterranean coast and from the mountains Consuelo Granda could see the German army retreating in great disorder northwards. She too was now able to come out of hiding in an Alpine village and moved down to Marseille where hundreds of Spanish Republicans met in the streets in an atmosphere of heady excitement. She had managed to locate David Granda and she moved to Riom where the couple settled down and eventually raised a large family in conditions of great hardship.

In Riom during the post-war years there were several hundred Spanish Republicans and the Grandas provide a fascinating insight into the anti-Franco opposition in this exile community. During the period up to 1951 the Republicans still believed that Franco might be toppled by international intervention or internal rebellion. However, the Republican opposition in exile was considerably weakened by geographical dispersal – some leaders were in Mexico, others in the USSR and France – and by bitter discord between Socialists, Anarchists and Communists. However, the Spanish Communist Party (PCE) and its leadership, located primarily in southern France, undoubtedly constituted the best-organised party in exile. The Grandas provide an interesting insight into rank and file activity in a Communist cell during these years. After the failure of the Aran Valley invasion the Communist strategy was to infiltrate militants into Spain where they were to join up with guerrilla fighters who had remained trapped in the mountainous areas of Aragon, Catalonia, Asturias and Andalucia. Although some 15 000 guerrillas may have been active during the period 1945–50, they were unable to provoke the general revolt that was expected: the Spanish peasantry and working class had been crushed and intimidated by mass killings and imprisonment, while starvation conditions made the struggle for survival the major preoccupation. One Asturian from Riom managed to get as far as his home town only to be arrested and imprisoned, as were many hundreds of others. The guerrillas, unable to establish the necessary support base in the local populations, became isolated in the mountains, tied down by huge civil guard forces, and were eventually reduced to a desperate semi-bandit existence. On her first return to Spain in 1954 Consuelo Granda was to hear how a last surviving group, which included a distant relative, had been wiped out only the year before by the civil guards in the mountains behind her home village. The decision of the PCE in 1950 to terminate the guerrilla movement indicated that the Communists had finally come to accept that a general uprising of the Spanish people against Franco was impossible.

Inside France, as David Granda shows from his own experience in the Riom cell of the PCE, the Spanish Communist opposition to the Franco dictatorship was further weakened and demoralised by Stalinism. In mid 1948 the Soviets branded 'Titoism' as a dangerous deviation in the Communist camp and the PCE leadership responded with a witch-hunt inside their own party against supposed American or Francoist spies, spreading a poisonous atmosphere of suspicion. These well-known Stalinist techniques were used to quell any critical debate within the party and to produce unquestioning submission to the leadership.[19] David Granda experienced the fatal consequences of Stalinist practices within the rank and file at Riom. One Spaniard from there had entered Spain in 1944 and been imprisoned, but managed to escape to France in 1950. On his arrival back in Riom his comrades, following the party line, treated him as a pariah and possible fascist agent, a treatment that pushed David Granda towards leaving the PCE. The disillusionment sown in the ranks of the exile community by such practices was compounded by international developments. Immediately after the Second World War the Allied powers had sought to isolate the Franco dictatorship through political and economic sanctions, but soon the growing Cold War created a climate in which the Pentagon sought to integrate Spain into NATO. The brutal repression of the Franco dictatorship counted as little compared to the American wish to build up military bases and strategic alliances to contain the Communist 'threat'. In 1953 the USA signed a military accord with Franco and two years later Spain was admitted to the United Nations. Even in France de Gaulle banned the Spanish Communist Party and some 160 members were arrested in September 1950. By the early 1950s therefore the Republican exiles had come to terms with the fact that the Franco dictatorship was well and truly secure. It was to maintain its vice-like grip on Spanish society for thirty-six years.

The decision of Consuelo Granda to return on vacation to Spain in 1954, and David Granda in 1956, was perhaps a tacit admission that the war against Franco was lost. Their account of the return to their home villages nearly twenty years after the fall of Asturias provides an extraordinary picture of Franco's Spain. For the inhabitants the reality of dictatorship had taken root insidiously over many years, but for the Grandas it was experienced as a fully-fledged phenomenon that contrasted grimly with the revolutionary Spain they had last known. For the first time they became aware of the enormous scale of the murderous repression and terror which had followed in the wake of the Nationalist victory. In Paladin David Granda found that villagers were strangely silent as to the whereabouts of those who had 'gone away' or been liquidated. His brothers Enrique and Paco narrowly escaped execution and after several years in labour camps were unable to find employment since workers were compelled to carry certificates of political reliability. In Valle Consuelo Granda found evidence of widespread and extremely brutal killings and beatings by falangist thugs. Nor, even in the mid 1950s, were the Grandas themselves necessarily safe from reprisals.

The Grandas were also struck by the terrible misery and backwardness of Spanish society. After the Nationalist victory a vindictive class of landowners and industrialists had a completely free hand to impose rock-bottom wages and conditions on a cowed proletariat. The isolation of Spain from the world economy during the Second World War and afterwards, because of international sanctions, led to an appalling collapse in living standards. Starving people scavenged for food and, in the rural south, were reduced to eating grass.[20] By contrast the Grandas arriving in 1956 in an ancient Citroën were regarded as rich. Above all and most depressing to the Grandas was an awareness of the extent to which many years of dictatorship and repression had affected people's attitudes; driven into a state of cowed ignorance, depoliticised and submissive, they seemed to be almost cut off from change in the world outside Spain, like people in a prison.

In 1973 David and Consuelo Granda decided to make a definitive return to Spain, a decision that was partly precipitated by David's being made redundant with the closure of the small aluminium factory where he had worked as a polisher since the end of the war. There followed eight unhappy years as the couple moved repeatedly between Asturias and France, unable to settle down in one place or another. General Franco died on 20 November 1975 and soon Spain was to make a remarkable and peaceful transition from dictatorship to an open and democratic society. However, these changes had come too late to make any major difference to the life of the Grandas. Like so many political exiles who have been compelled to live away from their native country for too long, return brought the painful awareness that they were alien and ill at ease in the very land which they had fought so hard to defend from the evil of fascism. In the end they finally settled in Riom; as David Granda concludes, for them the Civil War meant the loss not just of a four-year conflict, but of their country, of everything.

1 Village Life Before the Civil War – David

I was born on 29 December 1914. My father originally came from Aguera, towards the Asturian coast, and after he got married he worked as a carpenter in a large workshop at Trubia making or repairing carts. But later he rented a mill at Paladin, which is right next to my mother's village. And that's how we all came to be born there, in the flour.

The people in the region around Paladin are nearly all peasants; not big farmers, but poor people who have just enough to survive.[1] And it was all these small peasants who came to the mill to have their maize ground for making bread or porridge or to feed their animals. Because of their poverty – they were peasants with only two or three cows – the work in the mill was very hard because it's not the same to mill, for example, one hundred kilos in one go as to grind in small quantities. Each peasant would bring his small sack, one with fifteen kilos, another with ten, then one with twenty or thirty kilos and my father had to mill them all separately for each client and put the flour back into each owner's sack. He couldn't mix the flour of different people. It was incredibly hard work. That is why just to make a tiny return the mill had to work day and night; the stones had to grind twenty-four hours a day. For each Asturian measure of flour, a *copin*, my father would take a small cup called a *maquila* and put it aside in his barrel; that's how he was paid, in kind.

There were some periods in the year when there was more work in the mill; after the harvest especially there was always a lot to do because the villagers looked forward to this period to fill their stomachs. Before the maize harvest some people were so hungry or had such an urge to have a good feed on the new crop that they would cut it while it was not yet ripe, while the cobs were still too soft. They would leave the maize in the sun for a while and then put it in a sack and bring it to be ground. But instead of making a good flour the soft grain left a sticky crust which blocked up the mill stones. But my father invented a way of clearing this out with a very fine steel rod which he slid between the stones. However, the whole thing made a revolting mess.

The mill belonged to a wealthy neighbour called Alberto; he

owned a lot of land and houses, as well as the mill. We paid him in kind, thirty-three kilos of grain a month, but often we did not bring in enough to pay him and we had to buy it to make up the difference. My father would carry it in a sack on his back to Alberto's and empty it out and if it was short he would make up the weight week by week. But later Alberto began to go bankrupt and he began to sell off his properties, including the mill. The price was not high; it was a real bargain. My father wanted to buy it but while he was wealthy in children he was not in money; he had nothing at all. He tried to borrow the money, without success, and so it was bought by another man, a wealthy tax collector from Valduno called Antonio Suarez Magadan, and we continued to pay the rent in kind. This Magadan was a hunter and kept a lot of dogs and he said, 'You can pay the rent in maize so that I can make a porridge for my dogs.' So there we were when we were still small children helping my mother to work the mill because my father was usually out at work elsewhere doing carpentry, repairing houses and fixing new roofs, or working in a cartwright shop. My mother worked herself to a standstill, often frozen stiff from the damp and cold of the mill, just so that the landlord could feed his dogs. Because that's what it amounted to in the end; we were working for Magadan's dogs because the profit we made amounted to very little; just enough to make the evening meal of maize porridge.

That was our basic diet, maize. In the morning we had soup with maize bread and, on rare occasions, milk coffee; at midday it was usually cabbage and potatoes; and in the evening, the most common food of the region, a porridge made from maize flour, called *fariñas* in Asturias. To make that you boil some salted water and sprinkle the flour in while stirring; just like making wallpaper glue. And we ate it just like that or, if you were lucky, with a little milk. But there was a time of year when we got a good bellyful of food because the chestnuts were ripe. During two or three months in the year they were our basic food supply. All the chestnut trees belonged to particular families and since we didn't own any we rented some from an aunt. We would climb up the trees and knock the nuts down with long rods; they were then collected, placed in carefully made piles, and then covered over with brambles and heather. They might be left like that up in the mountain from October until almost Christmas, in the open and unprotected from rain or snow. When you went back the spiny case had rotted and could be easily separated from the chestnuts; you put them into sacks and took them home to store in the attic. A good year for chestnuts was a time for feasting and singing.[2]

By early spring the chestnuts ran out; they would never last through to bridge the gap before the new crops arrived. It was usually about the month of May which was the most terrible for hunger, but after that the agricultural cycle would restart. The cherries came and after that the pears and plums. That was our basic diet, maize and chestnuts; but our family, unlike some others in the village, was quite enterprising when it came to finding ways to fill the pot. At that time the stream was full of fish; all you had to do was to close the water sluices to the mill and go under the stone vault below, where the wheels are, and you would always find some trout.

It was during the 1914–18 war, or just before, that my father began to work the river coal. The River Nalón flows down from the coal mining basin at Mieres and Sama. In those days the mines didn't wash and grade the coal very well so that a great deal was thrown away with the waste into the tips.[3] Now, with the modern washing installations, little is lost and if you walk along the river bank today it's very rare to find any lumps of coal. But before, especially with the winter floods, the tips were washed away by the Nalón and the action of the river somehow graded the coal and left it in deposits on the river bed.

To raise the coal two boats worked together; a very big one which could hold two or three tons of coal and a small one just big enough to mount a windlass, a wooden drum for winding in the rope. The boats were anchored to big stones on the river bed, to keep them in position above the coal deposits. The heavy work was done by a man in the big boat with a eucalyptus pole about thirty feet long and pretty thick: I remember the first time we were sent to do that job we couldn't even lift it up to get it into the river. On the end of the pole was an iron hoop with a wire basket, like a sieve, which could hold up to a hundred kilos of coal. The pole was driven down into the coal on the bed of the river and then winched up by a boy or an old man who turned the windlass in the small boat. There would be coal and sand mixed together when you raised it, so the long pole was allowed to rest across the sides of the boat where you could shake the sieve about to wash out the gravel. But mixed in with the coal were small stones, scoria, which wouldn't burn and since it was heavier than the coal it would stay in a layer at the bottom. You lifted the good coal out with your hands and threw it into the bottom of the boat. All day long you did that, driving down the poling and raising it; some days you might take out 400 or 500 kilos, other times less, and on occasions you might fill a whole boat.

About 1914, during the First World War, the river coal began to fetch a very good price. I think that my father was working in a joiner's shop at the time and he built two boats and began to dredge for coal. A lot of people began to do the same: at that time the big bridge at Valduno had not been built, there was just a ferry, and it was said that you could cross the river, passing from boat to boat, there were so many. In order to get a decent price and to stop competition among themselves they decided to set up an association or co-operative. It was called the 'Sociedad de Carbones de Rio-La Valduna'. They rented a piece of land and everyone unloaded the coal there in one common pile. During the war the pile was enormous. From there the men carried the coal in baskets on their backs, perhaps fifty kilos at a time, and loaded it into railway wagons. The children helped too; I knew barely how to walk and I was already loading coal into the wagons. Since the wagons were so high, they put planks and up we went, our little baskets resting on a rolled up sack across the shoulders, just like coolies. But we were happy to do it; when the men were loading they drank wine and they would put a drop in our lemonade – we were pleased as punch.

The business of the co-operative was looked after by two men who were elected from the members. My father was the secretary and it was often he and another who went to arrange the sale with buyers at the port of San Esteban. The sale was made through a sample kept in a small bag and this was then analysed for the quantity of scoria and the calorific value. One time they built up a huge pile, enough to fill half a train, and when it was sold at a good price they climbed on top and drank to it with champagne. But they hadn't yet had the result of the analysis and several days later the buyers said they didn't want the coal, there was too much scoria and it needed to be washed again. That's how the association fell apart: it was said that there were a lot of people who didn't wash and grade the coal properly which was one of the conditions of being in the co-operative from the start. So, by the fault of some, all the others were losers and the co-operative ended. It's nearly always the case that associations like that collapse in that way, and that one was no exception.

In Paladin and all the little hamlets round about the great majority of people were truly poor. Each family had very little land, perhaps one or two hectares, and it was all divided up into tiny parcels. That's because there were usually lots of children and at the death of the father each one would inherit a small piece. And what's bizarre is that as soon as someone came into some land the plots were all further subdivided by walls or hedges. And it was all split up like that. But a lot of the peasants didn't own the land, or they owned so little that they had to rent some more at very high prices and when all is said and done there was not much left out of the crops at the year's end. But what was far more serious was that almost none of the peasants around Paladin owned their own cows. Since they couldn't afford to buy cows it was the *caciques* who paid for the cattle raised by the peasants. In Asturias the system was called the *comuña*. The rich owner would give a cow to a peasant to be looked after but whenever it calved and the calf was raised by the peasant and then sold in the market, half the price went to the *cacique*. In addition the peasant was always indebted to the owner for the original value of the animal. If, for example, you received a young cow at a certain price and then worked it for five or six years, when you went to sell it it might fetch perhaps half its original value, but you still owed the full amount. The owner never lost out; he always had to be reimbursed at the original price. And if the cow got ill and died by chance the *cacique* lost nothing; it was the peasant who lost all. Perhaps he would have to buy another cow, but he would remain indebted for the dead one. I have never seen such an injustice. Even when I was small I was aware of this: 'But it's not possible. If the cow dies she dies for everyone, no?' But no, she died for the *métayer* but she didn't die for the man who supplied her; he risked nothing. It was a kind of usury; like money which was borrowed at an extortionate rate of interest. And it was the great majority of peasants in the area who were forced to have recourse to the *comuña* system. The cow was absolutely vital to the peasant; not only did it give milk but it was also used to work the land, for ploughing and pulling carts.

In our small hamlet there were seven other households and I shall describe them in the order you would meet them coming into Paladin from Valduno.

The Ferro family had just a small piece of land next to their house; half was cultivated and half was a meadow with a few fruit trees. They sold the fruit and kept a few hens and sometimes a cow. For example, during the summer they might have two cows but as winter came on they got rid of them because they didn't have enough feed for the winter. And that's all there was to keep the father, the mother and two children.

Just across from them lived the family of Feliciano, who rented their house from Alberto. I believe that Feliciano married a woman who had a bit of money but instead of doing something with it they lived off it as long as it held out. Apart from that they had nothing at all; no land, nothing. There were two sons and two daughters and both the sons were packed off to Cuba because it was the time of the war in North Africa and the parents didn't want them to do military service. I don't think that they were very successful out there and one of them, Pépé, came back. When the little bit of capital had been used up they had absolutely nothing to live on. But in spite of their poverty they were a very proud family and the father always kept himself apart from the neighbours. Everyone knew that they didn't eat every day but the father was so proud he wouldn't accept any food if it was given to him openly. Sometimes when my mother made the bread she would send us at night to leave a loaf in front of the door; other times a basket of potatoes. When he opened the door he would take the food because he didn't know who had left it. People helped him like that in spite of himself, because he was so proud. One night his last daughter died: I think she died of hunger because what they had to eat couldn't have kept them alive.

Next was the Alberto family which lived in a big house just across the stream from the mill. They owned a lot of property; the house where Feliciano lived, the mill, and other land and buildings. Quite often the rents were paid in grain and after the harvest wagon after wagon would come loaded with leather sacks called *fuelles*. Alberto's house was big, like a fortress, and behind he had lots of land with fruit trees and where he kept cows. But Alberto was a rather unsteady type who tried his hand at all kinds of business and failed in most. In that family there were three sons and three daughters and all the boys – Alphonso, Clemente and Paco – went to Cuba.

The next house was that of Alphonso. He was the brother of Alberto and had married his brother's daughter Sarah, his own niece. For that he had to get a dispensation from the church. What a hypocritical set-up; perhaps all he had to do was pay ten pesetas to the priest. Once you've got a *dispensa* you are authorised to do anything, even to marry your own mother. The couple emigrated to Mexico, but I don't think things went too well and money was sent so that they could come back. They returned with a boy, Ismael, who was aged about eleven or twelve. He didn't add up to much either, the poor lad; he said he could throw a lasso and he was always with a rope trying to catch things, but without much success. When we were children, to have a bit of fun, when we saw Alberto walking along we would say to Ismael, 'Hey, Ismael, call your *tio y abuelo*', that's to say his 'uncle-grandad'. So he would call, '*Tio y abuelo*' and Alberto would chase us all over the place shouting, 'You little bastards'.

Next was the house of Carreno. People would say that the family there were 'de Casa Carreno', from the house of Carreno. But as is common in Asturias, that wasn't their real name and the family was called after the house. Living there was a very old woman called Tata who had enormous skirts which had been repaired so many times with little pieces of cloth that the whole dress was like a patchwork quilt. There were perhaps five hundred patches in her skirt and you couldn't tell the colour of the original.

That house knew nothing but misfortune. Tata was related to a man called Victor who came over from Cuba, rotten with tuberculosis. He married a woman called Perfecta and they had a daughter, Millagros, who died later from tuberculosis, and three sons whose name all began with an 'A' – Abelino, Antonio and Amadeo. The first to die from tuberculosis was the father. And when someone died in the family the mother, Perfecta, was to be seen next day walking around Paladin. She didn't cry or grieve or make any mention of what had happened; it was not as with some folk who spent years crying, not her.

The house which they lived in was more like a shed; the floor was made of beaten earth and it wasn't even flat, but full of holes, and at one end was a raised brick platform, the hearth where they made the fire. Just to the left of the fire was a door which led into the cowstall, and to get in the cow had to come through the kitchen. They slept in an attic up in the roof which had one small window. The house was damp and airless and those who had tuberculosis in that place really knew that they had got it. They didn't have much land, just three or four small plots – a morsel on the hillside just above my father's house, which was for the chestnut trees, two or three pieces just before getting to Valduno and perhaps another small patch near Volgues. But it was wretched, just enough to keep one cow. Since they couldn't afford to buy a cow they kept one under the *comuña* system which was so exploitative.

Then the three sons went off to seek their fortune in Cuba – it was the time when every one was emigrating – and they all came back disillusioned and ill. First Antonio died of tuberculosis and then Amadeo and that poor woman, Perfecta, was left alone with the last one, Abelino. He too was always ill and you would think that he was going to die any day. But what was strange about that woman – perhaps she had lost her reason – was that nearly all her children were dead; she had nothing, not a penny, and there were occasions when the neighbours paid for the funeral – but she would come down to the fountain to fetch water always singing. Often, when she was alone with the last ill child, we would go and give her a hand to cut the hay or to hoe the maize and that woman was always singing.

There is an old custom in Asturias called the *antroxo* which is still widely practised at Paladin; when a pig is killed you give a piece of meat to all the neighbours. From about the first of November onwards, throughout the winter, was the period when pigs were slaughtered and at that time Perfecta would come to the door to see if there was something for her. Everyone would give her a small basket of pieces; like that she had enough pork, cooked up with potatoes, to keep her going for a week or two.

Right next door to the house of Carreno was a slightly bigger one, that of Zapatero. Zapatero married twice; by the first wife he had seven or eight children and when they were already getting big he got remarried to a woman who was much younger than him and they had another eight children. The family was really wretched. Zapatero owned two or three pieces of land and he rented a bit from my aunt, but there was only enough meadow to keep one cow whereas he had two or three. He had enough land to feed four children, but he had eight. Well, that could be seen; the cows were skeletons and the children starving. He was in the same kind of position as my father, with a large family, but my father, although he didn't earn much, found other work or he did little jobs on the side and that enabled us to have a bit more in the larder, while Zapatero never brought in a wage from outside and all they had was a little land and two cows. I don't know how they managed to stay alive, except folk said that he would go at night into the fields of other people and cut maize to fill his *hórreo* or barn. Zapatero had a really vicious character, he was a real brute. He would take off his leather belt and holding it by the strap would beat his wife and children with the buckle end. My God, the screams that came from that house.

The last house was that of Carola or Carola la Taruca as we called it. The house was just a small hut like a shepherd's cabin, built into the side of the hill; it had a beaten earth floor and was very dark inside, just like a hole in the ground. It was so black that they would whitewash it. Since there was no electricity at that time they used acetylene lamps which worked on a kind of stone and when it had burned it was a bit like chalk. Well they would put this aside for several months and afterwards they would stir it up in a bucket of water and with that they painted the entrance.

The father was a very small man and people called him 'Manin'. He was originally from near Somiedo, towards the mountains of Galicia, but when he came to Paladin he and his eldest son had both been working as miners up in the mountains at Teberga. I've no idea why they gave that up to come to Paladin, to live in that shack. All they had in the way of land was a small garden alongside the house. Since they had no cows they had no means of getting manure for the land. Manin would go and cut some hay or heather and lay it in a bed on the ground and then he took a basket and collected all the cow dung and horse droppings left by the animals when they passed along the tracks. He would then pile the dung on the layer of hay or straw which he had prepared. Once he went very early in the morning, just before daybreak, to steal some straw from a field near Valduno where the wheat had just been cut. He made a huge pile of straw and carried it off home on his back. Well my brother-in-law Jerman used to come home from work in Trubia very early in the morning and what should he see but this pile of straw moving along with just two feet visible beneath. He knew that it was Manin de la Taruca stealing straw again from somebody else's field so he came up behind, without being seen, and set light to the straw with a match. The whole lot burst into flame and Manin was lucky not to have got burned up too.

The Carola family only had one small plot of land so they laboured for other people. When my father began to dredge for river coal he employed two of them to work with him. Later they had boats built for themselves and went their own way and that's how they made a living, selling coal or working the land for others. The eldest child, Celesto, married into the house of Villar, which is on the hillside across from Paladin. He was shot after the Civil War and the youngest son like-wise fell to the firing squad. There was another son called Jesús who was hopelessly ill with tuberculosis. He was a really easy-going type and come rain come shine you would see him going along the track from Valduno to Paladin always whistling; he was always cheerful. When he was in his twenties he liked to go and play a hand of cards in the bar like everyone else and people said that he was a drinker, which was not true because he didn't have the money. One day, because he was ill with tuberculosis, he began to hack up his lungs with coughing into a chamberpot and, as his father and mother were very ignorant folk, they said, 'That bugger is puking up wine again'. But he was bringing up blood and several days later he was dead.

They had a daughter called Oliva, the only member of the family alive today. She went to work as a domestic servant in the house of a man called Constante who had come back from South America loaded with money. He had lots of property in Havana and in a transport company at Oviedo. He was much older than her, but she was not bad looking when she was young so he married her. But during the October Revolution in 1934 he disappeared; he was shot by the *guardia civil* and his body was found in the River Nalón. But Oliva still lives in Paladin; she has built a new house alongside the hut they used to live in and she uses it as an outhouse for her brooms.

That's all the families of Paladin, and a lot of those people died of tuberculosis – that's how Alberto died and Esperanza, the wife of Zapatero, and lots of others. I think it was above all else a disease of the poor, a disease of poverty, because I've seen many who died like that in the village. The living conditions in the houses was terrible and the diet very bad.

Many of the people of Paladin were ignorant and believed in all kinds of superstitions: for example, if a dog howled in the night or if an owl hooted they were frightened because it was a sign that somebody would die soon. And if a cow fell sick there was a practice called *cambian el aqua* or changing the water. One day my Aunt Consuelo said to me, 'I want you to go to a certain place to see a woman, you give her this bottle of water, and when she's finished you bring it back.' The woman was a kind of healer and after she had done various things to the water you gave it to the cow which then recovered. But I went to the bank of the Nalón, near to the cemetery, and waited for about two hours – about the time it would have taken me to go and have the water changed – and then returned. My aunt was very pleased and gave me twenty-five centimos. She gave the water to the cow, but I don't know whether it recovered or not. There were a lot of beliefs like that, especially concerning animals and the evil eye.

The parish of Valduno, which includes Paladin, covers a big area and every Sunday people would come to church from miles around. It was almost obligatory for us children to go and my mother was very religious, but my father never went to mass. Perhaps he would go if a friend of his had died, to accompany the dead: but he never, never went to mass. I don't think that he was much of a believer but, whatever the case, he certainly didn't practise the faith. But he never tried to stop my mother from sending us to church. It was mainly the women and children who went; there were very few men and those were mainly the rich.

The church inside was in the form of a cross and on each side, to right and left, were two small side altars, one the Chapel de la Casa Nueva and the other the Chapel de Ardage and from there just up to the high altar was where the rich people sat, the *caciques* of the parish. The chairs which they sat on were privately owned; they belonged to the family, and the wealthier they were, the more splendid the seats. Some were really grand, covered in velvet, carved with the family name and with little cushions to kneel on. Behind them in the main body of the church was where all the peasants were; the poorer they were the further back from the altar, and the richer they were, the finer the chair. The old peasant women had a peculiar way of seating themselves on little wooden stools so that they were almost at ground level and, squatting like that with their big skirts spread out, they looked as if they were cut off from the waist. They all wore the mantilla. It was a strange sight. But what struck me most were the hands of those poor women: when you are small you notice the hands of old people in a different way. Their hands were covered in scars and hard like the bark of a tree. Perhaps they all had been picking chestnuts in the brambles and their old hands were all caloused. Years later, when I was in a concentration camp in France, I wrote a poem about those women – '*San Antonio del gocho*' or 'Saint Anthony of the pigs'. Those peasant women who were so religious, they didn't know the catechism or the history of the saints; for them what counted was St Anthony, the holy protector of pigs, and St John, and St Lazarus, who was shown with a dog licking his sores.

> Saint Anthony of the pig
> And Lazarus of the dog
> If you care for my Pastora
> And my Rubia
> Which is losing a teat
> I shall bring you some red poppies
> From the wheat field of the New Cueto.

Often the cows suffer from an illness in the hoof; they get cold when they lie down and they often lose a teat from congestion and can give no more milk. The poem is about the old women praying to San

Antonio and Lazarus, that if they take care of their cows – they commonly have names like Pastora or Rubia – and protect them from the illness they will bring them a gift of poppies from the corn fields near Valduno. Perhaps those old women did not understand the niceties of religion but they were good people, of honest faith. The wealthy people who went to church may have been better educated but they were a different matter altogether, a bad lot.

Even when I was young I was a bit of an unbeliever; in the eyes of my Aunt Consuelo I was a 'heretic' and *despegau* or too detached and cold. One day I said, 'The Good Lord. The Good Lord. I've never seen him. I've never seen God, so why should I believe in a thing I've never seen?' My Aunt said, 'And have you seen Havana? You believe well enough in Havana?' – 'Yes', I said, 'but there's folk who've come back.' And she began to chase me like nobody's business, to give me a cuff on the ear.

Gradually, as I got older, I began to feel opposed to the church. The parish priest who gave me my first communion, Juan Diaz, who came from Oviedo, was a good type, a great big likeable man who loved to drink cider – he died later from drink. He had a huge pot-belly and he loved cider more than anything; he would go into the bar and have bottle after bottle and he had a big stock at home. But then I began to see how things were because he didn't like anybody to miss the mass. He would get angry with those who didn't go and begin to shout at them right in public, in the middle of the road. 'You are a crowd of savages; you'll all go straight to hell. You were cutting hay on the Lord's Day.'

One Sunday we were loading coal into the railway wagons. My father was there with the other men and all us kids, each with a little bag tied on our back. And out from the church came the priest, followed by the choirboys and all the congregation, and after circling the church he went with a little sprinkler to bless the maize crops nearby; he blessed the fields and the houses. And we were working away when he came over to tell us off and by God, my father had a real set-to with him. The priest said, 'You work very hard for a Sunday.' My father replied, 'I already have the good fortune to work all week and on top of that I have to labour on Sunday as well. Am I not already burdened enough with that? Clear off; I don't stick my nose in your business; leave me in peace.' And then the priest tried to back off; he said to my father, 'It's not only those who go to church who are honest folk. I know there are some like you who don't go but I look on them as if they were church attenders, because just going to church is no sure sign of honesty. Indeed people like you may be less hypocritical.' The priest was trying to patch things up because my old man was angry, he was hopping mad.

From the 1920s through to the Civil War I think that the men went to church less and less.[4] When the Republic was proclaimed they even passed legislation that it would no longer be obligatory to pay for the church oil; because up till then the common people had to give money for the oil which was used in a fine copper lamp which hung in the centre of the church. And after that the priest threatened, 'If you want to come to mass you'll have to pay for the oil because the government has cut off the funds.'

When I was six or seven I began to go to the village school: that's one thing we can thank our old man for – we were a very large family, like most of those in the region, but while they rarely sent their children to school, we were all sent. My father taught us to read at home from an early age. I can remember learning the alphabet, not from a book but with the aid of a wooden board on which he had painted the ABC. This was handed down from one child to the next and like that my father taught us all to read. When we first went to school at six or seven all of us, except for Valentina, knew how to read already.

The school was built just after the First World War; at some time between 1917 and 1920. The school was right up in the mountains, high above the village, in a clearing surrounded by trees. That was because when the villagers decided to build a school they didn't want it anywhere near the houses; they said that the children would create havoc and cause too much trouble. There was a single classroom, like a barn, and upstairs the teacher's living quarters with two bedrooms, a kitchen and a small sitting-room. Since the building was on a steep slope it was set into the hillside and the walls at one end were very damp because they were below ground level; there was fungus growing there. There was no electricity and no heating.

Into that one room were crammed all the children from the parish of Valduno – from Premoño, Paladin, Purma, Volgues and elsewhere – boys and girls mixed together and aged from six to thirteen. There were never less than fifty in the class and sometimes sixty-five. You can imagine what conditions were like. We sat on very long benches, like church pews, with an inclined table to write on and small inkwells in holes all along. There were always arguments because we were crammed together; you had to keep one arm under the table and write with the other but you had no hand free to keep the paper still. Sometimes somebody would get both arms up and then there would be trouble, 'Please Sir, that one's got both his elbows on the table.' The teacher would say, 'Get your arm down, let your neighbour work.' Good God, nobody could work in those conditions. Since there were so many children in the school it was not possible that they all got proper attention. The peasants thought that if they brought gifts to the teacher he would give better instruction to their children, so there were lots who came with chickens, eggs and pieces of pork, and the teacher did take care to see that those whose parents made presents received closer attention. Us children would say among ourselves, 'So and so is the little darling of the master; of course his mother sends chickens.'

During the monarchy, before 1931, there were no lay schools. We were not taught by a priest but there were religious studies and on one wall was a large crucifix and opposite a picture of the King of Spain. The rich people sent their children to private Catholic colleges in the town and were taught by priests, but in the country ordinary people couldn't afford that. But we all came from poor families and at least we were on the same plane.[5] The school was a state school, but the facilities were rock-bottom. Each child had to buy their own books, so the books of my elder brother Enrique were passed on to me and then from me down the whole line of eight children. We had to bring our own steel-nibbed pens and chalks, but we could carve the penholders ourselves from hardwood and go to a small quarry near the River Nalón to look for chalks. All the learning we did was by rote, reciting from memory, but what was most backward in that poor school was the teachers. All the teachers who came to that isolated place up in the pine trees did so either because they were ill and needed the pure mountain air or because they were so useless that they couldn't find a position in a town. As a result the teachers were changing all the time; I think I had eleven in all. They were not paid much at the time and there is a Spanish saying, 'To be as poor as a schoolmaster'. It was a miserable living.

One of the teachers I remember in particular was a big fat man who came originally from the Canary Islands. He was so fat that he could hardly get upstairs to his apartment to go to the toilet. He got my father to make him a commode, a special seat with a lid and a chamber pot inside. Often during the lessons we saw his daughter come downstairs with a blanket and, wrapped up inside it, a chamber pot. He would put the pot inside the chair, cover himself up with the rug and have a shit right there in front of us. At the end of the classroom the teacher's desk was raised upon a little platform and that is where he would sit, like someone on a stage. We couldn't see anything, he was all wrapped up, but we could smell the shit, it stunk like I don't know what. And after a while one of his daughters would come down again and take the pot to empty it outside in the latrines.

There was another teacher called José Perez who was as thin as a rake and riddled with tuberculosis. That poor man, I don't know whether he was keen to teach us or not, but it was clear that he didn't have the strength because he was so ill and from time to time, when he went through a crisis, he would have to go upstairs and lie down. After Perez died came a teacher who must have had polio; he was very small and had one leg shorter than the other and a hand which was all twisted. He could write a beautiful hand in the 'English' style, which was much prized at the time. And that's what he taught us nearly all the time, how to write well; but as to teaching anything else he was incapable. Some years later my brothers met him in the market at Grado where he was selling wooden pitchforks and baskets which he had made. That was his real profession, making hay-forks and baskets. And then came another teacher called Leopold, and then Oliverio, and so it went on. You can imagine the kind of education we got; there was no continuity and you learned nothing at all.

Until I was eleven I went to school regularly but when you reached that age you were already big enough to start working a little. At that age us children would start working on the River Nalón, turning the windlass to dredge up the coal. One day or one week one of my brothers would miss school and go to work and then he would swop over with another and return to school. But when you reached fourteen you left school and began to work full-time.

About then, when I was fourteen or fifteen, a young teacher came who had his heart in the job, unlike all the others, and he agreed to hold evening classes free of charge if we would pay for the lighting. There was no electricity and we came to an agreement to cover the costs of an acetylene lamp. So each evening when I finished work on the river at Valduno, I went straight up the mountain to the school. That was only during one winter, from October to December, but I think that I learned more then than during the whole of my time at school.

There were a lot who went; the school was full, perhaps forty odd, and of all ages from fifteen to twenty-one and older. There were some who were already adult, who could neither read nor write, and who wanted to emigrate to Latin America, to Cuba, Mexico or Argentina. They were going out to seek their fortune or, as they approached the age for conscription, their parents packed them off to avoid military service. So they came to night-school to learn how to write a letter so they could keep in touch with their parents when they were abroad. There were lots and lots who came for that reason.[6] There was a book designed just for people like that, with model letters for each occasion and explaining how to lay it out and so on. And that's all they studied during the three months of school, how to write and sign a letter. Often the teacher placed a kid who already knew how to write alongside a fully-grown man to help him learn how to write a letter to the family. They became a bit dependent on us for help, but while we were aiding them we learned nothing at all. I remember helping one who had a beard who impressed me because he wore a waistcoat with a watch and chain. From time to time I would say, 'Look, that word means this', and he would take the watch from his pocket and say in a gruff voice, 'It's not yet time to go.'

Of course even when they did eventually write home from America their parents would often be unable to read the letter. In our hamlet, Paladin, I think that everyone could read and write, and everyone sent their children to school, even from the poorest families. But in some other villages, like Volgues for example, which is right next door, just the other side of the 'Lower Meadow', neither the children nor the parents could read. When my father was postman I would often deliver letters for him and people would say, 'Who is it from? Can you read it for me?' I would read the letter and often it was from their own children.

Sometimes those who came back from South America would come to inspect the school and to offer prizes to encourage the children. They were emigrants from the area; perhaps they had learned to write in the school before going abroad. On their return those who had made a bit of money would form a kind of association and come to visit the school. You would see three or four of these very well dressed men arrive; you could tell they were from America and were rich. We were made to do tests in front of them and they gave the winners some money. There would be first, second and third prize for boys and the same for girls. One prize was for arithmetic. There was a blackboard on each side of the classroom and the teacher would chalk up the same problems on each. Two boys were placed back to back; they went to the board and the one who answered all the problems fastest came first. Once I won a prize for general knowledge; they asked what was the capital of Asturias, things like that. But the biggest prize was for mathematics and when I won that they gave me twenty pesetas, paid all in one peseta coins to make it seem a lot. I ran down from school to Paladin like a rocket to show my parents; twenty pesetas at that time, that was quite something.

2 Stormclouds gather, 1930–1936 – David

The end of the monarchy in 1931 was a great event and I remember a man called Pedregal, who lived across the River Nalón at Anzo, firing a rocket to celebrate the new Republic. He must have been on the left from the very beginning because none of his children were baptised; it was the only family in the area that wasn't. And the people of Anzo said that the children were 'Moros' or Arabs because they were not baptised. That came from the time of the conflict between Moors and Christians in Spain. When we were kids we were stupid, we would shout at them across the river, 'Moros!' I think the father was the only man in the region who really added up to much because when the Republic was proclaimed the first rocket fired, the first flag flown was by him, Pedregal.[1]

As far as politics was concerned I don't think that you can say that my father was a militant; but he was to the left, he was a Republican. And the first Republican funeral ever held in that area was that of my grandfather. Under the monarchy, as later under Franco, most churchyards had a separate civil burial ground, a piece of land apart, for the atheists. But during the Republic they abolished the difference and my grandfather was buried in a civil ceremony, without a priest, and his coffin was draped with the Republican flag. It was a big affair.[2]

The years before the Civil War, during the Republic, were really harsh. Just to see the numbers of young unemployed around Paladin would make your heart ache, and it was the same everywhere in Asturias.[3] In the mining basin they began to put the workers on a three day week, the *aterceraos* as it was called, while there were huge piles of coal and none of it was being sold. What was going on was that the rich, the owners, were buying coal from abroad to put the miners out of work. In the factories it was the same, people were on a three-day week. It was a deliberate sabotage aimed at the Republic, to show that it was incapable of running the country and to disrupt the economy. And that's when the strikes began, strikes everywhere.

Asturias has a long tradition of workers' struggle. The general strike of 1917 was so big that the army had to be sent into Asturias and the whole mining basin was occupied. I remember one strike not long after the Republic came, perhaps it was in 1933, when the miners of Sama closed themselves up in the pit 'El Fondon' and refused to come out until their grievances were settled. And then there was a very important strike in the building industry at Oviedo and blackleg workers were sent from Madrid to break it: there were some enormous fights then. Then there was a strike in the docks and they refused to load or unload the ships and they sent blacklegs again. The men who came from elsewhere to break the strike were protected at work by the police, but the moment they came out from work and got separated a bit the strikers would be waiting with coal shovels and beat them terribly. In the lodging where the blacklegs were staying someone planted a bomb made from a box of nuts packed with dynamite.

There has always been a special link between the mines and the people on the land. That's because nearly all the coalminers are from a peasant background; nearly everyone who goes to work in the mine has some family in the countryside. At Valduno and in the District of Las Regueras there are lots of people who have sons or relatives in the mines at Mieres or Sama. And whenever there was a major strike in the mines they would send their children to be looked after in the villages. At Paladin and round about there were also a lot of people who worked in the factories at Trubia or at Oviedo.[4]

But it is true that a lot of the real peasants were a bit frightened of the left. If there was a strike they would not be active in support of it, or get mixed up in the struggles of the workers, or anything like that; but on the other hand they were not *against* the strikes, against the workers' fight. What got them worried was when the left was presented as an enemy of the Church. Because there were lots of peasants, like my Uncle Benjamin, who were really religious, and they would say, 'They want to destroy morality; to destroy the churches.' That's what the peasants feared most, that the anarchists would descend from the cities, from Gijón, with all their black flags flying, respecting nobody and a law unto themselves. That was a fear that the right exploited well, the burned churches, the massacred priests.

From the time when I left school at fourteen until I went into the army at twenty I couldn't find any regular paid work. The same applied to nearly all the young people around Paladin. In the big cities the young may have managed to find something but in the countryside those who didn't have any land to keep them busy had nothing to fall back on, only small jobs here and there for three days at a time, giving a hand to others. But a regular wage, never. In our family there were already three of us old enough by 1930 to bring in a wage, Enrique, myself and Paco; but not a job between us. Of course we worked on the river for coal, but a lot of the time it brought in a mere pittance. In winter when the river was in flood you couldn't lift anything and in summer, when the Nalón was very low and flowed slowly, you couldn't get anything either.

One day my father said, 'You're going to work with a clog-maker, I've already ordered the tools.' Every day I went on foot to Premoño to work as an apprentice, but I really hated it. A trade like that was worthless; perhaps today you can make a living but at the time it was something that everyone did and perhaps you would have to make three or four pairs of clogs in a day just to get by. I began to let things slide, I gave up the tools, and when my father saw that it wasn't working out he didn't insist. In the end all I ever made were two pairs of *madrenas* for my father and mother.

There are big factories at Trubia, not far from Paladin; one of them is a state arms factory and the other a general engineering works. I would have liked to have got a job there, but all the places were much sought after and you had to pull strings to get in, win the backing of some big shot, of a government minister! If anyone got a place there it was because he had someone backing him, wangling things for him: it was all fixed. If you went down there to look for work you might sometimes see a noticeboard offering places but if you enquired about it somehow they had always been taken. Those who could pull strings with the rich got in, but nobody in our family ever found a job. At Paladin there were only two who worked at Trubia. There was one who started work at eight in the morning and clocked off at two, but you would see him already back home by ten o'clock. If you asked if he was there because he was ill or something, he replied, 'No, I went to work, I stamped my card in the clock, read the newspaper a bit and then came home.' There was no discipline, no control, and he did much as he pleased. And I would say to myself, 'That bastard there brings in a good wage and look at us.'

With the coming of the Republic the Socialist Party began to organise meetings in the countryside through the Federation of Land Workers.[5] Well my father was not a very cultivated man but he could read and write and keep an account book so he was nominated secretary of the union which was a Socialist organisation. I remember that he had a rubber stamp marked 'Socialist Party' and during the Civil War, when he was a refugee near Aviles, he still had that stamp and union papers. And when he saw that the position was completely lost, that Asturias would fall to the Nationalists – it was the very last day, when I left by boat – he told me, 'I'm going to burn all this stuff'. He burned it because if he was found with that it was good enough reason for them to shoot him. And yet he presented no danger, neither for one side nor the other.

My father used to get a newspaper called the *Nueva España*; it was a regional paper and right wing. But he would get it free because he was a kind of local correspondent; if something happened in the area, perhaps somebody had fallen from a tree and died, he would write in. But later the Socialist newspaper *Avance* began to have a big influence. At that time, without any radio in the village, most of the political battles took place through the newspapers, each with its own tendency. Whenever we could we got hold of *Avance*. During the rising of October 1934 the offices were burned down by the Falangists of Oviedo and later in France I met quite a number of those who worked on the paper – they were all Socialists. But most of them, those who were unable to escape when Asturias fell, were shot. Javier Bueno was shot and a whole lot of others, just because they worked on *Avance*.[6]

At that time the two big parties of the left were the Anarchists, the CNT, which was strong in Gijón and at La Felguera, a mining town, and the Socialist Party. The Communist Party was really small. But I and my brothers and friends were not members of any organisation. In the countryside, in little villages like Paladin, there was no political organisation, no groups, no parties, nothing at all. Perhaps things were badly organised by the parties who concentrated all their effort in the big towns and especially in the mining district. That's where the best organisation was, with paid-up members.

In our everyday discussions we were perhaps more anarchist in tendency than anything: that everything needed turning over and remaking anew. But in spite of the absence of any party the political divisions of right and left were as clear as you please. We were like uncarded militants; if, for example, there was a discussion in the bar there might be somebody there who was to the right and everyone would know it, and he would know that the rest were on the left. No one there would hold a party card, but in the discussions that made no difference and the divisions were clear. It was as clear as day who was to the right and who was to the left. On the one side were the workers, the wage-earners, and those who had nothing; and on the other those who owned some property, were Catholic and supported

CEDA.[7] It was as simple as that, without any refined ideas.

In little villages like Paladin and Valduno the politics of the right were organised by the most important people, those who had plenty of land or money, *los caciques*. There was the priest, the secretary to the mayor, the doctor, the local tax-collector; people like that. During an election, even under the Republic, they would visit everyone and buy votes, and the more miserable and propertyless the people so much the better because they were so much the easier to bribe. They were promised a mattress, things like that. There was one election in Asturias, that of 1933, which was called the *Electiones del Chorizo* because that's what was on offer – sausages.[8] During the 1933 election at Paladin voting took place in the school and a group of right-wingers were waiting outside to interfere with the old people as they went in. They might have their voting card for a particular candidate all ready in their pocket, but those on the right would say, 'What have you got there, let's have a look. Ah, but it's not that one you want, it's this one'. And they would alter their voting card right there in the doorway of the school. So the old people had to be closely watched by the young, because they were often senile and easily influenced. They tried to do that to my grandfather, to tell him that his voting card was no good, but someone from our family was to hand and said, 'What do you mean it's no good? I gave him that card myself and it's perfectly valid.' The right was always up to tricks like that.

The region of Paladin and Valduno played a big part in the Revolution of October 1934 because a lot of the arms used by the miners during the uprising were hidden in the church of Valduno. There was a boat which was often referred to as the 'Phantom Ship', but its real name was the *Turquesa*. It came into San Esteban de Pravia, a port at the mouth of the Nalón, at night-time carrying arms and they were hidden in the roof of the church. At the end towards the river, next to the altar, was a small room where the priest kept his things, the vestry, and there was a space above the ceiling and they hid lots of guns there as well as in some haystacks close by. Not many people knew about it, but the whole operation to bring in the guns clandestinely at night was organised by Cornelio who was in touch with the miners' leader, González Peña.[9]

Cornelio, one of the leading Socialists in Asturias, lived in our parish; his father was the sacristan of Valduno and their house was next to the church. He was a short, bulky man; he had little, short legs, broad shoulders and his head was set into his body almost without any neck. Cornelio went to Cuba, like his brother, but for some reason he came back to Valduno. He didn't have much money, just a patch of land which he worked and some cows. He already had a reputation as a Socialist because he sometimes wrote articles for *Avance* and I remember that after one piece, to show how fearless he was, he wrote, 'Signed and underlined with the barrel of a gun'. Whenever there were elections he would engage in propaganda for the left and he himself stood in the local elections; I think he was district councillor on several occasions.

In October 1934, I think it was the third or about then, a lot of men came to Valduno to pick up the weapons. People were saying, 'What are they doing here, all these men?' They had come for the weapons to take to Oviedo, and from there they launched the attack upon the capital with a few guns and dynamite. Most of the men were coalminers and Socialists, because the union was almost exclusively controlled by the Socialist Party. And they were expecting Madrid and Barcelona to rise at the same time, because when they started out the whole thing was supposed to be a general strike, a general armed strike, to take power for the Socialists. But Barcelona didn't reply to the call – there was a bit of fighting and soon order was restored – and the same thing happened in Madrid. Well the Asturians continued fighting and it went on for just short of three weeks and Oviedo almost fell.[10]

There was a man from Premoño, near Paladin, called Jovino, but he was known to everyone as 'Mano Negro' or 'Black Hand': it was probably a nickname he'd had since school, because at school everyone has got one. He came from a very poor family; the only time they ate well was during the chestnut season. Well Mano Negro went off to Oviedo, his clothes all in rags, and when he came back he was wearing new shoes, a new shirt, a suit and gloves. He looked really elegant. 'That's it', he said, 'Oviedo has been taken.' But it wasn't true and one or two days later the whole thing was over.

A few days after the fighting had started at Oviedo they began to form a red army. A Socialist from near Paladin came along; he said, 'OK, I've been sent by the Socialist Party, by the leaders. We must organise a Red Army and everything.'[11] So we held some meetings in the porchway of the bar at Paladin, but since everything was soon over we didn't have time to get a force properly organised. But we were all set to get enrolled, to make up a company. But when those bastards, the regular army, arrived and swamped the whole area the plan was quickly dropped. While the radio was saying, 'Oh, but there is a revolution in Barcelona too', we knew that it wasn't true because we could see the soldiers before our very eyes. People were disheartened, 'Well the other places haven't taken up arms.'

The army came in; there was General Franco, General López Ochoa, Yague and the African Army, the 'Tercio', which is like a foreign legion.[12] The whole of Asturias was invaded in a military operation. When the army column came in from the west, through Aviles, in order to enter Oviedo, they took ordinary civilians and put them as a shield in front. And they advanced like that, with the army behind. Well the miners couldn't fire on their own people. There was a lot of fighting and one woman became famous, a heroine of the October Revolution, Aida de la Fuente, because she stayed at the machine-gun to the very last, until they managed to kill her. And after there was a bloody repression, a real massacre; the 'Tercio' disembowelled women, put hostages in front as they advanced and sowed terror. They killed a lot of people and 30 000 were taken prisoner and beaten up or tortured. In the prisons the soldiers and the civil guards formed a double line, a *'tuba de la risa'*, and to make people talk they would be forced to go down the middle where they were smashed around. When they came out they were half-dead.

During October, when the Republicans or revolutionary miners first entered Oviedo they stormed the Bank of Spain and took millions of pesetas from the vaults. The money was put in milk-churns and hidden in various places. The civil guard swamped all the region round Valduno; all the river plain near Valduno was thick as flies with them. People asked, 'What are they looking for?' Well they were searching for the money everywhere and just next to Paladin in a small wood they discovered some churns in a fox-hole, with perhaps two or three million pesetas inside. And a little higher up some more. At four o'clock in the morning they took Cornelio's brother Constante – the one who had come back from Cuba so wealthy – down next to the cemetery and he must have known where some of the money was hidden. And almost certainly after they had located the money they shot him because two weeks later his body was found miles down-river, almost at the sea. He could only be identified by his shirt, the buttons of his shirt, because he was half-eaten by fish. Cornelio was also arrested and tortured.[13]

One day during that time I was going along the *carrilona*, the cart-track which goes from Paladin to Valduno, when a group of civil guards came up. I was with my father at the time. One of them said, 'Where are you going?' I replied, 'Over there, to the river. I work there.' He said, 'Come here', and they put handcuffs on me and then, 'Let's go, you're coming with us.' My father said, 'But he hasn't done anything.' 'Ah, shut your mouth.' My father went back to Paladin and they led me to the bar at Valduno and there were other men arrested too, and they held us there, all of us handcuffed, alongside the counter. The owner of the bar, a man called Luis, said to the lieutenant in charge, 'I'd like to give them a drink; can you free their hands?' But the lieutenant – his name was Julian Galachi and he came from Navarre – said, 'They can drink as they are, with both hands.' And he could see that my handcuffs were too tight because I kept trying to turn my wrists round inside. He had eyes just like a snake, 'Oh, so it's too tight!', and he got up and with a key locked them even more until they were biting into the flesh. And Luis put a lit cigarette into our mouths and Galachi told him, 'They don't need to smoke, eh.' And the other civil guards were sitting at a table having a snack.

Afterwards Galachi took us along the fields by the river; several of us were in front with him in the rear. They wanted to find the rifles from the *Turquesa*, from the Revolution, which they thought were hidden at Valduno. He said, 'The river is black, but if it became clear we would see your gun, eh? The river must be full of them. Where did you throw yours?' 'Mine? But I haven't got one.' He said, 'Oh yes you have; that's for sure. Oh yes, nobody's got a rifle, but you all have.' In the fields there were straw stacks from after the maize harvest and he made us pull them down. 'Come on, come on, over with that and see if there are any hidden guns.' But there was nothing at all.

Afterwards they took everyone off to the prison in Oviedo. But my father arrived just in time with a letter from a man who lived in the *Palacio*, the big house above Paladin: he was married to the daughter of the house and was some kind of lawyer or magistrate. He said in the note that I came from an honourable family, that he would answer for my behaviour, and so on and so forth. The lieutenant who was in command said, 'OK, we're going to let you go, but you must keep your ears open and if there is anyone round here with a hidden gun you must inform us.' 'Yes, sure', and I cleared off home. But the others, my friend Corcino, his father, a man called Eduardo and his brother Laviano, and the rest were all put in prison.

Many years later, long after the Civil War, I met Corcino in the bar near the bridge at Paladin. He said, 'Hey now, do you remember when they rounded us up?' 'Yes, and you? Did they take you to

Oviedo?' 'Yes', he said, 'they never asked me my name and I was never judged. And you should have seen that prison; they tied my arms to a pole, as if I was on a cross, and hung me from the ceiling like an aeroplane. Sometimes I spent the afternoon like that.' He was laughing. They call that torture the 'aeroplane' in Spain. 'But you were lucky', he told me. And there were thousands of people held like that for seventeen months and they never asked them their name or brought them before the courts. There were some prisons which were veritable torture blocks, like the prison called 'El Hecho' at Mieres, where they committed all kinds of atrocities. They would scatter rice on the ground and make prisoners kneel on it, without trousers, and hold a coin to the wall with their forehead. And some say that they took the bottom out of a chair and they made men sit on it while they burned them with candles underneath. When I was in a concentration camp in France I met an Asturian, a barber, who had had his testicles pulled off with pincers.

Soon after the October Revolution I approached my twentieth birthday and at that age you had two options, either to go into the army or emigrate. Military service was obligatory for all men, but a lot of people didn't want their sons to go into the army because of its bad reputation. I think they were especially afraid they would be sent to fight in North Africa, in Morocco, because a lot came back with malaria and other diseases. So when the time for conscription drew near the peasants would scrape some money together – they might sell a cow or a field – to send the son away to South America. Those who escaped service like that were called *prófugos*; when they got to America they would have to stay a good while because in Spain they were considered to be deserters. There were some, like the son of Feliciano of Paladin, who returned too soon; in his case he was tried and condemned to six months' military service.

But of course that was not the only reason for emigration, thousands would go to America to seek their fortune. There was no work in Asturias and the depression was very severe. Today Spaniards emigrate to Northern Europe but at that time they all left for South America, for Cuba, Mexico, Buenos Aires; a few to Chile or Brazil. There were passenger ships, the *Christopher Columbus*, the *Havana*, the *Maria Christina*, which had regular crossings from La Coruña, Vigo and Gijón. Those who left usually had a contact over there already; there were relatives or other Asturians who would send for them and sometimes pay their ticket. There was a man, originally from Paladin, who lived in Havana at a place called

Guanavacao; he owned a big store and when someone in the region, from Paladin, Valduno or Volgues, wanted to send a child abroad he would post the money for them to come over. Afterwards they would work for him and pay off the debt, the price of the ticket. That system was a kind of exploitation too. A lot of those who emigrated came back with holes in their pockets; the family might have to sell a cow to pay for their return. Yet there were some who made their fortune – a fortune by the standards of the time – and were able to buy a small house and a cow or two.

In our family we had an uncle at Havana, at Cieglo de Avila in the Province of Camaguey; he was my father's brother and my godfather. And I think that there was a time when there were plans to send Enrique over there. But nothing came of it and both he and I faced up to the prospect of our military service; not that we were unwilling to go, because we were kicking our heels about in Paladin. It gave us a chance to get out.

I was posted to Burgos and when I got to the barracks they cut our hair to the scalp, just like convicts. I remember that when I first arrived the conscripts from all the other regions of Spain were already there; it was only the Asturians and the Basques who were late by three days. When the other conscripts saw us come in they said, 'That's the Asturian revolutionaries, they've just come out of prison'. It was not true; I hadn't been in prison. Well they had already issued uniforms to the others and the companies were nearly all formed, but there were four or five of us still in civilian clothes and we had to stay several days like that, dressed in peasant clothes.

There was a Galician soldier, a volunteer who had been in the army for years and he was not even a corporal, just a private, and he began to look for an argument with me and a Basque: 'Yes, you come down from there and you think that you can overturn the government and everything and make a revolution; what do you know about it?' He began to insult us and I got in a fight. The soldiers' beds were just two iron trestles with three planks laid across and a mattress, so I grabbed one of the trestles and as I swung it he half turned and got a terrific blow across the hip. All hell was let loose. I was put under arrest and taken to the guardhouse to be locked up. An officer said to me, 'You know that here, when you enter the barracks, you leave your balls at the gate.' 'Why's that?' 'There's no fighting here; you're lucky that you are not yet in uniform otherwise you'd spend a month in prison.' I spent a day and one night locked up and then rejoined the company.

Discipline was harsh and the conditions pretty rough. What was hard to take at first was the food, it was nauseating. In the morning they gave us what they called coffee, but every time you had a drink it made you run for the toilet, it gave you diarrhoea, just like a purgative. And for dinner, in the canteen, there would be a corporal and five or six men to a table, and they put a pot to share out. But it really stank; the first few days I couldn't stomach anything. They would say, 'Today it's *callos a la Madrileno*', tripes done in the Madrid fashion, and you would see the snout of a cow or a pig floating inside with the hair and all. It was disgusting.

At that time the Civil War was just round the corner: looking back I don't know whether I can honestly say that I saw it coming, but things were very tense. What was surprising was the way in which we were pushed through our training in double-quick time so that we could take our oath to the flag. Normally it would take perhaps four months of training before you were sworn in and in our case we did it just after arriving. I think the reason for that was that elections had been called for 16 February and they expected a lot of trouble; they wanted all the soldiers under the flag. So every day, day in day out without fail, we were taken to the rifle range for firing practice.

During the spring and early summer of 1936 there were so many political demonstrations, threats and armed attacks. At Valladolid there was a big demonstration at the cycle track, the velodrome, and one man was killed. In my company there was a soldier from Valladolid called Balvino who was in the Falange; he said, 'All those trouble-makers, those bastard communists, we're going to kill them all.' There was also trouble in Burgos and you could see the Falangists demonstrating in the streets, they were well organised. Then, as I've said, we conscripts were all sworn under the flag in double haste because trouble was expected. We were also involved in army manoeuvres around Burgos; we had to capture the city. We were sent up into the hills above Burgos, beyond the airfield at a place called 'La Cartuja' where there was a big monastery. From there we went on an exercise to capture the capital, just as if it was the real thing, and inside Burgos there was another force of defenders who prepared artillery barrages against us up in the hillside. And us, the infantry, we had to capture Burgos. Perhaps all that was planned in readiness so they would know how to defend the city because Burgos is a very important military centre, full of regiments.[14]

In my company there were two officers who were left-wing and I heard, years later, that they were both shot in the first days of the Civil War. One of them, a big fat man called Alfredo Ibanez Frias, had a *remplazo*, a batman whose job it was to do all kinds of chores: even if the officer lived off-camp he would go and do domestic tasks, his shopping and so on. Well the *remplazo*, a man called Salvaterra, told me that he was given instructions by Frias that if he ever came to his house during the night for any reason he was to knock at the door in a special way, with a code. The officer was already afraid and almost certainly knew that there was something in the wind.

The captain of the company, a Galician called José Alonso Alonso, was right-wing, a nasty piece of work. Everyone called him *El Hueso*, the slave-driver. Whenever he got an opportunity, when all the company was assembled for a lesson in theory, he always brought politics in and the question of Spain. The name of Spain was treated with total disrespect. He would say, 'When you hear someone speaking well of England it's an Englishman; if you hear someone speak well of France, it's a Frenchman; but sad to say, when one hears someone speak badly of Spain, it's always a Spaniard.' Well he said that the Spanish were not patriotic, but that Spain was the most wonderful country in the world. He would praise it to the skies. And you could see that the other left-wing officer, Pedro Nogal Alonzo, was not at all happy when he spoke like that; it showed in his behaviour and he clearly wished that the captain would shut up and clear off. Alonzo was a very kind man, and fatherly towards us. He was already old, at least fifty-five, and he had spent his whole life in the army just to reach the grade of lieutenant. We all regarded him as left-wing and he too was shot when the right seized control in Burgos.

I worked in the steam laundry with two other soldiers, one from Santander called Martin, a religious type who made me visit all the churches of Burgos, and another from a poor peasant family near Burgos. The peasant told me, 'I volunteered for the army because there's not enough to eat at home. My parents have a bit of land, but not enough to feed everyone, so I went into the army.' And in June they began to give summer leave and his came due. He said, 'Listen, if I go right now I can't help my parents with the harvest, it's too early. If you can take my place I can go later.' I wasn't due any leave but said, 'All right, if we can arrange it; as far as I'm concerned the quicker I can get away the better.' So we went to see the officer and he said that it was in order, I only had to have the agreement of the peasant and I could go. I was given a train ticket to get me home.

Waiting for the train at Burgos station I chanced on my brother Enrique who was also coming home on leave from his regiment at Logrono. When we reached Valduno my father met us at the station.

The two of us were in uniform and I remember people saying to him, 'You must be proud to have two sons as soldiers.' But we were a terrible sight, a real eye-sore!

I don't think that in general people expected the Civil War to break out when it did. There had been lots of rumours but nobody took them seriously, in spite of the tensions which existed. But then we had been living with that tension for a long time. What is strange is that so many soldiers were given their summer leave of forty-five days, like myself and Enrique. Perhaps the rebel generals intended to start the coup d'état a little later because, as it was, they found themselves with half the soldiers at home. But then there was the assassination of Castillo and of Calvo Sotelo so perhaps the rebels found their plans overtaken by events.[15]

I had forty-five days leave at Paladin and three days before it was due to end the Civil War erupted.

3 The War in Asturias – David

When the coup d'état took place on 18 July word soon got about through the press and radio.[1] Enrique and I didn't know what to do because according to military instructions, which are read out to all soldiers, if something abnormal like that occurs you must rejoin your regiment as soon as possible. But I couldn't go to Burgos because the trains were not running; we were completely cut off and couldn't go anywhere. In that situation you were supposed to place yourself at the disposal of the nearest government authority, so Enrique and I went to report to the townhall of our commune at Santullano. 'We are soldiers on leave.' 'Oh', they said, 'there's nothing we can do about that, you'll have to go to Trubia. You'll find out there sure enough what to do.'

At Trubia, which is only five miles from Paladin, there is an important ordnance factory and there is always a company or detachment of soldiers to guard the place; they belong to an Oviedo regiment called the *Milan*. When we got there we found the captain in charge and he told us that the government, the Minister of War Casares Quiroga, had disbanded the army. Like that the soldiers could disobey the rebel commanders and stay out of their hands. 'Well', said the captain, 'you can do what you like; you can stay here, you can go home, or you can go to the front – as you like.' Well there were already a good number of men in the Trubia factory, they were sleeping in the magazine of the works waiting for something to be organised, and we were unsure what to do. However, at that moment we came across Cornelio Fernandez, the Socialist leader from Valduno, and he said, 'I'll take you both as an escort, as a bodyguard, but you can keep your uniforms on because that looks much better.' We both wanted to get rid of our uniforms. Well Cornelio was just driving around from one war committee to another in a big American car, a Chrysler Imperial, which he had requisitioned, trying to look important but not actually doing anything to help organise the war effort. But one day we went up to the Oviedo front and I managed to get away from him.

What happened when the generals began the uprising was that Aranda managed to take Oviedo for the rebels. During the first day or two the news reports said that the military had risen but that a lot of the officers had remained faithful to the Republic and that reassured a lot of people. It must have been on the very day after the rebellion broke out in Africa, on 18 July, that I was on the highway which goes from Galicia to Oviedo, just across the river from Valduno, when lorries came past full of civil guards. They raised their clenched fists and shouted, 'Long live the Republic!' But that was a trick, an organised plan. Normally the civil guard are scattered about in small towns and villages; there are barracks or *quartel* where four or five live and from there they go out and patrol the countryside. Well Aranda wanted to concentrate them all in Oviedo and they got through like that, shouting, 'Long live the Republic! Everyone must defend the Republic!' We were not too worried by events because we thought, 'Crikey, if the civil guard are on our side this time there's no problem, no danger.' And from all the west of Asturias, the region towards Galicia – Luanco, Grado and elsewhere – the civil guards passed through into Oviedo. In the mining region the people were more suspicious and at Sama they cut the road and wouldn't let them through, but the great majority of the civil and assault guards got into Oviedo. Aranda was reputed to be a Republican, a freemason and a friend of Prieto, the General Secretary of the Socialist Party, and that lulled people into a false sense of security. But we were duped and there was Aranda and a big force entrenched in Oviedo.

Well after riding about in the car with Cornelio for two or three days, doing nothing in particular, I thought to myself, 'This can't go on.' One day we went up to the 'circle', the Oviedo front, when we were stopped by a group of miners at a place called Biedes. They said they were not very many to guard the position so I said, 'Right, I'm staying here' and Cornelio agreed, although he still kept Enrique and Vicente, another soldier on leave, as escorts.

At Biedes I found myself with a group of about twenty miners. We were just below a big mountain on the outskirts of Oviedo called Naranco, at a crossroads, and there we mounted guard day and night. They said, 'It's through here that Aranda is likely to try and break out, to open a route from Oviedo to Aviles.' The men at Biedes were nearly all old miners; they had already taken part in the Revolution in 'thirty-four. They were real experts in the use of dynamite and they showed me how to use it; they said, 'If it's a lorry you throw a packet like this'; there might be three sticks of dynamite in a bundle. 'If it's a car you throw one and a half sticks or two sticks.' There were little bundles already prepared which you carried in small bags. You had to be very careful because the fuses were very short, all timed at around thirteen seconds: 'You've just got time to light the fuse and you throw it.' I had a terrible headache all the time; the miners said, 'Oh, but that's the dynamite; it's nothing, it always gives you a headache.'

Those miners were very simple men but very determined; they believed in what they were doing with an unshakeable faith; it was fantastic. I liked them a lot because I, for example, was twenty-one at the time and those men of forty-five or fifty would speak to you as if you were their own age; they treated you like an equal. And they were euphoric; they had real faith. I've often heard it said that revolutionaries make war because they love to rebel for its own sake, because they like discord; it's not true. They were more conscious of the serious implications of what they were doing than anyone else could be. They said, 'Here we are staking our whole future; we're risking our freedom.' It was truly magnificent: all or nothing.

I stayed at Biedes for about two weeks, but nothing ever happened. We just stayed on the spot, sleeping fully clothed, in the open or on the floor of a small dance-hall in a nearby bar. But one day Cornelio appeared and said, 'You know that the Anarchists are destroying all the churches in the region; they come and burn them down. Today they are planning to go to the church of Trasmonte in the Las Regueras; we must go and protect it.' What a military exploit for Republican soldiers, protecting a church! Well we agreed and I went with my friend Corsino, from near Paladin, and with José Manuel (who today denies that he was ever in the war because he's a fool and fell victim to what happened after the Civil War when nobody wanted to take responsibility for what they had done). And we went at night in cars requisitioned by the militias up to Trasmonte which is only seven miles away. When we got there we found a lot of refugees, old people, women and children, who had already fled before the forces of Franco which were advancing from Galicia. They had come from the west of Asturias, from around Grado and further off, Cabruñana and those parts. They were crowded round the church and were looking for somewhere to sleep. We told them. 'All right, the Anarchists of Gijón want to burn the church and we have come to protect it, so now it's safe and you can go inside.' So we stayed for a while and the refugees went into the church and settled down to sleep.

Corsino said, 'Even so, we should look and see what the priests have in the way of wine, what they use to put in the cup at mass.' And we had a look; there was Malaga wine and it was good. And we respected everything, nothing was looted. But the Anarchists must have known there were militias protecting the church because they never turned up; there was no trouble there. And I think it was a good thing because to destroy buildings like that, old churches which are very fine, is a thing which only people without any sort of values can do.

I stayed with the miners at Biedes for two weeks and absolutely nothing happened; there was no attempt to break out. And we began to realise that the serious threat was not from Aranda but from the Francoist forces, the column advancing from Galicia which was getting nearer all the time.[2] Everyone was saying, 'What we have to do is stop that column.' So Corsino, José Manuel and I said, 'Well what are we doing here? Let's go down there.' So we volunteered for the western front and were sent up to La Espina.

At that time there was no proper military command, just a kind of freelance militia. We were all volunteers and groups were formed named after the leader, for example 'El grupo de Piñón' or 'El grupo de Otero. There were old men, young kids, women, stonemasons and miners – a real crazy mix – and with no proper uniform. People were dressed in their working clothes, in blue overalls. And we went up the road towards Galicia to take on regular army units equipped with rifles, machine-guns and artillery.[3] All I had was a hunting gun and the others were equipped with anything they could lay their hands on: there was no standard equipment and everyone had to find their own bullets, otherwise they went short. I was with one man who had a really magnificent rifle, a Remington; like the one Buffalo Bill had. There were a lot of guns which were captured when the Simancas barracks at Gijón fell and there were even weapons which had been hidden during the October '34 Revolution and which began to resurface, but in general there was a real shortage. At the front there were occasions when there was a line of combatants in the trenches and behind a second reserve line of men without weapons. They were waiting to pick up the guns of those who fell dead. Yes, for a long while it was like that in Asturias, hunting guns and dynamite.

When we got to Grado, which is on the road to Galicia, they were organising battalions to go up to the front. Next to a garage I saw a man called Demetrio from near Paladin who was sharpening a long piece of iron on a huge grinding stone, the kind which you see in farmyards and which you turn with a handle. I said, 'What are you doing with that?' 'I'm sharpening this to make a sword.' It was just a length of iron and the sparks were flying. 'There's not many guns', he said, 'but I'm going to be well armed, eh?'

In Grado things began to get well-organised and I was put in a group led by a tailor from there called Piñón. We set off and arrived after nightfall up in a mountain called Espina and the leader decided that we should go down into a pass and wait. We were right at the bottom in a cleft between two peaks and we stayed in position there for two or three days. All we had to eat was a helmetful of nuts and one leg of ham between ten or twelve men, but the local wine was clear and strong.

To our right was positioned a company of assault guards, a kind of Republican police, and one morning at about ten or eleven o'clock we saw them high above making a signal to us with a flag. Then bullets began to fly, pinging all round us. Then we saw that the assault guards were telling us to retreat, but there were some who said, 'Those bastards up there; perhaps they are not really on our side. We'll stay put.' The assault guards were retreating because they were in a much better position to see than us and the enemy was in the process of outflanking us on the other side of the hill. By the time we realised what was going on the assault guards had retreated and disappeared from sight and we were getting trapped in on our left. One of those in command said, 'OK, let's go; we're pulling out', and we began to move back as they fired on us. Bullets were flying everywhere. There was one exposed spot, a narrow passage, where we had to get out one by one. A man made a sign to us from behind a stone wall when to make our run. 'Wait till they have fired and then move!'

Well we managed to get out and we went up into the mountains during an August heatwave; we did twenty kilometres like that in the mountains. I remember coming to a place called Santa Eufemia; there's a little chapel there, and it was as hot as hell and my feet were hurting because my boots were too tight. We asked some peasant women to give us something to eat and drink and they came with big jugs of milk. For that they were magnificent – perhaps they would have done the same for the Francoists, eh? – but we were well treated. All there is to eat up in those mountains is ham and bread, but since we had been eating ham for three days all we wanted was the milk. Where we come from we are big milk-drinkers. A peasant woman gave me a big glass of milk and I drank half and poured the rest in my boots. She asked, 'Why did you pour it into your boots?' 'Because the boots are too small and I think that my feet are going to explode!' 'Oh, my poor son', said the little old woman. We were armed men and you couldn't say that they were afraid. No, quite frankly, they were helping us.

From there we finally came down near the town of Salas and there was one hell of a débâcle going on. Between Salas and Cornellana there is a long, flat stretch of road, the road from Galicia to Oviedo, and there were hundreds of people fleeing from Salas. There was chaos and some militia men who had stopped in the town were seizing the opportunity to loot the shops; they had emptied everything into the streets. There was an enclosure for the horses of the militia and I and Aniseto from Valduno went and took the last one, a black horse which had cast a shoe on a foreleg. Aniseto had seen an abandoned machine-gun and he said we ought to take it, so we both mounted the horse along with the gun. I was riding in front with the machine-gun, which had the tripod missing, lying across the horse's back. Well that poor horse couldn't move very fast and sometimes to make it shift a bit faster I lifted the gun and let it bang down onto his back. But the poor animal was limping.

We got away as fast as we could and after a while we reached Cornellana and there everyone was fleeing in panic; it was a real stampede. People were shouting, 'The column is coming! We are being encircled!' At Cornellana we found the tailor Piñón who had organised our group in Grado and when he saw us he began crying like a baby: 'I thought you were all killed in the pass, that none would come back alive.' It's true some of them didn't get out alive. He was babbling away.

At that moment there was some dispute as to what we should do. A lot of militiamen were saying, 'We'll go to Oviedo; we'll go and take Oviedo.' They spoke as if they were just going to walk over there and take it, like plucking an apple from a tree. 'We'll go to Oviedo and take it; we'll sort this end out afterwards.' From there Oviedo must have been a good eighty miles. But others said, 'There are already enough people at Oviedo. We've got to hold back the fascist column; it must be stopped here.' There was a miner there called Otero who was quite a big number, a political leader in the Socialist Party in Sama de Langreo, and he said, 'Listen comrades we must not go back to Oviedo. We've got to get organised and go up into the mountains: they must be stopped.'[4] There was real chaos; there was still plenty of wine and drink about and you could see lots of drunk militiamen and from time to time one of them would fire a shotgun in the air from the middle of the crowd. It was pretty dangerous.

Those in our group said, 'What shall we do?' 'We'll go with Otero.'

So we dropped Piñón because he had shown us he was useless and joined up with Otero. The leader put Aniseto of Valduno in charge of our group from the Las Regueras district. Aniseto knew that I had been in the army at Burgos and had been trained to use an automatic and he said, 'The first automatic rifle we get hold of will be for you.' I said, 'You had better find it first before making any promises.' There we were with our odd collection of rabbit-guns, old rifles, a Remington; bits and pieces.

From Cornellana we climbed into the mountains all afternoon, up to a summit at Santa Eufemia near Salas, and established a line there during the night. I remember that a professional soldier, all dressed up in uniform with stars and everything, arrived at dusk. He was drunk as a lord and asked if there was anything to drink; he wasn't concerned about the situation at all, he was completely drunk. The men began to murmur, 'That one, eh?' Everyone was suspicious of the professional soldier.[5] All he did before leaving was to say, 'Right, you place your line along here.' We were concealed just below the summit of the mountain and it was decided to position an advance guard just over the top to watch out for the fascists if they approached.

We were sleeping under a huge beech tree when suddenly – bang! bang! bang! – the Francoists began firing at us as if we were rabbits. The idiots who were in the lookout must have fallen asleep or they didn't see the others who had managed to get up to the top of the mountain and were firing down on us. There was pandemonium but we managed to get out. I was bleeding from below the jaw and someone said, 'I'll tell you what, the wound is very deep.' 'No, it's OK.' 'No, it's too deep, you'll have to go and get it patched up.' I was taken to a first aid post next to the road; it was very badly organised. They said, 'We can't do anything here, the wounded have to go to Grado.' So I was taken by car to the hospital at Grado which had been set up in a house requisitioned from a marquis. And who should I find in the ward but my brother Enrique. I said, 'But what on earth are you doing here?' He said, 'What am I doing here? A tree fell on top of me!' He had been with a field-gun up in the mountains, firing on the advancing column, when a small Republican aeroplane – one of those light aircraft which are used for advertising, they fly about with a long banner advertising goods – mistook them for the Francoists and began to fire upon them. It dropped some small bombs and one fell alongside the gun, tearing up a tree which came down on top of the soldiers. Enrique was black and blue all over with cuts and bruises. I said, 'Is everyone all right?' He said, 'No, there's one of the gunners lying over there who is on the way out.' There were so many wounded in the hospital that they were sending the less serious cases home; they came in for treatment now and again. So after I had been seen to I was sent back home to Paladin; that must have been in September.

The Civil War had only been going a few weeks and I began to see how fast people can become corrupted in such a situation. As soon as the war broke out war committees began to spring up everywhere, it was almost spontaneous, in all the towns and villages.[6] There was one section of each committee which looked after military affairs and another, the *abastos*, which administered the food supply. The *abastos* had to find supplies for the soldiers as well as those who were working, the ordinary people in the locality who were in need of food. The committee would send out militiamen to requisition from the farmers and others – potatoes from one, a pig from another, rabbits, a barrel of cider, and so on. They were paid with an IOU, a voucher which would one day be reimbursed for money by the Republic.

The war had only been going for perhaps six weeks and I could see that things were deteriorating; there were those who had been unimpeachable and very honest before the war, but the moment they were in a position of responsibility and controlled sums of money or food supplies they began to be corrupted. For example, I went to the committee at Valduno with my friend Aniseto; they had set up a supply centre in the tax-collectors house, but it was more like a bar inside. We were asked, 'Do you want something to eat?' 'Why, have you got something?' 'Yes, we've just got a meal ready.' We said all right and sat down and the place was full of women; they were women I had never seen before; I don't know where they came from. Aniseto and I were given a huge meal and we talked to the girls and we realised that the whole thing was rotten, that the place was a kind of brothel. We said, 'What's going on here?' Those who were running things began to make excuses: 'Oh, these are honest folk; that girl over there has come to . . .', and so on. It was a good job that Corsino was not there but still up at the front; he would have given that lot a burst of the machine-gun! Yes, to see that after only a few weeks was quite disillusioning; to see people losing their honesty right at the start.

While I was recovering at Paladin I worked under the orders of the war committee, helping with the requisitioning. The committee received an order to round up all the guns it could from the huntsmen. A list was drawn up of all those who were known to have guns and they were all reactionaries, because those who were left-wing couldn't afford to own a gun. I went with some other militiamen around the villages and in one place we came to the house of Juan de Valle who was right-wing but a good man and very likeable. And we thought, 'My God he loves his gun more than his children; why should we take it away from him?' We arrived at his door and presented the order of the committee; he said, 'Oh, you've made a trip for nothing, my gun isn't here. It needed repairing and I sent it to Oviedo.' 'All right, that's OK. Your gun is in Oviedo.' We didn't want to take it from him. Even if he had said, 'I've hidden it; I don't want it messed up', we would have let him keep it because he was a stout, honest man. And nearly everywhere we went it was the same story: there were no guns. They were all people we knew, local folk and we didn't collect a single gun.

A few days later I was told, 'We have to go and requisition potatoes for the army', and blow me if another didn't say, 'I know, let's try your uncle.' My Uncle Benjamin lived at Casuco, a hamlet just down the road, between Paladin and Valduno. He was a brother of my mother and a wealthy man; he had married a woman who had lots of money and land. He rented out land to poor peasants and exploited them through the *comuña* system. He was very right-wing, one of the *caciques* who went hunting boar and voted for the right. On top of that he was a real skinflint. Well the organisers of the war committee asked me if it bothered me to go to his house. I said, 'Listen, it's not me who is giving the orders round here, it's you. I'm not afraid of him; what difference can it make to me if he's my uncle?' So I went off with a horse to his place and he came out: 'What do you want?' I said, 'Listen, you must give me five hundred kilos of potatoes for the war committee.' In all we had to get in three or four tons of potatoes from various neighbours. 'What!', he said, 'And is it you, my own nephew, coming to demand this? Aren't you ashamed?' 'But it's not me who is giving you orders; I've never asked anything from you in my life, it's the war committee.' 'Well you tell them my potatoes aren't lifted yet.' 'Well it would be better for you if you dug them up because if not they're going to come and help themselves.' Of course he dug them up himself!

I stayed at Paladin for a short while in September but soon the Galician column captured Grado and the whole surrounding region and there was a real stampede to get out. My parents took refuge near Aviles.[7] It was then, because of the disorder and the Francoists getting closer to Oviedo, that they began to speak of a general militarisation, the setting up of a regular army. Up until then we had all fought as volunteers and there was a real mixture of people in the groups, young, old, women, all types. It was a bit anarchic. For example, there were moments when a Socialist militia was in a certain area and they would say to an Anarchist group, 'We must go over and relieve a militia because they have been at the front for a long while.' They would say, 'Oh no, we are not going to relieve those.' You see there was no discipline. So by an order of the government the forces were organised in a regular way, with battalions, companies and commanding officers. When that happened there were a lot of soldiers, especially the older men who were say fifty years old, who said, 'Right, if we are to be militarised I'm going home. I don't want to be a regular. I want to defend the Republic, but as a volunteer, not as a soldier.'[8]

There were a lot of women at the front, they carried rifles and fought just like the men. But it was decided that their place was in the canteens or hospitals, not in the trenches, and they were sent away from the front. There were also young kids and they were also ordered to leave. In my company there was a young boy and when he was told to go home he said, 'No, I don't want to.' 'But yes; we can't let you stay here.' The poor kid was really sad, he just didn't want to go home, so we made a collection among ourselves and gave him the money. 'Here you are, go off home with this. When you are a little bigger, if the war is still going, you can come back.' And he went, but he didn't want to.

When the order to militarise came, Corsino and I went to a recruiting centre in Aviles to get enrolled. From there we were sent to Gijón to join a brigade which was in need of men, the Maxim Gorky. Since Asturias was completely cut off from the rest of Spain they were unable to equip us with proper uniforms so we were still dressed in workers' overalls, but everyone was given an armband. There had been moments during the early battles when we couldn't tell who was on our side, it was a real mess. But after being reorganised we could recognise each other more easily. We were now regulars, on a pay of three hundred pesetas a month. Wherever possible the commanding officers were former professional soldiers who had remained faithful to the Republic, but soon they set up a military academy near Gijón for the rapid training of those who were promoted from the ranks.

Corsino and I had only just reached the barracks and joined up with the Maxim Gorky when, the very same afternoon, it was said that there was a shortage of volunteers for the front at Escamplero. The Francoist column had already passed Grado and was pushing along the Nalón Valley towards the arms factory at Trubia, in fact right through our back yard. Escamplero is up in the mountains not far from Paladin. Corsino said, 'That's down our way; let's go.' We left Gijón the same night; we had only arrived that afternoon and we were already off to the front again.

We were a short while up at Escamplero and then we were moved a small distance to the village of Biedes and there we were stuck in the trenches, full of mud and shit, for sixty-nine days. Nearly all the time that I was at the front I was with a Frenchman called Charles Chapuis, a good old boy who had worked in a circus. He would say, 'Me, I've come here to fight', because he was left-wing. He called me 'Chico'. 'Chico', he would say, 'you stick with me and you'll see how we make war.' He was very likeable; he could have been my father and he certainly knew how to fight. One day a whole consignment of rifles arrived; we were told they were Mexican but I think that they were really Czech, they were really good guns.[9] Chapuis had just an old gun and when he saw the new rifles he threw it away and grabbed one. The commander, Tomás, said, 'Watch it, wait till we give you one because we have to record the number.' He replied, 'This one is mine, nobody is going to take it away from me.' 'What! We don't want any indiscipline here.' 'I'm here because I choose to be; I'm French and nobody can force me to stay. If you don't like it I'm clearing off.' 'OK, keep your rifle, but let me take the number down.' My God, he was pleased as punch with that gun.

We were dug into trenches in a field of beetroot and down below the line was a meadow with a little spring. And Charles Chapuis would say, 'I'm going to have a wash; if you see the enemy taking aim you fire, OK?' 'All right.' Well he would go down there every morning, take off his shirt, and his bald head shining like a calabash. And as soon as he was in the hollow the others would start firing and me at them. 'Fire! Chico; fire!,' he would shout.

From time to time we would exchange shots with the other side like that or we would shout across to the other trenches, sing songs or hurl insults. We would call out, 'Gallegos!', and they replied, 'Asturianos!' The Francoist army facing us had marched in from the west, from Galicia, and the Galicians have a bad name in Asturias, so we would taunt them about that. You see the Galicians from the coast, the fishermen and sailors, were on the left; for example, the Anarchists were very strong around La Coruña. But those from inland, the peasants, were most of them on Franco's side. And it was always the Galicians who came as blacklegs to Asturias to break the strikes in the mines and on the railway. After the 1934 October Revolution when there were so many men in prison it was they who came to take their jobs. So there was a traditional animosity and we would shout insults at each other across the lines.[10] They cried, 'Asturianos! Communistas!'; they said we all wanted to be deputies and to be dictators. And we would say, what if we were hungry and they owned everything which we desired? And then one of them might ask, 'And you, where do you come from?' Of course we would never say where we really came from; if I was from Paladin I would reply, 'I'm from Grado.' Then we would ask them the same thing, 'And you?' One time there was a man on the other side whose voice I recognised when he said his name was Reinelio. When I said I knew who he was he replied, 'No, no, no, you've made a mistake, that's not me.'

Most of the time we were stuck in the trenches but one day the '*El Rapin*' battalion was engaged and it was trapped and we could see from our position that the Moors, the North African regulars, were coming up in force to attack them. We said, 'Christ! The reinforcements will massacre all the men down there'; so we were sent to make a diversion. It was four or five o'clock in the afternoon and three or four men were left behind to guard the trenches. Since I had no soles to my boots and the meadows were deep in water the captain said to me, 'OK, you stay here.' But there was one soldier, Jesús del Carucheo, who whenever he had to go into battle would piss and shit himself and he said, 'I'll give you my boots.' I said, 'Hand them over.' I put them on and went with Charles Chapuis. We were all loaded down with hand-grenades which were clanking away as we ran and in a meadow I dropped a grenade and turned round to find it. But the enemy were firing on us and Chapuis shouted, 'Chico! Chico! Leave the grenades, leave the grenades; run!' We climbed up to a little rocky hump which had some bushes and undergrowth and we got behind a rock and began firing on the column which was coming to attack our battalion. The battalion managed to disengage but the little mound behind which we were concealed was in the middle of an open, flat space and afterwards we couldn't get out because they had positioned a machine-gun. But at night they sent men from our side to guide us out; we heard a whisper in the dark, 'Pssst! This way', and we got out one by one. It must have been three or four o'clock in the morning when we reached the trenches.

After a while everyone began to get a bit demoralised; we had been in the trenches for too long and the food was very bad or there wasn't enough. Behind the lines the battalion had a kitchen, a canteen set up in a house, and there were women to cook. But there was never enough food, so there were always groups of us going off at night, without permission, to get hold of eggs, a cow or a pig. And we were filthy and tired of being in the trenches. And somebody would say, 'Oh, there's such and such a battalion which is always near the coast, over there near Aviles, in a place where the enemy will never try to attack. They can come up here and replace us so that we can get a bit of rest.' We were fed up with it. In the end our commander said, 'OK, there is only one thing to do, a group of you can go and see the general commander at Onievra. But no playing at silly buggers, eh! You can put your case calmly.' So a group of representatives from our battalion went to see the commander at HQ. 'Listen, we are covered in lice; we've been in the trenches two months and it's about time that we had a break.' He replied, 'We'll do what we can; a battalion will have to replace you but they are all at the front.' In other words here were no reserves. But in the end, at Christmas, they sent a battalion, the *Azana* or the *Sangre de Octubre*, to take over our positions and we went down to Gijón for one night. But almost immediately we went back again to replace another battalion so they could come down in turn and everyone had a little time off for Christmas.

When we got to Gijón we were covered in mud and our clothing was in a bad state. It was cold and we asked for warmer clothing, but there wasn't any to be had. And there was one soldier who said, 'I know what we can do, we'll go to the Calle Corrida (one of the principal streets of Gijón), and we'll take the coats from those who come out of the theatres; they are not up in the mountains, at the front.' I didn't go and take anything from anybody but there were some who went. 'Hey you!' they said, 'where do you work?' 'In an office', or 'In a hospital.' 'OK, you don't have need of your coat.' They came back with leather jackets or good coats: the next day there was a real stink in the press.

One of those in a position of command in our battalion was called Fernando; he owned a carpentry works in Llanes. And there were some men in our unit from the same town who said, 'That bloke is a bastard; he was friendly with all the Falangists in Llanes.' So when we were at Gijón for that one night on leave we all got together in a bar; the man was removed from command and we had to find someone to replace him. And because I had been at Burgos someone said, 'But there is a professional soldier here, Granda.' 'No, I don't want to take the job; but there's another regular here.' 'Who?' 'Acelino.' Acelino must have been about sixty years old and had served ten years in the foreign legion. He said, 'I'd like to do it but I can't write and do things like that.' I said, 'I'll help you; you command and I'll take care of the paperwork.' So it was agreed, but it was rather funny because Acelino was a very small man, but he took himself very seriously in his job and was very proud.

After our one night in town we went to the front and not long afterwards the Republicans planned a large-scale offensive. The Francoist forces, the Galician column, had forced a passage right up the Nalón Valley and entered Oviedo on 17 October. The only way in and out of the city was along a tiny road which passed through the mountains above Paladin: lorries with supplies rolled along it day and night, without stop, into Oviedo. The plan was to cut the corridor with a pincer movement; some forces would come in from the south side of the Nalón, near Trubia, and the others would push from our positions at Escamplero on the north. And we were to join up and cut the road.[11]

The attack was to begin at about ten minutes to five in the morning and just before the advance we were given three days' rations; half a slab of chocolate and some bread. And, blow me, I was so hungry that, like the others, I scoffed the lot in one go and just after it was announced, 'You must not eat too much because if you get a stomach wound it's very dangerous.' We were given a measure of spirits which we called '*salta parapetos*' or 'over the top'. It was so awful it would drive you crazy and you would go anywhere after that! Well just before five o'clock we all sank a big shot of that and over the top we went.

Where my company had to attack, at the Pico del Arca, there was a little plain, flat as a table, and at the far end a little rocky hill surrounded with barbed wire which was the enemy position. Well the commanders of our regiment – it was a Communist regiment – decided that there would be a flag for the company which put up the best show in the attack. It was a way of encouraging us, like a competition. Everyone wanted to win that flag. The commander of our company said that it was us who would attack the position at the end of the plain. It was suicidal to go in there, real madness, but it was us who took the risk and we set off towards the enemy positions.

I was in the leading group that went in to cut the barbed wire and I had cut through several strands, with the others coming up from behind ready to pass through, when there was an explosion. The enemy had heard us and everything let rip. I think that the very first shot which they fired got me: I went to raise myself from the ground and 'Bang!', I got hit in the left leg. There was a soldier there called Boall, a former policeman, who dragged me behind a boulder and the real battle began. The place was full of injured soldiers screaming, 'Mama! Aiee! Aiee!'. The weather was terrible and I was pinned down there for five hours by the enemy fire. It wasn't until ten o'clock that they managed to drive the Nationalists back over the hillock and could begin to get the wounded out. I was taken by stretcher to the trenches, but the first-aid men could do nothing for me, nothing at all. From that point there was at least two kilometres of mountains to descend by mere sheeptracks and they carried me down to the road where big lorries, which had been requisitioned as ambulances, were waiting. When the medical aids saw any case which was too serious to wait they were sent off immediately in small cars and one said, 'This one can't wait till the lorry is full, go and put him in a car.' My leg was – puagh! – all in pieces and they took two big pieces of wood from the canteen of the general staff which was close by, and placed one on each side like a splint. And I was taken down, lying in the back seat of the car, to the hospital at Aviles.

When we arrived I was lifted out in a courtyard; I remember it was concrete and it was there that you were undressed before going up into a ward. But I was wearing blue overalls which were still loaded up with handgrenades and as I was lowered down one of them rolled away across the concrete. The two stretcher bearers dropped me in the yard and ran off like nobody's business. 'But you silly buggers! It won't explode', I shouted. I had not lost consciousness. 'It won't explode; you have to lift the pin first.' What a carry on. Then someone came and removed the grenades and I was taken up to a bedroom. A doctor came and had a look at me; he said, 'Puagh! There's nothing that we can do, no, nothing.' Well when he said that I looked at my leg; it was black, completely black. My God, terrible.

Apart from nuns, who changed the beds and so on, most of the nursing of the wounded was done by girls who belonged to the Communist-Socialist Youth. They were always very vigilant and if they saw that a wounded soldier was not being treated properly they reported it to a defence committee. That was because everyone distrusted the doctors; it was said that some doctors were fascists and up to no good, that if they found the chance they would amputate a leg where it wasn't necessary or let someone die deliberately. Perhaps that was true in some places, but it wasn't like that everywhere. And I remember a girl who came and looked at my leg; she said, 'It smells bad already'. So she fetched the doctor who came and said, 'Well he must be got ready.' I thought they were going to operate to patch me up, but when I regained consciousness, blow me, I began to feel for my leg with my hand and – bouahhh! – there was nothing. That is when the dramatics began; I began to throw everything in reach, everything on the night-table. One male nurse, Abilio, was hit by a glass: he said, 'But he's gone crazy with the ether, with the chloroform; we'll have to tie him down; he's gone mad.' I was crazy because I realised they had cut my leg off. Well they tied me down to the bed until I had calmed down a bit.

The wound began to get badly infected and it stank the place out so badly that they had to transfer me down into the yard, on the concrete. Before the war the morgue was there, but alongside they had put up a kind of hut made of planks to receive those who had gangrene, because they reeked so badly. There were a few beds there and the place was full of bloodstains. There were four of us there with gangrene. One of the soldiers came from Santander, but his friends came, got him out through a window, and took him off in a car to Santander so he could die at home. Because that's how it was, they were just leaving us to die. They gave us something for the pain and said there was nothing to be done. But Enrique had been in the same battle as I, with the artillery, and he heard that I was in hospital, and so he turned up with my father. Well when they saw how things were, that the people in the hospital had abandoned the three of us with gangrene to die, they kicked up a fuss and got the wheels turning because just after that the doctors really began to look after us.

There were three of us in the shed; myself, Ricardo and Benavides. Ricardo had an arm shattered by a grenade and had to have it amputated because of gangrene. He was a Galician, a bad lot and a thief to boot, but the other, Benavides, became a good friend of mine and years later was to help me a lot when I was starving in the French concentration camps. Before the war Benavides had worked in the Herrero Bank in Oviedo, but afterwards he was sent to run a small branch out in the country. But he had a bust-up because the left there, the Communists or the Socialists, wanted to control the bank and they were up to no good and, as director, he wasn't having it. He said, 'In that case I'll go to the front!' And he did. But he had no military experience; he had never touched a rifle or revolver or anything like that in his life. One day during an attack someone showed him how to throw a grenade, 'Look, you pull out the pin; you wait a little. Don't throw it immediately because they can chuck it back.' So he took a grenade, pulled the pin, and 'Bang!', he blew his hand to pieces.

A nurse and a nun would come nearly every day to the shed where we were and snip away the rotten flesh with scissors, until the wound was clean. I had my leg amputated near the knee and every day they cut away a little basin of flesh. But we were not put to sleep or given an anaesthetic. There was a nun, an old woman called Sister Françoise, who would stay with us all night: nobody else dare come in there because of the stench. And she would stay there all the time; you could hear her frock as she moved about or she would often sit and hold my hand, or come and give an injection. I think that she was a fine person. We would swear like troopers, but she never said anything. Well the nurses didn't give up and in the end they won; they stopped the gangrene of all three of us. Afterwards we were taken back up into an ordinary ward and given the best food because, as they said, 'You have been saved from a very nasty thing.'

One day the surgeon who had carried out the amputations came along with an assistant surgeon and a woman with a typewriter. The doctor said, 'Well, do you know what you had?' 'Yes, gangrene.' 'Yes, but which kind? It was gaseous gangrene. It was very difficult to keep you alive, but now you are saved you must tell us everything about your treatment. Because we didn't expect to save you and we've managed to save a bit of you, eh? And since the treatment worked so well we want to take notes so that other hospitals can be informed.' We were like guinea-pigs. Well what they had done, because there was no disinfectant available, was to treat our wounds with petrol and it proved very successful in stopping the gangrene. But it burned the healthy tissue, so they made up a pomade with a petrol base and it was that which had such an amazing success. As a result our wounds began to heal.

That was about April or May of 1937. Then, since a new offensive was being planned, we were told that we would have to be moved to Santander because the hospital at Aviles was close to the front and would be needed. So we were taken by lorry to Pola de Sera and on from there by train to Santander. There we were put in a casino, the 'King's Casino', which had been turned into a hospital. In Aviles the three of us with gangrene had been a little spoiled; we would say, 'Oh, it's really hurting badly', and they would give us a painkiller called 'Panphoton' and shots of morphine. Well the first nights we were at Santander the nurses would not give us injections so that we could get to sleep. We were in real agony, but after a while things got better.

I had only been a few weeks at Santander and it was then, it must have been around May 1937, that I saw the *España* sunk, a big Nationalist battleship which had been one of the best in the Spanish fleet. From the balcony of the hospital you could look out over the port and one day an English merchant ship began to enter. We were all cheering because it was very difficult for any ship to get through the fascist blockade to bring in arms and food. But all of a sudden we heard two warning shots fired by the *España* and the merchant ship stopped, hesitated and then began to manoeuvre to turn round. Then two light aeroplanes flew out from a field near Santander called Albericias and we saw them making out toward the *España*. Then suddenly we heard a huge explosion, 'Broom!'. Just then, out on the horizon, we saw a big English ship on patrol; it was said to be the *Royal Oak*. All of a sudden the *España* began to lift her bow and then it plunged down; it must have taken only twenty minutes to sink. We were all shouting with excitement, 'She's sinking! She's sinking!' Several small boats went out and began to pick up bits and pieces of the superstructure, flags, anything floating, and a destroyer, the *Velasco*, arrived to pick up the survivors who were swimming about. Several days later a cordon of soldiers was placed along the beach because every ten yards you would see a pair of feet floating up and then the body of a dead sailor. There were some people who said that one of the planes had put a bomb right down the funnel of the *España*; it was one of those rumours so common in wartime. But there were others who were more expert in the matter, who had been sailors, and they said, 'That battleship could not have sunk like that unless it was hit by a torpedo. It must have been a torpedo. When the *Royal Oak* saw the *España* firing on an English merchantman it must have sent a torpedo.'[12]

It was also while I was in Santander that we heard the news that Guernica had been bombed; that the whole town had disappeared, wiped off the map. I remember reading in a paper an account by a journalist who wrote, 'I found nobody among the piles of rubble and the smoke, just a doll, the remains of a half-burned doll. Where can she be, the little girl who owned that doll, because there is nothing,

nothing left alive.' From the very first day people said that it was Franco's air force which had destroyed Guernica. But at the time Franco was telling the whole world that it was the Republicans who had bombed the town. But it was not true, it was the German air force, and the ultimate responsibility must lie with Franco's Northern Command.[13]

From time to time I got news of my battalion, the Maxim Gorky. While I was still in hospital in Aviles I had met Acelino, the little old man who had been put in charge of our company; he had come in with a minor wound. I asked him what had happened to the rest of them in the battle after I was wounded. He said, 'What others? There's no one left.' They had been nearly all killed or wounded. Apparently the offensive had succeeded in cutting the route, but they were forced to abandon it soon after. Later what was left of the battalion had been involved in a second offensive in the same sector. Acelino said, 'We found the place full of rotting corpses down there, the bodies of the blokes we hadn't managed to get out.' From Escamplero the battalion was pulled back to a place near Oviedo called El Pardo. 'But', he said, 'half the battalion is kaput or they are wounded like you; there is almost nobody left.' Then some time later I met another soldier from our brigade, a miner from Carbayin. I saw him in the street and I said, 'Well and how is the Maxim Gorky?' He said that from El Pardo the battalion had been sent to Bilbao where it took part in the defence against the big Nationalist offensive. He said, 'We all came out in one railway truck; you can guess what was left.' When they retreated from Bilbao there were only twelve left from a whole battalion.[14]

The area in which I fell was a real slaughter-house. The enemy had sustained huge losses too in the same zone around Valduno and Escamplero. Years later, when I returned to Spain, I met some peasants from near Valduno, from Premoño and Ania, who told me that during the war they had stayed behind on their farms when the Nationalists advanced and that they had been forced to go with their ox carts to take out the dead, because there were places in the mountains where a lorry or ambulance couldn't get through. The fighting had been very heavy and the shocktroops were always the Moors, the Arab regulars from North Africa. When they were mown down they were replaced by another wave. The peasants brought out cartload after cartload, piled high with bodies. Afterwards they were buried in an Arab cemetery; you can see it today if you go beyond Grado on the road to Galicia.

Things were quite comfortable at Santander and then, suddenly, the silly sods on the other side began to advance; they took the Basque country and Santander was flooded with soldiers in retreat.[15] The Asturian government issued an order that all the wounded Asturians who were in Santander should be evacuated to the west. The doctors told me that I was making good progress and that it was stupid to move me then because my treatment would be disrupted. But anyway we were shoved on a train for Luanco on the coast, but finding out that there was no alcohol there – by that time it was already in short supply – but plentiful in Infiesto we arranged to be put down there instead. At Infiesto there was plenty to eat and we were allowed to go into town – I was just beginning to use crutches – and it was true, there was lots to drink. Well the first few times I went out into Infiesto I felt really low, to see myself like that, with one empty trouser-leg trailing on the ground. I must have been depressed; I think that all those who lose a limb go through a difficult period like that, when they have to readjust to what their life is going to be like in the future. One day I said to myself, 'Shit, this can't go on.' So I tried to finish myself off. But some idiot of a girl there, a nurse who came from Grado who knew my parents, somehow managed to tell my family and they were really distressed. One day my father appeared; 'Ah', he said, 'not that. It's not true, is it?' He was not too happy when he went home.

It was just then that I met Consuelo. I was not too sociable at the time. One day I was on a balcony upstairs, next to the room where I slept, and I saw her. She was only a kid of fifteen years, but she was grown up for her age, already a young woman. Well she was doing something nearby and I was reading when she said, 'You. Why don't you go out with the others?' 'Oh, I get out OK.' 'Oh rubbish! You go out but when you come back you're drunk.' So we got to know each other a little and one day she said, 'You know there is a cinema in town; if you like we can go to see a film.' That's how things began; I went one evening with her to the cinema and we became friends, we were courting.

4 The Civil War in Asturias – Consuelo

THE COMING OF THE WAR

It was in 1917 or 1918 that my mother emigrated from Asturias to Mexico. She came from a very large family of nine or ten children. When my grandmother died my grandfather had got remarried to a woman called Andrea who disliked the children of the first marriage; she couldn't bear to have them in the house. So my mother left for South America, at the same time as her sister Araceli who got married on the boat out and settled in Buenos Aires in Argentina. When my mother had got to Mexico and managed to save a bit of money she sent it home to bring over her two brothers and her sister. The sister, Serafina, later returned home and lives in Infiesto and one brother, José, is living in New York. He went there from Cuba when Castro came to power. The youngest brother, Fernando, went over to Mexico with another man from Infiesto and together they set up in business. They had a canteen near a silver mine and one day the revolutionaries arrived, I don't know whether it was Zapata or Pancho Villa, and he went off with them to make the revolution. But he was captured by soldiers and hung.

My mother got married to a Mexican, but two years later my father died; he was found one morning dead from a heart attack. Well my paternal grandparents wanted my mother to stay in Mexico – she was living with them at the time – but she had made up her mind to return home. She preferred to be single and independent, even if things were more difficult. So she came back to Asturias, to Valle near Infiesto, with my sister Angelina and me. Perhaps she thought she would be able to stay with her father on the farm, but he wasn't going to have that. He said, 'You can leave the children here but you, you can go and find work.' My mother went to find work in Madrid and we were left with Andrea, my grandfather's second wife, who was a spiteful and harsh woman. She never gave us a crust of bread; she fed her own daughter and nephews well, but we were pushed outside. My sister was very small at the time, but she remembers too how we were treated. Andrea would push us outside and lock the door while they were eating and we looked in through the window to see what they were having. We didn't know what it was to taste chocolate or white bread: I was eight or nine when I had chocolate for the first time.

My mother never came to see us, she worked all the time as a cook in Madrid. She sent money, everything she earned, and shoes and clothing, but we were like outcasts. If my mother sent material Andrea would make things for her daughter, while we wore her old dresses. Certainly somebody must have told my mother or written to her about all this because she came and found a job at Infiesto in the 'Casa de Secorro', a kind of popular infirmary. She had a small flat there and so we were able to live together for the first time, but since my mother couldn't get by looking after the three of us I had to work too. I washed the floors, did the shopping, cleaned the surgery and the staircase – everything.

I went to school at Cardes, a village near Valle, from the age of five to eleven; that's all. But well before the age of eleven I already missed school to help with the work. When I could read and write my mother said there was no more point in going. I went to school when there was no work to do. My mother would say, 'Well today you've got no work to do so you can go to school.' I didn't help her because there was no school, it was the other way round, I went to school when there was nothing to do.

I was nine years old when the Republic came in 1931 and I remember being in the road and it was almost dark and a man said, 'We are now a Republic; we've won.' Then a girl came along the road carrying a big Republican flag.

But I remember the events of 'thirty-four much better. On the eve of the 1934 Revolution I was staying in Oviedo with a friend of my mother – I was there for the festival – and in the afternoon my mother phoned to say that I should come home immediately, on the very first train. And the next day at five o'clock in the morning the Revolution began. In Infiesto it went on for about a week and we were closed up in the house; each morning we didn't know if we were going to find the miners occupying the town or the police and the army.[1] Just before the army arrived the workers who were involved in the Revolution were out in the street and a lot of them were strangers to us, they were outsiders.

Then the army and the police moved in and the town was occupied. I was in the street outside our house when I met a nephew of my mother's, Ismael; he was about eighteen years old at the time. He said to me, 'Here, take this into the house and look after it for me.' It was a packet. 'What is it?' 'You just look after it.' So I took it and put it on the dresser in the kitchen and then I forgot all about it. Several days later our house was full of soldiers and officers, sleeping in the corridors, everywhere. All the houses in Infiesto had been taken over for billets and there were soldiers with every family. I said to my mother, 'Oh, there's some shopping of Ismael's here.' She said, 'What is it?' 'I don't know; it's a packet he gave me.' When she opened it up it was full of sticks of dynamite.

Ismael had been involved in the Revolution and wanted to get out of Infiesto, to escape into the mountains. But just near our house, which was on the edge of town, was a police control point and that's why he gave the packet of dynamite to me. He was lucky not to get caught with it because there were soldiers and officers everywhere. Ismael was never arrested. He hid up in the mountains in a hut and up there he got to know a girl who looked after the cows and she became pregnant. But her father had been in the civil guard and a year later, in 1935, he was able to use his influence to get Ismael pardoned so that his daughter could get married. Ismael was never charged or put in prison. The girl and he got married and they are still living up there, near Espinaredo.

In the infirmary my mother had always aided the poor, all those who had not got enough money to pay for medicine or injections, so she had the reputation of being a friend of the workers. Well the prison of Infiesto was right opposite the Casa de Socorro and all the revolutionaries who were taken prisoner were put in there. At night the head of the prison, who was a friend of my mother's, came to fetch her and smuggled her into the prison without the knowledge of the police so she could tend those who had bullet wounds or who had been beaten up. At night my mother gave injections, disinfected wounds and helped all those who were seriously ill and we carried over mattresses for those who had broken backs or who had been hung by their feet and beaten.

During the period of repression, in late 1934 and 1935, my mother got into trouble with her boss, the doctor in charge of the infirmary, who was a fascist.[2] He knew that she had been into the prison to give aid because some neighbours gave her away. Before the elections of February 1936 he said to her, 'Listen, I don't want you making any propaganda in favour of the left; if you campaign for the left you will have to quit your job. I want you to vote for the right. If you vote for the left and they win you'll be out.' Well my mother said nothing, not a word. When the election campaign began in 1936 I went with some other girls, with Gavina and her friends who were much bigger than me, to distribute leaflets. We walked along the railway line as far as Villamayor and all the villages in the direction of Nava, to attend meetings and to hand out leaflets. We went on the railway track so we wouldn't be seen because the fascists patrolled the road in cars and attacked those who were on foot. One day the brother-in-law of the doctor gave me some right-wing leaflets and I tore them up and threw them away and he came to tell my mother's boss. The doctor had quite an argument with my mother about that.

Well when the elections came the Popular Front won and since the director had told my mother that if this happened she must go, she said to him, 'You can look for someone else, I'm going.' 'Why are you going?' 'Because we won the elections; I'm off.' 'Oh, no.' 'Yes, yes, I'm leaving.' 'But it was only said to frighten you.' My mother did not have another job, she had nothing, nothing at all; she preferred to go and live in an old house which she had bought and repaired. My mother had an inheritance from her father when he died and she sold that bit of land to buy a house and to furnish it. So we left the clinic and went to live in the house at Valle. And we were there during the months of May, June and July – my mother earned nothing, we ate as we could – and in July, when the Civil War started, the first week that the wounded began to arrive in Infiesto, they came to get my mother.

THE CIVIL WAR

Somebody from the War Committee came to the village; he asked me, 'Is your mother at home?' 'Yes.' 'Is she in work at the moment?' 'No.' 'Good, so she can come, we have need of her.' And he told me, 'You can come too; we need your help', because he knew that I helped my mother with the work of the infirmary. I was only fourteen, but if I told anyone I was that age they laughed because they all thought I was seventeen or eighteen; I was big for my age.

My mother and I both went down to Infiesto and the War Committee told us to organise a hospital for the wounded who were beginning to arrive from the Oviedo front. A big villa with large grounds on the edge of town had been requisitioned to serve as a hospital and my mother was given a lorry and two militiamen to go and round up beds and furniture. They installed about thirty beds, bedside tables, chairs and all the other things needed in a hospital, linen, crockery and so on. I went along with a friend to help my mother and there were such scenes when we went to the houses to requisition material. We would arrive at the homes of the right, of the fascists, and my mother showed them the order from the War Committee; 'There we are, you will have to give us twelve sheets, twelve pillow-cases and face towels.' 'Oh no, we haven't got any of these things. We are not fascists.' But they were all fascists, the whole lot. Then they would say, 'You are nothing but thieves.' But the militiamen were armed with rifles and when they saw that they were scared and they handed over the stuff. They took out those heavy bunches of keys that they keep in big bourgeois houses; they opened the cupboards and took out sheets that had never been used, all new. The militiamen then gave them a receipt so that they could eventually reclaim the money. We spent all day requisitioning and on into the night; lorry-load after lorry-load. Some of the beds which we collected were quite magnificent, all in carved wood.

Well the accusation made against my mother years later, when the fascists came to power, was that she had stolen all these things. That is why my mother would never return to Spain from France because they accused her of stealing and taking the things home: she had made a lot of enemies. But that was not true, she never took anything home; on the contrary, at the beginning of the war, before going to requisition from the bourgeoisie, we went to our house and my mother kept back just four sheets for each bed and everything else she took to the hospital. She took a mattress and, above all, linen. When the fascists took control they accused my mother of stealing things for her own house, but we had given almost everything we had from our home.

The hospital was run with the help of several volunteer nurses from Infiesto and from the moment that everything was ready in August it was full of wounded soldiers all the time. Every day the doctor from the infirmary came to the International Red Cross Hospital as it was called and my mother helped him in the surgery. Although I was young I gave a hand too; I was not frightened by the injuries because I was already used to that kind of thing and had seen stomachs being opened and arms cut.

But then problems started when a woman was appointed as director. She was a useless figurehead; she did not know the first thing about hospital work but she was left-wing and looked imposing. My mother was good at her job as a nurse but she was not capable of managing the hospital so this woman was appointed over her head and she wanted to run everything her own way. She began to lay on big dinners for her men-friends. The hospital was supplied with food by the people; the peasants would bring rabbits or eggs, everyone gave something. The militiamen went into the villages, 'Can you give us something for the hospital?' If they gave nothing they would be requisitioned anyway. But they were always asked first. One person would give a sack of potatoes, another a ham or honey. Well that woman began to lay on banquets for her friends in the army, the battalion commanders, using the food which had been given to the hospital. That is all she did, sit in a room on a settee guzzling big dinners. Everyone began to complain, 'But this is not a restaurant, she can entertain them in her own place (because she owned a restaurant in Infiesto); this place is for the wounded; we are not working for the guests of Señora Blanca.'

Then my mother said, 'Right, I'm leaving, I did not go and requisition sofas for the friends of this woman to sit on. I'm going.' She went to see the head of the War Committee and said, 'Right, if there is some place where I can be useful send me there; I don't want to stay at the hospital.' 'Where do you want to go?' 'To the front if you like; it's up to you.' He said that he could arrange that but when my mother said she wanted to take me too he said that I was too young. 'No, your daughter can't go because it's too dangerous: it's in the front line. You go and perhaps she will be able to join you later.' There was another woman from Valle who also wanted to go to the front with my mother but they would not let her because she was married and with two very small children.

They made out a pass for my mother and with that she had to go to the International Red Cross centre at Sama de Langreo, to be sent to wherever she was most needed. They sent her to the front line, the Oviedo Circle, close to the water reservoir at Los Areneros. But when the Arab troops broke through the seige of Oviedo in October she and the others were forced to retreat to the village of Santa Madero. They had been forced to get out so fast that my mother lost all her medical supplies and she sent a militiaman, a neighbour of ours from near Infiesto, to our house at Valle to fetch some sheets. He said to my Aunt Enriqueta, who was looking after me, 'Well her mother says that Consuelo is to come with the linen and that she can stay with her.' My Aunt would not agree to that, she said that my Uncle Antonio could bring the linen instead. But in the end it was arranged that I should go and off I went with the militiaman. We had to pass round by the hills on the outskirts of Oviedo, by Manjayo and La Torres. It was close to the front and we made our way up to Santa

Madero protected by a hill. The fascists were just over the other side. I arrived, bringing the packet of linen, and my mother said, 'Well you can stay here if you like; the front is nearby and we are short of stretcher-bearers here.' In the little church at Santa Madero was a medical post, with doctors, and there was a shortage of stretcher-bearers because all the able-bodied men had been sent up to the front. So there I stayed; we slept wherever we could, in the *hórreos*,[3] in barns and houses.

From the emergency medical post at Santa Madero the wounded were taken down to Trubia where two big houses had been turned into a hospital. I joined up with two young men to make an ambulance team. The driver, Antonio, came from Lada near La Felguera and the ambulance, which was a delivery van, belonged to his father who manufactured shoes. When soldiers came to requisition the van his father said, 'Ah no! Not on my life. There is no way that you can have my van; there is only one condition on which you can take it and that's if my son goes along as well to look after it, otherwise you can't have it.' They said, 'OK, let your son come.' He would rather see his son go to the front than that his van should come to some harm! But the son was not too happy to go along. The other lad, Marcelino, was his friend and went along as mechanic, although he didn't know anything about engines. They were only young lads, about eighteen, and the three of us made a team.

The van had been made into an improvised ambulance so that it could carry three stretchers on each side, but it had not been very well done and in all the bends going down to Trubia the stretchers would fall down and the wounded men had to be laid on the floor. So while the other two went in the cab I was always in the back of the van to look after the soldiers. Sometimes we would make seven or eight trips in a night, depending on the extent of the fighting. One day we were going down to Trubia when an aeroplane, just a little thing, began to machine-gun the vehicles on the road. The two lads in front were really scared and the van began to hurtle round the bends too fast. We were really loaded up in the back with wounded men; there were five or six and me, seated on a box between two stretchers. One soldier, who had a wounded arm, was sitting on the floor and in one bend the door suddenly opened and he shot out through the back. I began to shout and bang, 'Stop! Stop!' They halted and Marcelino got out; he was scared stiff and looked quite ill. I said, 'We've lost one.' 'It's not true; I don't believe you; it's just to mess us around. Let's go Antonio.' 'Well you can count them, there's one missing. The door opened and he fell out.' 'We'll carry on and pick him up on the return trip.' 'And what are you going to do afterwards? We'll have to turn round again to take him down to Trubia.' So he reversed in a little country lane and went back and sure enough the soldier was there, sitting on the side of the road, holding his arm. *'Me cago en Dios! What are you buggers playing at?'* Antonio didn't budge from the steering wheel, he was always scared, a very timid person, but Marcelino said, 'Didn't you see the plane?' 'Yes, I saw it.' 'Well then; this isn't an ambulance you know, it's just a van. Get in then and stop complaining.' I took him under the arms and helped him to climb in. He asked me, 'You travel around with blokes like that?' 'Yes.' 'You must be crazy. Why don't you go home; haven't you got any parents?' 'No.' 'Well that's clear enough; if I had a daughter like you who went around with blokes like that!' But Antonio and Marcelino were very kind, they were like brothers to me. They always treated me like a boy, not like a girl. Afterwards we got in some trouble because the soldier reported us, but since he was not too badly injured we were let off.

Some time around mid-November came an order that all the women working at the front be recalled and that all those who were of good conduct be employed in the rear while the others – because there were some prostitutes – be chucked out.[4] My mother and I received an order to go to work in a hospital in Gijón. We slept in a hotel called the 'Little Palace' in the Calle Corrida and went each day to the hospital which was at Somio, just outside Gijón. After a while we were sent to work in a hospital for the treatment of scabies; at that time scabies was spreading everywhere. All those who were infected had to be washed down and then we scrubbed them with brushes and put on an ointment and we repeated that every day until it cleared up. But no matter where we worked we always slept in the same hostel, and everyone – stretcher-bearers, nurses and doctors – was on an equal footing and there was a very good spirit of friendship. There were no goings on between men and women, we were all pals. I've never experienced such a spirit of comradeship anywhere else; we all helped each other and there was a wonderful atmosphere. Everyone was willing to make sacrifices: when they needed stretcher-bearers for the Bilbao front a lot from there volunteered and many of them never came back.

After Christmas they began to make preparations for the battle of 21 February, the one in which David fell; hospitals were being set up everywhere in Gijón. All the nurses, assistants and stretcher-bearers were told to go and make mattresses to equip a hospital which was being set up in a convent, the Patronato St José. I don't know what they had done with the nuns because there weren't any there. The place was huge inside and there was a chapel with an organ. We worked from morning till night making mattresses stuffed with maize leaves; we sewed them up, set up the beds and got everything ready for the offensive. And when the day of the battle came we were posted two assistants to each floor under the charge of a nurse.

In the courtyard they had installed a crematorium oven to burn all the dressings and the arms and legs which were amputated; nothing was buried. Each Sunday we were supposed to take it in turns to burn everything. Well the older women were crafty, they didn't want to do that job and since there were three or four of us young girls they said, 'Ah, the young ones can do it.' But I didn't give a damn; it didn't turn my stomach at all to burn a leg or dressings; it was all the same to me. I also went to work in the medical tribunal where all those who had been ill or wounded were examined to see if they were fit to return to the front. I was used to seeing naked men there; it didn't concern me at all.

There was one soldier who had been very badly wounded; he looked just like a skeleton from a concentration camp. There was pus oozing from the wounds on his knees and his shoulders; it was coming out all the time and nobody wanted to be with him. He was in a room by himself and no one wanted to nurse him. I didn't have much work at that time and was asked to go and care for him; he was all wrapped up in cottonwool and from time to time I had to change the dressings. I was only fourteen years old but I was quite used to hospital work.

One night in April my mother was on night duty with a male nurse who was in the Communist Party and they were asked by the left to keep an eye on the doctor because he was under suspicion. The nights that he was on duty he amputated the arms and legs of the wounded as soon as they arrived from the front. Those fascist doctors would cut off a hand or an arm for no reason at all.[5] That night, when the wounded began to arrive, the doctor was asleep and when he eventually woke up my mother was tending one of the soldiers. She said to the doctor, 'It's nothing; I've already seen to it. I've cleaned it up and we'll take the dressing off tomorrow. It's nothing.' The doctor said, 'Let's see – no, no, no, come on, let's take a look. Remove all that.' My mother removed the dressing and he said, 'Ah, the arm will have to be cut off straight away.' Well the other nurse and my mother looked at each other and said, 'But no, it's not serious.' 'But you don't know anything about it; I'm the doctor here. I'm the surgeon.' So he cut off the arm.

My mother and her friend went to the Communist Party to denounce him. But two days later the male nurse received an order to go to the front and my mother likewise to go to the hospital at Infiesto. The whole affair had been passed on to the Medical HQ, but the doctor continued in his post because in the headquarters there were fascists and they were able to hush things up, to cover it over.

My mother and I returned to the hospital at Infiesto: I remember it was the date of my birthday, 21 April. That was at the time of the battle of Bilbao and there was a lot of work because of all the wounded. They had laid a siding with a platform so that the trains came right into the grounds of the hospital and the soldiers were taken off directly. During April and May there was a lot of work; sometimes we rested during the day because a train was due to arrive in the night. Things were badly organised because it was the same personnel who worked both during the day and the night; there was no shift system. Each nurse had thirty-one to thirty-five patients to look after and that meant a tremendous amount of work, making the beds, helping the wounded to dress and so on. The hospital staff slept down the road in the infirmary where my mother used to work. Sometimes we finished work at four in the morning and we had to get up at seven, so we would sleep under the trees near the road. We were too tired to go back to the residence for the sake of only two or three hours sleep. Then in May there was an epidemic of typhus and there were several deaths in the hospital, both among the staff and the patients. I was given an injection but it made me very ill for a month.

In June, just before the fall of Santander, all the wounded soldiers in the east were evacuated to Asturias. I had a friend, Anparo, who looked after a ward of Basque and Asturian soldiers who had come from Santander and because they could sing very well we would go there in the evening to listen and to sing with them. It was in a little annexe hidden behind the main building, a pavilion, and the bosses didn't come there very often so it was nice and quiet. One evening I went there; it was night-time and the lights were out, but you could see by the moon as if it was day. There were big windows looking out onto the grounds. There was a soldier from La Felguera called Leyva, along with his friends, and we sat on the bed singing. And down at the end of the room, in front of a window, was David lying across the foot of a bed. I said, 'Who is that over there?' One of them said, 'Oh, leave him be; he is always in a bad mood and complaining and he doesn't want to sing. Leave him be.' 'Very well', I said, 'but why is that? Doesn't he know how to sing?' 'Yes, but he doesn't want to. Leave him in peace; he is always in a black mood, complaining for nothing. If you bring him over here you can call it a day, he'll start a row.' 'Oh, but it makes me feel bad to leave him all alone over there.' So Charo said, 'Go and get him.' So I went over and said, 'Why don't you come and join us; come on!' 'Go on, clear off! Have you ever felt the end of a stick?' He had a walking stick and a crutch. 'Have you never been hit before with a stick?' I said, 'No. Why?' 'Clear off.' 'All right, damn that then.'

So I went back to the others; they asked, 'Well, what did he say to you?' 'He wanted to give me a good hiding with his stick.' 'Well that will teach you; he is a trouble-maker; he's going through a bad time.' So we carried on singing and didn't pay him any more attention. We left him alone.

One day I was in my ward on the ground floor, feeding the wounded, when the door was bashed open with the blow of a stick. It was David. The soldiers said, 'But who is this; he doesn't belong here? Chuck him out.' I said, 'What's the matter with you?' He got just as far as the first bed, which was empty, and fell onto it in a heap. He was drunk; so drunk that he couldn't stand up. The soldiers were shouting at me, 'But what the hell is he doing here? He'll puke up everywhere; throw him out.' 'No he won't. I know who he is, he's from upstairs.' 'Well he can just go back up; call his nurse.' There was an old man there called Chico who must have been over sixty; he said, 'Little one, do you know him?' 'Yes, since two or three days.' 'Right, we're going to take him outside.' There was an arcade. 'You know what we are going to do, since his nurse has gone home? We're going to look after him ourselves. Go to the kitchen and get some black coffee and salt.' So we prepared a full pot of coffee mixed with salt and we held him up while I made him drink, and he was burbling in a drunken way, 'They have killed my brother; my poor mother's dead.' We made him drink and then got him up to his room and into bed.

Afterwards we found out that on that day he had thrown himself under a lorry to try and kill himself, but the lorry braked in time or managed to avoid him. Two or three days later I was on the balcony of a room which was empty; I was writing postcards to the soldiers who had written to me. He came in and sat in a big armchair and we began to talk. I asked him, 'But why did you throw yourself under a lorry?' 'Oh, because I've had enough. I'm useless, nobody can get on with me. My life's finished.' He gave me a whole sorry story, a real plateful. I said, 'But you know that there is no reason to lose your head; there are plenty of others like you and they lead a happy life.' 'But I can't hope to get married, to have a wife.' 'But yes of course you can marry: me, I like you a lot.' Well he began to laugh, 'No. You, you're too young.' Well it was me told him that I loved him; he never said anything to me, and he still hasn't! 'Well I love you a lot', I said. Perhaps if I said that he would be happier. And then we began to go out together.

Not long after that Santander was taken by the enemy, and my mother, since we all had Mexican nationality, went to the Mexican consulate in Gijón to get the authorisation for us to evacuate. At that time only the women and children refugees from Bilbao and Santander and foreigners could leave. It was on 6 September, a month before the Asturians evacuated by sea, that we left. We went down to the 'Old Port' where there were two fine ships, painted all white, but they were already full. So we took a taxi across to the other port where there was only a coal ship. My sister and I had wanted to go in a white steamer, but there was nothing doing. We were the first to go aboard the coal ship because all the people who had arrived earlier had gone onto the other two boats. We had to climb down into the hold and there must have been a foot of coal-dust left in the bottom after the coal had been taken out. We took some planks to lie down on. It was about seven o'clock in the evening and soon after I fell asleep.

5 The Fall of Asturias – David

By October the enemy was getting closer and closer day by day. Asturias was completely cut off and the Nationalists were advancing from the east; they were through Santander and coming into Asturias. Consuelo's mother worked in the hospital and when things got bad she took Consuelo and her sister, Angelina, and left by boat from Gijón. Since they held Mexican passports the mother had decided to go there.

I stayed in Infiesto for a little longer, but eventually things became too hot. We were almost in the front line; the Army of the North had retreated right back to Infiesto and every day wounded soldiers were coming in from the lines close by.[1] It must have been about a week before the war ended, before Asturias finally fell, that the director of the hospital told some of us that we were to be moved to Sama de Langreo in the mining region. He said that we were still of some use to the war effort, even the limbless. 'Useful for what?' we asked. 'Now you are well recovered you are nice and plump; you are going to go and give blood.' I said that I was not opposed to giving my blood but that I wouldn't go inland; I wanted to be close to the sea in case we had to get out suddenly. The director said that nothing was going to happen; but there we were, with the fascists almost on top of us. There were some Basques in the hospital who did not believe him because they had retreated all the way from Irun. They refused to go to Sama.

Well at about three or four in the morning some buses arrived and they began to load the Basques into them to take them to a hospital at Villaviciosa which is on the coast near Gijón. There was a hospital for those who had almost recovered and from there soldiers were sent to military headquarters for clearance to go back to the front. I took my little bundle of belongings and went to wait with the Basques to board a bus. But I was seen by a hospital administrator who said that I had to go to Sama with the other soldiers who were in my ward, that I was being stupid. 'Stupid or not', I said, 'I'm going to Villaviciosa.'

When I got to Villaviciosa there was incredible chaos. The hospital was an old cider factory and there was a shortage of everything. In the refectory when I asked for a spoon they said, 'Shit, there's no spoons here! There's nothing left at all.' In the afternoon I asked to see the doctor and he turned out to be a small, rather likeable Cuban. I told him that I wanted to leave hospital and go to the military tribunal at Gijón so that I could be cleared, get a disabled serviceman's pass, to go home. He said, 'But you are not completely mended.' 'Yes! Yes! I'm OK.' He said, 'All right, let's have a look; take down your trousers.' And after the inspection he said, 'No, no; you can't go yet.' But I insisted and in the end he gave in. 'You take responsibility for any complications.'

I took a bus to Gijón, intending to stay overnight in the barracks of my regiment, the Maxim Gorky. When I arrived I was told that there was nothing to eat. 'Shit, a soldier of the regiment and you've nothing to give me?' But they agreed to take me over to the hospital of the *Patronato* for the night. I ate in the kitchen late at night – everyone else had eaten – and there was just me and a Basque who had just come from the front. There was a bench to sit at the table and he said, 'Don't get too close to me, the lice are falling off me. Sit a bit further away. Look!' And true enough he was crawling.

The next day I went to the Medical Centre in Gijón where they kept the records for the whole army and sure enough they found my record with the day I had fallen in the attack and everything. With that I went before a medical tribunal, a committee of doctors, and I was given a paper marked 'Evacuation'. 'OK', I was told, 'with that you go to the port commission in Gijón docks and you can leave on a boat when there is one.'

But I didn't want to leave Asturias without seeing my parents at Aguera and so I went to the Langreo station in Gijón to catch a train for Aviles. I remember waiting in the station with three or four people, men and women. I was very hungry and on the platform was a big sack, like a bag of beans. We began to open it and, blow me, it was full of peanuts! We just hurled ourselves on them, filling all our pockets. At Aviles I stayed overnight in an army centre and the next morning sat on the edge of the road until someone stopped to give me a lift to Aguera.

At Aguera were my mother, father, younger brother Jesús, and Valentina. When I came through the door it was the first time that they had seen me on crutches and they all began to cry. They said, 'Well there we are, you're here.' I went to sit down and they rushed to get a chair for me. 'But no,' I said, 'I can seat myself. Well how are things?' 'Things are bad; to find something to eat we have to go to the headquarters of a battalion which is at the front close to here. What they give us to eat for one day or a week we polish off in one hour; we've almost no food at all.' 'OK, I'll go and see if they will give something to me.' I went off with my brother Jesús, so that he could carry anything which they might give me. It was a brigade from Santander. 'But what are you doing here?' they asked. 'My family is here; I've come to find something to eat.' Well blow me, they began to pile so much on us, Jesús could hardly carry it all. When we got back to the house Valentina and my mother said, 'Waaahh! You've brought a lot to eat!'

I told my parents that I could not stay because the battalion had stopped paying me – I hadn't received anything for three or four months – and I needed to find it. At that time the Maxim Gorky was miles up in the mountains, high up in a pass at Pola de Lena, above Mieres. That is where the paymaster was and I decided to go and find him. So I returned to Gijón and then made my way to La Felguera in the mining district, where I stayed with a friend. I finally got a lift in a lorry up to Pola de Lena. The paymaster said that he couldn't give me all my back-pay because there was not enough money, but he gave me the wages for one month. When I got back down to La Felguera, to my friend's house, he said, 'Don't you know they are trying to get everyone out by boat! The fascists are already in Villaviciosa! We've got to get out of here really fast. My friends are looking for a vehicle right now.'[2] We all piled into the back of a small lorry; there was standing room only and they drove like crazy along the twisting road to the coast.

We reached Gijón at nightfall and we began to go round looking for people that we knew, but they had all gone. At the offices of the Socialist newspaper *Avance* we found someone. He said, 'But what the hell are you doing here, get to the port. Everyone has gone from here. Jesus Christ! The fascists are here; they've arrived. You've got to get out!' We went down to the 'Old Port' of Gijón and all hell was let loose. Everyone, men, women, children, soldiers, were in a panic, pushing and fighting their way to the quayside. Some were shouting, 'It's all over, they've freed the prisoners. The fascist prisoners have been released and they are in the street,' The Fifth Column had opened the prison gates. 'The army is here! They are coming! They are coming!' It was pandemonium.[3]

In the port everyone was trying to get onto a little coal ship, a collier. The steamer was keeled over on its side and it turned out that it had been bombed and was taking in a lot of water. A team of Basque metalworkers was trying to repair the hole in the side by welding on a metal plate. The boat could not get out anyway until the tide came up to float it off. Everyone was trying to get on the ship and a battalion, the *Batallôn de Defensa*, made a cordon so that women and injured wouldn't be crushed. But what with the general panic and the people screaming that the fascists were coming, things were out of control. The soldiers wanted to get away too. Some people were trying to climb up the sides and were falling in the water. It was sickening. The man I was with from La Felguera managed to scramble on board and found himself a place up a mast, but I was stuck there. With crutches under my arms and stuck in the crush near the gang plank I couldn't budge forward or back. Then a bloke up on the ship reached down the stock of a rifle and shouted, 'Grab that!', and he hauled me up. Once we were on deck we were told to go down into the hold to make space on deck. There was a lot of water down below but I managed to perch myself on one of the iron girders running along the side of the hold. I stayed down there a day and a night and when I came on deck we were at sea; the ship had come out on the tide at three o'clock in the morning. In all there were 1800 people on that little tub; women, children, wounded men, soldiers.

On deck I found a friend of mine from Gijón, Valentin Gonzalez; he had a bullet lodged in his foot near the ankle and it was all swollen up. We found a corner to sit but every time someone pushed by they banged my bad leg; it was unbelievable. The coast was patrolled by Francoist ships, so the steamer headed straight out into the ocean, far out; but in the end they had to come back in to the coast again because there was no proper captain or pilot aboard and the men at the wheel could only navigate by land sightings, from lighthouse signals and by hugging the coast. Well after a long while in the open sea they turned in to the land and we thought that we must be far north, right up near France. Then someone shouted, 'But that's Santander!' We were only a short distance up the coast and that part was all in fascist hands. So out we headed again for the open sea.

Then the man who was stoking the boilers found some dynamite mixed in with the coal and people were saying that there was a fascist squad on board. Everyone began to demand to see the identity cards of the others. When someone ordered Valentin to show his papers he pulled out a revolver. 'And yours?' Then the man who was at the steering-wheel began to complain that the rudder would not function properly. It was thought that the tiller rods – the steering system worked through bars running along each side of the hold – must have been blocked by people sitting too close. They were ordered to stay clear, but there was still something wrong and after searching they found that a piece of wood had been jammed into the steering system to block it. After a good search they found five fascists; they had French and English currency, guns, the lot. And one man, who was dressed in a gabardine, threw himself overboard. I don't know whether he was one of them or just crazy. Anyway the Asturian leaders on the boat said to some soldiers, 'Right, you take care of these characters.' Later, when we were on a train taking us from Bordeaux to Barcelona, I asked someone, 'Well, what happened to those men?' 'Oh', they said, 'they stayed behind.' I think that they were bumped off; yes, for sure.

The little coaster we were on, the *Maria Elena*, was listing badly during our voyage through the Bay of Biscay and things got gradually worse. By the time that we reached the mouth of the Gironde to go into Bordeaux she was right over on her side; you could almost touch the sea on one side while the other was high in the air. We could only make very slow progress and we tried to attract attention so that a tug could come and take us into Bordeaux. There were dozens of other little boats, fishing smacks, from northern Spain going past us up the river, but we couldn't make any headway. People began to get anxious, 'Oh, they are not coming, they are not coming. The boat's sinking!' And our ship was hooting and hooting and there was nobody in sight to help us. Women were crying and wailing and men were saying, 'Jesus Christ! What's going on?' Everyone was in despair. Some people made a ball of rags, soaked it in petrol, and set fire to it at the top of a mast; it really burned like crazy. Eventually a pilot came on board and we moved upriver. It is a long way up the estuary to Bordeaux and we were moving very slowly, all listing and tilted over. The pilot reached a place in the river where he said that we would have to wait because we would have to have a medical inspection before disembarking. We told him that we couldn't wait, that if we didn't get into the quay we would go down. We could see the land on each side, we could see houses and everything. In the end they realised that we could not wait and that we really were sinking and agreed to land us without the medical inspection. We put in to a quay and as we disembarked there was a big police cordon; we had to pass between two lines of policemen, like a corridor, into a railway station. And just after we got ashore people began to say, 'That's it, the boat has sunk.' Yes, it was true; it was taking water very fast and within an hour or two the *Maria Elena* sank at the quayside.

6 Escape from Asturias – Consuelo

I fell asleep in the hold of the ship and when I woke up, it must have been about eleven o'clock or midnight, it was packed full with people. They all had to get down into the hold by a rope ladder, the old, the sick, everyone. It was all black with people crammed in there and all you could see were rows of heads, like crates of melons, with everyone sitting because there was no room to lie down. My mother said, 'Don't get up because you'll never find a place again.' It was bursting at the seams; as soon as one person stood up, another took their place. All night they were loading people onto the ship and so I settled down and fell asleep. The next morning I heard the cry of a baby close by; my mother said, 'A woman, a fisherman's wife, has had a baby during the night.'

We went out to sea and we were five days in the hold of that ship. There were no toilets, no water, nothing to eat. There was a stock of water on board but they didn't give any to us, not even for the babies; it was just for the crew, four or five men who were locked in the cabins with some women. Even the babies and the sick could not have a cabin; we were all together in the coal, in the dust.

When we had gone to say goodbye to my Aunt Rosario before leaving Infiesto she had given us a bag of potatoes for the journey and that is all we had to eat for five days, a little bag of cooked potatoes. Every night people were dying.

A fascist ship, the *Almirante Cervera*, was patrolling the coast and it fired some shots; they shouted through loudhailers, 'Put out your lights! Extinguish your lights!'[1] We were really scared and the other two ships from Gijón, which were behind us, were stopped and taken into Santander. And every night we were fired on by the fascists, just to frighten us. But during the day, since there were English ships patrolling, they cleared off. One day an English ship told us, 'You will have to turn around and head east to find Bordeaux.' The man who was navigating our ship didn't know what he was doing and we had gone way off course, too far to the north. We had to come back down the French coast and eventually we arrived in Bordeaux.

Well after five days lying in the coal-dust and without being able to wash we were all black like Senegalese. There were no proper toilets, just an arrangement of planks up on the deck and now and then someone would come and sluice it down with a bucket of water. But by the time we got to Bordeaux there was vomit and shit everywhere. At Bordeaux a man came aboard and said, 'No, no, you can't get off yet. You will have to wash.' But all that they brought onto the ship for 3000 people was one barrel of water. People were fighting to get washed. I remember that there was a wounded soldier who had lost a leg and he was standing back, like me and my sister, watching them all push and shove to get washed. He said, 'Don't you want to get washed?' 'But of course, but I'm not going to fight to do it.' 'You are right, we can wait.' But when the others had finished washing the water was thick and black like tar. Half of us there didn't wash at all. My sister made her handkerchief wet and dabbed her face but it didn't make any difference. We were both black as negroes.

A man came up the gangway with a basket of bread and before he could get on deck the women threw themselves at him. When he saw all those people fighting to get at him he just dropped the basket, turned tail and fled. I managed to grab a small piece of bread, but can you imagine that, one basket of bread for 3000 people? Not many got a taste of it. Finally they made us come ashore and from the gangway we went straight into a kind of warehouse or shed where we were given an injection, for typhus or whatever, and a cup of coffee. Then waiting on the other side of the shed was a train and we went straight into the carriages and the doors were closed with lead seals.

The train went from the port, through Bordeaux to Toulouse, and there the police opened one of the doors on our carriage and put onto the train four young Asturians who had managed to escape to France in a tiny boat. And all along the way, each time the train stopped, the *Secours Rouge*[2] were waiting and pushed through the windows tins of condensed milk and little cheese slices wrapped in silver. It was badly organised but at least we had something to eat.

From Toulouse we were taken across the Pyrenees to Puigcerda in the north of Catalonia. There we were shoved into a carriage which had been damaged by bombs, it was just like riding in cattle trucks, and taken to Ripoll in the Province of Gerona. And then on by lorry to Mollo, right next to the French–Catalan frontier. In that village, Mollo, the people were all fascists, the whole lot. The Anarchists had come from a town nearby, Campradón, and had taken the priest away and killed him, so they put us in his house. We were all women and children, except for a few old men, because all the older boys and the young and middle-aged men were separated from the women and sent to a different place. There was a lieutenant at Mollo who was in charge of the frontier guards and he said to us, 'Listen, here the village is hostile towards refugees. Nothing has been properly arranged yet for you but be patient and everything will be fixed.' Up there the peasants didn't have ration cards, they could go and buy freely in the shops, but if you didn't speak Catalan, like us refugees, they wouldn't sell you anything. We were a long time without bread but later my sister learned to speak some Catalan in order to go and buy bread. We wanted to get out of that place.

In December we were able to move to Campradón which is a spa town of about 1500 to 2000 people and that is where we stayed until the fall of Catalonia a year later. In Campradón the Catalan bourgeoisie had lots of little holiday villas but since most of the owners had escaped into France they were empty and that is where they installed the refugees from Santander, Bilbao, Asturias, Madrid and Valencia. But the local people who had stayed behind were right-wing. Later in a concentration camp in France I met the mayor of Campradón who was an Anarchist and he told me that he had received an anonymous letter threatening to liquidate him if he took care of the refugees. He said, 'I would have preferred to die rather than not to give them help. I couldn't refuse aid to refugees and to find them shelter.'

During that time we were very hungry; even when my mother and I began to work in the hospital at Campradón we didn't get fed. My mother and sister searched everywhere in the countryside for food, but they didn't find anything. One night we went to steal turnips and cabbages from the fields; there was my sister and I, another Asturian woman called Julia, and a Basque, Esperanca. Sometimes we couldn't use torches to see because it was close to the frontier and the assault guards were patrolling the roads. We had to find things by touch and sometimes we thought we had picked potatoes when it was beetroot. We filled a whole sack and emptied it into the bath when we got back. We boiled up soup with vegetables and salt, but there was no meat or fat in it. Nor was there any wood or coal for heating, although the winters in the Pyrenees are very severe. There was one time when we had hardly eaten anything for a month and it was bitterly cold and we stayed in bed nearly the whole time to keep warm and to keep our strength up. We were all together in one big room and three of us to a bed; Julia, her mother, her niece and son in one bed and my mother, my sister and I in another. We only got out of bed for a little while in the evening.

One day I went to Barcelona with a woman called Carmen who had lost touch with her husband, an assault guard, during the fall of Asturias. She wanted to go to Barcelona to see if she could find him but since she didn't like to go alone she asked my mother if I could go. We managed to get a pass, because at that time you couldn't travel more than a few miles from where you were living, and we went to Barcelona and began to ask in all the barracks. When we reached the *Karl Marx* barracks a political meeting was taking place and we stopped to listen: I was looking along all the crowded balconies above to see if I could find David. There was no sign of him, but Carmen managed to find her husband.

Then coming away from the barracks, as we were crossing the park, I saw Leyva, David's friend from Infiesto. He said, 'Consuelo! What are you doing here?' 'And you?' We got talking and he said that if I came along to the *Luna*, a bar in Barcelona, about two o'clock that afternoon I would find David. And sure enough he was there and after a while Carmen and her husband went off to eat in a restaurant and David's friends went too and we were left alone. We stayed there talking on the terrace of that café from three in the afternoon until four in the morning. David was drinking beer all the time and I was so hungry; I could see other people tucking in to plates of food and I kept thinking, 'Isn't he going to ask me if I want to eat?' I didn't have the courage to ask him although I was starving. At four in the morning I had to leave to meet Carmen and her husband in the Catalonia Square so that we could catch the five o'clock train back to Campradón. When they found out that I had not eaten anything they kept on teasing me all the way back, 'Ah, what it is to feed on love and roses and fresh dew!', and so on.

I came back to Barcelona on one other occasion to meet David. We had arranged to meet at the top of the Passo de Garcia but somehow he didn't turn up or we missed each other. Then in July, just before the Battle of the Ebro, he came to see me in Campradón. But after he had moved to Vich he wrote to say that he was giving me up, that I was too young, that he had no future, that I could find a better man who had two legs, that everything was finished and we had lost the war. I was not to think of him any more; he didn't love me any more and I should not write. Julia said, 'Hey then, don't you write to your Asturian any more?' 'No, he doesn't write any more.' 'Ah', she said. 'Oh well! So much the better; give him up.'

Then came the fall of Catalonia and the general retreat. Since David was closer to Barcelona than us I was always expecting that he would come. I thought, 'Well, perhaps he'll come to Campradón and he'll stay with us and we can cross the frontier together.' But on 29 January we had to get out of Campradón; David never turned up and we lost track of each other. I was not to see him again for five years.

7 Catalonia in War – David

When we got to Bordeaux I had not eaten for four or five days. The *Secours Rouge Français* had organised some food; we had to line up and we were given a hunk of bread and a piece of cheese. I tore off a piece of bread with my teeth but I couldn't swallow anything at all because I had been without food for so long. But afterwards I got into another queue where they were handing out coffee with milk and after I had drunk some of that I felt better and was able to eat a little.

A team of Spanish Republican doctors appeared and they told all those who were wounded or disabled to get into a separate line. We were to be taken on board a Spanish transatlantic liner which was moored nearby and which had been converted into a hospital ship. I refused to go, although the other disabled soldiers were keen enough. I said that there was no way that I was going back on a ship after our last little adventure. But a doctor insisted that I go and told me to show him my wound which had just a gauze dressing and a piece of plaster. He examined it and said, 'You must stay here.' But I was quite firm, I was not going to give way, and I insisted on going with all the others to Barcelona. In the end he gave in, 'All right, if that's what you want.'

We went onto a station platform to get into a train and the whole place was sealed off by a cordon of police on both sides. I wanted to buy some cigarettes before getting onto the train but a policeman would not let me, 'No, no, no. *Allez, allez, allez!*' And as he said that he took a packet of cigarettes from his pocket, a packet of Gauloise with about ten or fifteen cigarettes, and gave it to me. A policeman! The train set off for Barcelona and all day long we travelled through France. When the train stopped at Toulouse we were allowed to get off onto the platform but it was sealed off on all sides by police, the whole station was cut off. I had a five-peseta coin and I went to a newspaper kiosk to try and buy some cigarettes. The man who was serving said, 'No. Here, you can have a packet of cigarettes, but keep your money for the Republic, she needs it. Keep your money.' He was kind.

When we crossed the French–Spanish frontier near Port Bou we had to go through a tunnel; one end of it was in France and the other in Spain. When we were inside the tunnel the train stopped in the dark and people began to say, 'What's going on?' It turned out that

Nationalist aeroplanes were waiting to bomb the train as it came into Spain.

It was getting dark when the train stopped at Figueras, instead of going straight on to Barcelona, as we had thought. We were taken to the Castle of San Pablo which was a clearing-point for all the refugees coming from the north. It was the same place where all the volunteers for the International Brigades were first sent to on arrival in Spain. The place was full of them, dressed in ordinary civilian clothing, and when they saw us arriving, especially as there were a lot of disabled and wounded soldiers among us, they all lined up in ranks and saluted us. 'Ah', I thought, 'things are getting better here already.'

We ate and slept in the castle and the next day took a train to Barcelona. At that time there were thousands of refugees arriving in Barcelona, all the evacuees from northern Spain, and as the trains came into the station there were welcoming committees waiting to take care of them. But we must have been in one of the very last trains because there was nobody at the station to direct us. We didn't know where to go, all adrift in the city, but my friend Valentin, the one with a bullet in his foot, said, 'I know Barcelona a little; we'll head for the centre.' We went to a big square in the centre, the Plaza de Cataluña, and we were a terrible sight, all black with dirt, unshaven and badly dressed. We began to look for some kind of relief organisation and a woman came by, a Czech nurse dressed all in leather, who showed us the way to the headquarters of the United Socialist Party. There we were given something to eat and then taken to the hospital of San Pablo. There we were nice and comfortable; we had a shower and were given a bed and those who needed attention for their wounds were seen to.

I could not stay in the hospital for long because the beds were needed for wounded soldiers arriving from the front. They told all of us who were virtually recovered that we would have to go to Valencia but that idea didn't appeal to me at all because the enemy was advancing and threatening to cut off the whole southern zone.[1] I refused to go and was told that in that case I would have to put up with living in the barracks. After a spell in the barracks, where I contracted scabies and had to get hospital treatment, I began to look for a room to rent. In the Asturian Centre I was told to go to the headquarters of the Eastern Army because it was there that they kept all the records of the Army of the North. There I was given my army pay, which was a fair bit because I was given several months back-pay, and with that I was able to rent a room. Since I could eat in the canteen of the army barracks and travel free until nine in the evening on public transport or get into the theatre or cinema with no charge I had most of my money to spend as I liked. I had money in my pocket to go out on the town a bit.

At first I found life in Barcelona very demoralising. In Asturias we had been encircled for a long while; there was only one way out, by the sea, and there was almost nothing left in the way of food and supplies. Everyone was on the same level and there were no distinctions; we all ate lentils. But when we reached Catalonia it was like landing on a different planet. You could eat in first class restaurants which had a full menu. All us soldiers from the Army of the North would say, 'Blow me, we come from over there where we have been nearly starving for sixteen months and here life's just like normal, as if there's no war; what the hell is going on here?' The shops were full of goods and you could just walk in and buy whatever you wanted – shoes, clothes, anything. There were tailors' shops where people could go and have a suit made to measure and you would see army officers all dolled up in fine uniforms while all of us in Asturias, regardless of rank, wore boilersuits and there was just a little badge to mark the rank.[2]

On reflection I suppose that you could say that it was normal that things should be like that in Barcelona because the front was so far away and then, in a city of two million, there's bound to be more resources. But in Asturias the war was more of a reality; things were harder and you knew that it was no game. Just imagine what it was like to be in Asturias, completely surrounded: the people fought, they resisted, till the very end, till they were driven onto the beaches. They were still embarking at Gijón when the fascists closed in; it was war to the last bullet. And then the contrast, arriving in Barcelona where life was normal, as if there was no war. Well that demoralised a lot of soldiers who arrived from the north. They would say, 'Oh, but if things are like that I'm not going back to the front.' And there were some who didn't go but took themselves off to the *Barrio Chino*, the red-light district, or just shacked up somewhere. For them the war was over. Later on of course things got more difficult in Barcelona, there were shortages and it began to look like any other town in wartime.

The other thing that demoralised us was the difference from Asturias where there was real unity of purpose. Unlike other parts of Spain, the Socialists, the Communists and the Anarchists had managed to reach agreement; there was a united front, the UHP, the

Unión de Hermanos Proletarias.[3] All the parties were united together under the Council of Asturias, the government set up during the Civil War. Everyone was in agreement about what we were doing and how we were doing it and there seemed to be more equality because we all wore the same clothes and ate the same food, but in Catalonia there were real divisions.

As far as the war effort was concerned I think that the Communist Party was best organised and it was they who said that in a war, faced with a disciplined enemy, we would have to be efficient. Because a disciplined army could only be beaten by one that was even better organised; that things were lost if everyone fired in a different direction. We needed to have a united effort. But in Barcelona the CNT, the Anarchists, were very strong and all the industry, transport and so on was controlled by them. They had collectives on the land, right up in Aragon. But they ran things as they liked; the government had no say. But how can you let a factory, for example, manufacture one size of shell when what the government wanted was something else? What was necessary was a single command and the question of how things were to be run after the Civil War needed to be left aside; the winning of the war came first. I think that the Communist Party was quite right in this matter.[4] Undoubtedly it buggered things up in other ways, but for the question of discipline it was the most strict.

In Aragon there were moments when, for example, the Anarchists would say, 'All right, we are going back to Barcelona today', and then they would quit the front. And on other occasions they would say, 'Today we are going to die to recover this scrap of land', and they would all get killed. Because you cannot say that the Anarchists were cowards, on the contrary they were real hotheads. When it came to fighting they really fought. But at other times they said, 'Well on this matter we won't listen to the government.' They wanted to make war and revolution at the same time and that was not possible. But when it came to the creation of the Fifth Army for the defence of Madrid it was the Communist Party which organised things with real discipline and saved the capital.[5] Then when they committed those stupidities with the attack on the POUM, and Stalinist purges were carried out inside the party, that blackened their good record.[6]

Each political party wanted to use every opportunity to build up their own strength to the disadvantage of others and that made for divisions. If the Communist Party wanted increased aid from the Soviet Union the Socialist Party was frightened that it would help make the PCE stronger. The Socialists also said that the foreign powers, France, Britain and America, feared the PCE and that we couldn't get their support if there was a Communist majority. So they sought to limit the number of important government posts held by Communists. But the PCE for its part said that if things carried on like they were under the Socialists the war would be lost in two days. Once a Messerschmitt was captured on the Eastern front and Prieto wanted to give it to the English and American experts to study, while the PCE wanted it for the Soviets. So there was a hell of a row, just over a bloody plane.

Each party was trying to recruit as fast as it could. When I went to the front at Escamplero, up in the mountains, we were almost in full battle when I was told, 'Come here; what's your name? Look, we are a Communist battalion, here's your membership card.' Everyone had to have a Communist Party card and if you asked why they said, 'Because us lot, the Maxim Gorky, we're Communists.' That's how I was made a member, right in the front line. And in Barcelona you could see things like that going on all the time. One day I was sitting in a tram when a bloke asked me if I had been wounded on the Eastern front. When I said no, in the North, he said, 'You know that we have already organised a League for the Disabled. You go to a certain address and they will verify your record and issue you with a card.' So I went along and was given an identity card with a photograph and with that I had the right to so much tobacco, to travel on the tramway or in the underground, or to go to the cinema free. Well several days later I met another man who asked, 'Have you been registered yet as a disabled soldier?' I said yes, but when he saw my card he said, 'But no, there is another organisation which is better than that. Ours will give you more tobacco than the others and they give out food parcels too.' It turned out that there were several rival associations for the disabled. I asked him what the hell was the point of that. It turned out that he was in an Anarchist association and that they refused to have anything to do with the government organisation because it was 'bourgeois' and bureaucratic.

I was living in a rented room, along with some other Asturians, when the fascists began to bomb Barcelona. It was in March 1938 and the havoc was terrible, people were killed like flies. The first heavy raid went on for ten days and the centre of Barcelona, around the Plaza Palacio, was blown to smithereens. Each day I went with a group of four or five Asturians, who had rooms in the same building as me, to eat in the barracks near the park. On one occasion there were so many people trying to get off the underground at the Luna station that I couldn't get out of the train on my crutches, so I told the others I would go on to the terminus and get off on the return train. Well when I finally got out at the Luna stop I saw a terrible sight; a bomb had fallen right next to the entrance to the station as the crowd was leaving; it was a sea of blood. I found one of my friends and when I asked him where Jesús was he said, 'Oh, but we found Jesús; he'd got no head. You were lucky not getting off when we did because nearly everyone died.'

Another time I was crossing the central park to go and eat. A woman was coming towards me when I heard a whistling noise – 'phuuiii' – so I grabbed hold of her fast and pushed her to the ground. She began to shout, 'You silly bugger; what do you think you're doing? You animal . . .' She thought that I was attacking her. And then – boom! boom! boom! – bombs began to fall all around us. After it stopped she said, 'Oh my God!' 'And if you were not lying flat you would have been cut in two.' And afterwards she began to apologise.

Usually sirens went off when an attack was due and people went into the underground or into cellars. But it got so overcrowded below that a lot of people just stayed where they were, sitting in the cafés, or wherever. One day coming back from the canteen I came past a restaurant near the Francia station that had just been hit by a bomb. It had been full of people and there were pieces of body, of women, children and men, in the street.

During all that time the fascist radio claimed that only military targets were bombed and the Committee of Non-Intervention went along with that. But it was not true; the Germans and Italians were already engaging in a total war, a psychological war aimed at demoralising the civilian population. They bombed the city centre not because there were any military targets but to create panic.[7]

Towards the end of 1938 all the disabled soldiers were told that they had to leave Barcelona and we were all brought together in the *Garcia Lorca* barracks at Vich, some sixty kilometres away. The government thought that the sight of so many wounded men in Barcelona was having a demoralising effect and it was true that no matter where you went, in the tramcars or wherever, the place was full of men on crutches. So the whole bunch of us was cleared out of the city. There were some hundred to one hundred and fifty disabled at Vich and life there was quite comfortable; there was a little library of books to pass away the time. But while I was there the war effort began to go very badly and it was said that Prieto wanted to make peace with Franco.[8] As a result the PCE and the PSOE, the

Socialists, were at each other's throats and the Communists began to campaign to recruit a hundred thousand volunteers for the front. I and a lot of others at Vich were taken by Communist organisers down to Barcelona to help recruit volunteers; we manned tables in the street, decked with flags and slogans. There were very few enquiries; sometimes we would be there for hours on end and only one would volunteer. The whole city was full of tables like that and we never got anywhere near the hundred thousand. After one week we returned to Vich. And I thought to myself, 'How do they have the gall to place disabled men in the street to recruit? Just to see us must scare people stiff. If anyone was to volunteer why, in a few days he might be looking like us.' We were a charming bunch of recruiting officers – armless, legless, mangled and crippled soldiers of every description. Perhaps they just could not find anyone else to do the job.

Life was quite tranquil at Vich, but in Barcelona things were getting worse from day to day and by January 1939 we could see that it was all over.

8 Exodus across the Pyrenees – Consuelo

One morning at five o'clock – I think it was the 27th of January – a policeman whom we knew and who lived in a house just opposite came to tell us, 'You had better pack your things because you are refugees and tomorrow the Fifth Column is going to rise and kill everyone, especially the refugees.'[1] There were fascists in hiding, in the walls of houses, under staircases; they were waiting for the moment to emerge. The house where we were living was full of refugees; there were at least fifty of them sleeping in the corridors and wherever they could find space. We told them they had to leave because the Fifth Column was going to rise and we began to prepare our suitcases.

At that time I was recovering from flu and I hadn't been to work in the Camprodón hospital for two weeks. I decided to get out of bed and to go there to see what was happening. All the nurses had gone, all the staff, everybody, and wounded soldiers were lying outside on the pavement. The army was in full retreat and ambulances were bringing the wounded soldiers from further south, dumping them on the pavement and going back for more. The road was full of injured men from the Barcelona front. I went up to one of them who was sitting on the ground and asked, 'What are you doing here?' 'There's nobody here to tend the wounded, no one; they have all left except for a woman in the kitchens and one doctor upstairs. Do you know how to change a dressing?' I said, 'Yes.' So I went to the surgery and there was a queue of soldiers right along the corridor; they were waiting there. Perhaps they thought that there were doctors inside. There was a disabled soldier there who had lost both legs; he knew me and he said, 'Don't go in there because you will never be able to get away; look at the queue that there is!' I said, 'Well, all the same I'm going to change a dressing for a soldier over there.' Both his arms were wounded near the elbow. So I went into the surgery and attended to him and after him there was another and then another and the next morning I was still giving aid. I could no longer stand up, I had no more strength left, because I was weak from the flu. And the soldiers were saying to me, 'Go on, get out.'

Those who were unable to walk couldn't get away, they were trapped. The Republicans had cleared a route from Camprodón through the mountains to the frontier, but from there to the first French village there was nothing, not even a track. It was very mountainous with deep ravines. The vehicles went up as far as the frontier and there at the pass they had to push them over the cliffs to make way for others coming up behind. The cars and lorries, as they arrived, were put in gear and sent down the ravine. So the wounded who could walk could carry on, but the others were blocked there.

We set off from Camprodón with a small handcart: there were eight of us altogether, four women, two children, another young woman and me. I was sixteen at the time. We piled all our things on the cart and began to push it for mile after mile, continuously uphill, into the Pyrenees. And the further that we went the harder it was to push so we began to discard the suitcases one by one. 'Right, what if we dump this suitcase? Yes, chuck it off.' And then further on we opened the suitcases and began to sort out the less valuable things to discard them. 'Right, this has got to go.' And like that every half mile. We just couldn't go any further; the road was climbing up and up and up. Lorries were going past with the wounded.

When we got to Mollo, the village where we had stayed when we first came to Catalonia, we lost my sister. The evening before we left Camprodón my mother had sent her and a friend ahead with a suitcase as far as Mollo so the journey would be easier the next day. When we reached Mollo my mother sent my sister up to the village to get the case from the house of the people where she had left it, but when she came back she said, 'The suitcase isn't there. As we didn't seem to be coming the people left and they took our case with them.' All our most valuable things had been put in that case. I think that my sister must have gone ahead to see if she could find the others with the case but after that we lost her, and my mother never saw her again.

We carried on; the track was all mud, mud up to your knees because the thousands of people going past had churned up the snow and earth. When we reached the top of the mountain we had to wait because the frontier was not yet open; that was January 28th and it didn't open until seven in the morning on the 29th of January 1939.[2] There were thousands of people up there on the mountainside stumbling in the snow.

An ambulance driver called 'El Gordo' saw me and asked, 'Where is your mother?' 'She is just over there.' 'But no, your mother's not there.' I said, 'Yes, she was there, on the side of the road.' My mother thought that I had gone somewhere else; she had moved and there I was, lost; my mother lost and my sister lost. Night was falling and there I was all alone – well not alone, with thousands of others, and we were stuck there unable to pass over the frontier. I had to sleep there on top of a pile of paper. A lorry had come loaded with paper and tipped the lot down a ravine, so I took some of it and made a bed. About eight or nine in the morning – the frontier was already open – I heard a voice calling, 'Consuelo, what are you doing there; are you asleep?' It was the army driver 'El Gordo' and he was laughing, 'What, you slept there?' 'But yes.' 'But don't you see what you are sleeping on?' I said, 'No', and turning round I could see they were Republican banknotes. A whole lorry load had been brought from Barcelona. I was sleeping in a pile of bank notes and I had covered myself up with them. There were people who emptied out their suitcases and filled them with wads of notes; they dumped their clothes on the side of the road. I watched them and thought, 'Oh, I'm not going to take any, it's not worth the trouble.'

Anyway I had lost my suitcase; all I had was a string shopping bag which I had found in which I carried a pair of high-heeled shoes and lots of little Christmas presents that I had been given by the wounded soldiers in the hospital. Before reaching the frontier I had lost my ordinary shoes in the mud and I couldn't walk in the high-heeled ones; they were in the bag and I was barefoot when I crossed into France. On the French side of the frontier there were journalists waiting and photographers who wanted to take my picture. They said, 'Stop there! Stand there!' I said, 'Oh, go to hell! For God's sake.' All along the way I came across wounded soldiers from the hospitals where I had worked. There was one who must have had a stomach operation or something like that and he was being pushed along in a wheelbarrow, and they were going down the mountain like that, in the ice, with a soldier who was in a serious condition.[3]

Before I got to the frontier there had been an assault guard up on a lorry which was full of boxes. He asked me, 'Do you want some soap?' 'No, that I can do without.' 'Do you want some peanuts?' 'No' 'And concentrated milk?' 'Yes.' 'So he gave me two tins of condensed milk and some hazelnuts and I put them in the string bag with my shoes. After crossing the frontier it was all downhill and descending I came across two wounded men who were trying to make a fire in the snow with little bits of wood and sticks they had collected; they wanted to heat up some snow to make hot water. I asked them, 'Do you want a tin of milk?'; so I gave them one. They recognised me but when I saw myself later in a mirror I don't know how they were

Exodus across the Pyrenees – Consuelo

able to; I'd slept in the open, my hair was all plastered down with the rain and stuck to my body down my collar.

After I gave the soldiers the milk I carried on; I walked all day and then night came and it began to snow. The ground was all churned up mud and snow because so many people had gone by. You could hear children crying out in the night, 'Mummy! I'm lost!' Further on a woman was giving birth in the snow; children were sliding, falling down in the rocks; it was terrible, a nightmare, something quite horrible. It is difficult to imagine how awful it was, the crossing of the Pyrenees. I had been walking all day and I was feverish; I began to shake and feel delirious. Then it was night and I still hadn't reached the village in France, so I collected together a lot of abandoned suitcases – they were lying everywhere – and made a circle. It was just where the trees began, on the edge of the forest. I made a ring of cases and put two flat on the ground in the middle to lie on and I curled up there, without any covering. I remember once taking my hand from my pocket and I could see there was lots of snow drifting down. And then I heard voices crying, 'Mummy!', and all the names of the saints' calendar being shouted, 'Rodolpho! Paquito! Josepha!' You could hear voices like that all night, like a nightmare. And all the time people were going past close by, dragging themselves along, on all fours, wounded men who were losing their bandages: terrible, it was horrible, horrible.

There was an old woman who was sitting on a suitcase near me, holding a little child. She talked to me at first, 'I'm waiting for my daughter with two little children, but I don't know where they are, so I'm not moving from here.' Then she wrapped herself up in a blanket along with the little girl; the feet, the head, everything. I had nothing to cover me. And a long time after, I don't know how long I had been there, but after a long while I couldn't move, I couldn't take my hands out of my pockets, I couldn't move my legs, I was freezing and I didn't have any shoes. Then I felt somebody tugging at me; it was Julia, the Basque woman who had lived with us at Camprodón. She had lost her nine-year-old son and was looking for him. But she came across me instead and she didn't want to leave me there because she knew me and wanted to get me down to the village. She was a little woman, much smaller than me, and she took me by the sleeves of my coat and dragged me down the mountain on her back, right down to Prats-de-Mollo. But my legs were dragging on the ground. She held me like a sack of potatoes and as she went along she said, '*Hija de puta*. Daughter of a whore; to save you I lose the chance to find my son. Why didn't I leave you to die up there?' But I couldn't reply; I could hear her but I couldn't speak. And she was saying, 'Cursed be the hour I met you, you bitch; because of you I have to abandon my son who may be dead from the cold in the mountains.' Well I wanted to say to her that she should leave me, but I couldn't speak. Then I saw lights, coloured lights, like the beginning of a town and I said, 'Look, there's a fair.' Julia said, 'I shit on your mother; a fair! a fair! Daughter of a whore.' All the way down she went on like that. Perhaps there were coloured lights left from Christmas; anyway they certainly looked coloured to me.

At the bottom the road went along the foot of the mountain and then there was a bridge and on the far side a church. When we reached the bridge, I don't know what time it was but it was still dark, policemen appeared on each side of the road and came towards us. They said, '*Oro, Oro*. Gold, gold.' Julia let out a yell of rage, 'Shit for you!' They waved us past, '*Allez, allez*. Go on.' They took us over the bridge to a school which was in a meadow alongside the river.

There were Senegalese guards at the school and inside there was straw on the floor for the sick to lie on. In the yard outside it was snowing or raining; I could see the drops coming down. Julia told them to give me something hot and they boiled up some coffee in a big iron cauldron, like the ones they use to cook up pigs' feed. I was given a bowl of coffee and milk and when I tried to drink it I sicked it up; I don't think it even reached my stomach. Then I was laid down in the straw just as I was, with my clothes soaked through. All the very ill people were put in the school apart from all the others who were in the field, outside in the rain.

Someone said to me, 'Hey, is that you?' It was a wounded soldier from the hospital. 'What's the matter with you?' 'I don't know; I can't move.' 'But you will have to get out of that coat.' 'But no, I'm not taking it off.' 'Come on, you must.' The others there dragged it off me by force and hung it on a nail; it was made from a blanket and it was dripping water. Underneath I had on a new dress which had been made during the war and the water had made it shrink so that the waist was up under my armpits and it was so tight that I could hardly move or breathe. They cut the dress open at the back with a razor blade and there I was, in the month of January, in just a black slip and nothing to wear. A French girl called Mimi gave me an aspirin and then they covered me up in straw. I was lying between two Basque soldiers; all the wounded there were from the hospital at Camprodón and I knew all of them.

Exodus across the Pyrenees – Consuelo

The next morning Julia came; she said, 'The guards won't let me leave, but I'm going to make a run for it. I've got to find my son.' She went into the field outside the school; the mountainside was right above and she began shouting, 'Eduardo! Eduardo!' After some while there was a reply, 'Mummy! Mummy!', but Julia couldn't see him because of the trees. 'Eduardo!' She jumped over the wall right in front of the eyes of the Senegalese and someone explained to them, 'It's a woman who has lost her son.' So they didn't fire on her, they didn't try to stop her, not a move. She crossed the bridge and in a while she was back with her son. Julia had lost her mother and her niece too, but she managed to find them two or three days later.

I eventually found my mother; she was ill and had been put in another school nearby. But my sister was still lost and we never found her. She had ended up in another village and there were so many refugees flooding in that they put them in lorries and moved them elsewhere. If she had been ill she would have been put with one of us, but she was taken off in a lorry to the Gard region. My mother never saw her daughter again.

We stayed five days in that village and after that time I was able to get up and move about and my mother was waiting for me. I hadn't got anything to wear but Julia took a black Spanish shawl, one with a fringe, which she found drying on a wall and she gave it to me. I was in my underwear, with a black, fringed shawl and barefoot. And during that time they didn't give us anything to eat; I don't know why, whether there were just too many people and not enough helpers. I can't remember having eaten. I was waiting on the pavement outside the school with my mother, ready to be moved elsewhere, when an open lorry came past and there were people on top throwing bread and oranges into the crowd. My mother said, 'Run! Quick and grab some bread.' And I ran fast after the lorry and I got a loaf and up on the lorry there was a camera filming the people reaching out their hands to catch some bread. Years later my mother went to see the film *To Die in Madrid* and she said, 'You are in the film. Do you remember when you ran behind the lorry to get some bread? Well it's there, in the film.' I went to see it and the film is shot from inside the lorry and I'm there behind, reaching up my hands.

From the village of Prats-de-Mollo we were taken in lorries to a station and then by train to Valence, and I was still barefoot and without a dress.

9 Across the Pyrenees – David

Towards the end of January we could see that everything was collapsing and our leader, an Asturian called Antonio, who had lost both his hands except for two fingers, said that we needed to get hold of some lorries to take us to the frontier. He went to see the commander of the headquarters at Vich, a man from Santander who was disabled too, and he explained that if the Nationalist forces moved in fast we couldn't just walk across like the others. He told Antonio not to worry and that we should have our lorries. But blow me, nothing seemed to happen and right at the end, when the fascists were already in Barcelona, we still had no lorries. So Antonio, the head of our barrack, said we would all go on crutches down to the army headquarters, which we did and we refused to budge until they found us some transport. Immediately they found some small lorries and we were taken up to Puigcerda, close to the frontier. We thought that we were about to cross over but things were not that simple because the frontier was closed on the French side; they wouldn't let anybody through. So back we were taken and dumped in a former hotel at Regina and there we were without any transport again.

There we were, stranded, and the frontier was only two or three miles away, but for us it could just as well have been one hundred. Everyone was asking how we were going to get across when we had only crutches. In the end we managed to get in touch with some Asturian lorry drivers who were with the army transports at Puigcerda. They said, 'We've put some lorries in a garage all ready to go. All we have to do is fill up the radiators with water (they were emptied because of the severe cold); don't worry, those lorries are being kept just for you.' We waited but everyone was anxious and on edge because the enemy was closing in: 'Jesus Christ! When are we going?' Nobody could sleep. There were some soldiers who tried to force their way over the frontier, but they were driven back. But at last one night word came that the frontier was open and the lorries turned up. 'Come on! Come on! Everyone on board; we're off.'[1]

It was the 9th of February 1939 when we crossed the frontier; that was the famous passage of the Pyrenees, when the Spanish refugees came across the mountains.[2] That was something quite criminal,

Across the Pyrenees – David

terrible. It was a disaster; a great flood of people, women, children, soldiers, driven on by the fear of the fascists just behind.

Once we had crossed into France there was a huge jam at the police control point and all us disabled soldiers had to get down from the lorry. We were searched one by one and the frontier police – they could nearly all speak Spanish – were saying, 'Gold? Have you got any gold?' 'Gold?', was the reply, 'Yes, shit and lice.' We climbed back up into the lorries and were taken to a railway station at La Tour de Carol.

There you could see the extent of the disaster; thousands and thousands of people, most of them living out in the open, in the snow and ice. Us disabled soldiers were taken to a railway depot, a great big shed where the railway line ran inside, and a lorry-load of hay was thrown down for us to sleep on. The first day or two, before the food supply began to get organised, there was nothing to eat and outside the snow was lying one or two feet deep on the ground. As the Spanish army came over the frontier it drove a lot of sheep with it and they had been penned up close by. At night there were men who would creep over in the dark, past the French police guards, and kill one to bring back to eat. That's how we first got some food, by stealing sheep, stealing sheep which belonged to us. Everything was taken from us by the police: lorries, guns, horses, sheep, and after that you couldn't touch a thing. I remember that as the soldiers arrived at La Tour de Carol they were disarmed and the police began to stack the weapons in the tunnel for foot passengers which went under the railway lines from one platform to another and it was completely full. And all the Spanish transports, lorries, vans, ambulances, were parked near the shed where we were. The drivers were removed and a police guard was placed on them and any materials they were carrying.

I managed to get into one lorry and found a piece of lard and in another, a mobile library, I took two fine books, one on natural history and the other on politics called *The Miscarriage of the League of Nations*. But a gendarme came and told me to put them back. I argued with him, 'But these books belong to us.' 'No, no. They are not yours. All this stuff is under French control; you don't have the right to take anything.' 'But this is a Spanish library; this is ours.' He said, 'No, no, no; give me those books', and he tore them away from me. But I had hidden another in my shirt so I managed to get away with that. *'Allez! Allez!*. Back to the shed.'[3]

After a while they began to organise the food. A cooking range was installed between the railway lines, and an Andalusian – he had lost a leg – acted as cook. We were given pieces of beef and he boiled them up whole and we ate that and drank the stock. The cold was terrible; it was like Siberia, and we had nothing to protect us but straw. And in the shed along with us were women and children and civilian men, and all around us thousands of soldiers camping out in the snow. Often when we woke in the morning, when we looked across the tracks to a line of trees, there would be men hanging there by the neck. A lot committed suicide like that, especially the old peasants. The old men used to wear a long flannel band wrapped round their body to support their kidneys and they hung themselves with that or with their belts. One morning I saw two old fellows hanging by their flannels. Ah, my God.

We were a curious spectacle for the French; you would see cars driving up and people inside looking at us. There were not many journalists, mainly tourists. A lot of cars had skis attached to the roof and someone would say, 'You see over there, that's the rich people.'

One day a train wagon full of loaves arrived and it was unloaded into lorries to be distributed to all the soldiers and other refugees. With us there was a sailor and a café waiter from Barcelona who said, 'Don't worry, we're going to get some bread for you.' They went over to where the train was being unloaded by Spanish soldiers into lorries; it was completely surrounded by police guards. One of the two offered to help and he climbed up into the lorry, while the other stayed outside the cordon of police. When the guards were not looking a loaf would come flying over their heads, quick as a flash, and was caught by the other. Those two were really artful. And every time a lorry was loaded they would come back with two or three *miches*, the big round loaves you get in the south of France. I don't know how they got away with it, right under the nose of the police.

With us there was an Arab, a Moroccan, a former toreador, who had crossed the lines to the Republican side. He had been wounded and was badly crippled. He set up a little stove and fried up pieces of bread in oil and we would eat that. Once, while he was cooking, a policeman came and said, 'You will set fire to the straw.' The Arab said, 'No, no.' But the policeman said, 'Yes, yes. Clear off!', and he gave him a shove so that he would get back from the stove. But the soldier was carrying a stick to walk with and, by Christ, he struck the gendarme one almighty blow; he fell like a log. Some other police came and took the Arab away, but several days later he was back with us.

On another occasion I saw the Durruti division arriving. From the station you could see a little road running close by and the division came along there, all in formation and singing.[4] There were quite a number of us disabled soldiers watching them go by and when one of them realised we were there he shouted, 'Hey look! The disabled soldiers are over there.' They seemed to have plenty of food with them and they began to throw things over to us. A big cheese came flying over towards me and when I caught it on my chest it sent me back onto my arse. One of the soldiers in the column had a fine Alsatian dog – perhaps that dog had been with him right through the war – and the police came towards him to take the dog and to disarm him. One of the policemen gave the dog a boot in the belly and it began to whimper and the soldier grabbed the gendarme and with one punch sent him flying. He was taken away out of the formation. The division was taken a little way further down the road, to camp in a small wood. They were out in the snow with nothing to eat or keep them warm, but during the night you could see enormous fires burning over there. They tore branches from the trees and made great bonfires; it was burning magnificently and it must have been good and hot. What astonished the French policemen was that they could get green wood to blaze like that; they said, 'Those men know how to keep warm all right; they could even get water to burn.'

Since trains still came through the station at La Tour de Carol from time to time there were some refugees who tried to escape on them and there were some who managed to get away in spite of the cordon of gendarmes. Then came a time when the French authorities began to separate all the women and children from the men and sent them away by train to other parts of France. There was a train packed with women and children ready to pull out and another disabled soldier and I thought we would try and hide in one of the carriages. 'Come on, let's try and get on and we'll hide under the women's skirts.' We didn't have any idea where it was going, except that it was headed for the interior of France. Well I climbed up and the women began to complain, 'No, no, no. You can't stay here because if they find you it's going to make a lot of trouble and they will make us all get out with our kids. You are going to get us into trouble.' They were bawling away. We climbed in one side and came straight out on the other and back to the sheds.

We were at La Tour de Carol through February and then, one fine day, we were put in a train and told we were being moved to a camp where we would be better off. It turned out to be the concentration camp of Septfonds.

10 Refugee Labour – Consuelo

From Prats-de-Mollo we were taken by train to Valence. We were herded into a ruined factory which had no roof and it rained and snowed inside and we slept on straw. It was a big place and there were thousands of us. There were no toilets and people shat wherever they could; everywhere you went you were walking in water and shit. It was as cold as Siberia and there were no blankets, not even for the children. There were women who gave birth there in the middle of the crowds of people, without any kind of bedding or linen, and the new-born babies were wrapped up in shirts or pieces of blanket; it was terrible. There were no doctors, no nurses, nothing at all. We were like animals; just like a herd of cattle.

We were there for two days and some French women came and said something, 'Bla bla bla bla'; we didn't understand a word. Then they came back later with boxes of Gruyère cheese and enough old clothing for about twenty people, although we were in our thousands. People were fighting like dogs for the clothes. I was sitting on a wooden box and one of the French women must have seen that I was nearly naked because she held up some clothing and then threw it across to me. It was an old grey winter dress, full of holes, and it came down to my ankles but at least it was warm. But I was still barefoot.

When the time came to leave they blew a whistle so that we would get into lines: it was already starting, the forming up into lines, the regimentation. People were saying, 'Where are we going?', because nobody told us a thing. Ever since leaving Asturias my mother had been hoping that we could go to Mexico. She would say, 'When we get to Bordeaux we'll ask to see the Mexican consul', and at Valence she still believed it was possible. 'We will demand to see the consul.' As if all she had to do was snap her fingers and a consul would come running; and we hadn't even got any identity papers or money.

We were all formed up into a line to go through the streets and as we walked along I looked back and saw a huge column; there were thousands, just like the endless lines of prisoners that you see in films. Some carried small packets, others babies; barefoot, dirty, with tangled hair, filthy. As we went through Valence women were standing on the pavement or they came out of the houses to watch

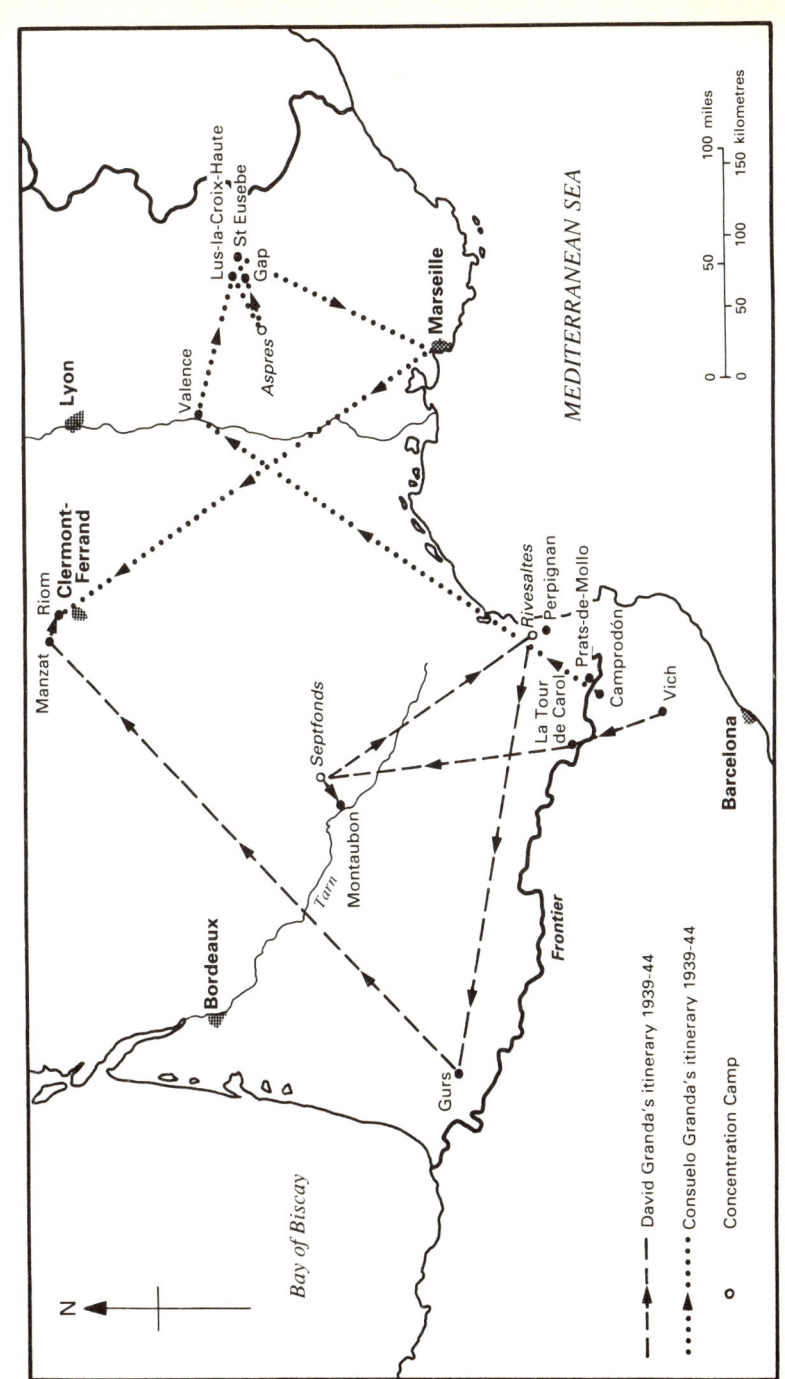

MAP 2 *The itineraries of David and Consuelo Granda*

and some of them were crying. I said to myself, 'Well blow me, we must look a pretty sight.' When you are in that situation you don't see yourself in that way, as pitiful. You feel yourself to be better than the way you appear to others. A woman came out from a shop and gave us a bar of chocolate and she was crying.

From Valence we went by train to Lus-la-Croix-Haute, a small village up in the Alps, in the Drôme. The journey took two days; every time another train came past we pulled into a siding and we would sit there for five or six hours, and then we would move on another twenty miles and stop again. We were given nothing at all to eat and the carriages were unheated and freezing cold because we were up in the Alps in winter. At each town or village we came to the train would stop and a small group of refugees would get out, depending on how many the municipality wanted to take.

It was dark when we finally got to Lus-la-Croix-Haute. In that region, high in the Alps, there is snow for five months in the year and when we reached the little station you could see a big wall of snow on each side of the road. About twenty of us got out and some of the old women began to cry. They said, 'Oh my God, where are they taking us? Where are they leaving us?' We were shoved along by the policemen using their rifle butts, as if we were animals – '*Allez! Allez!*'

The policemen took us about half a mile to the village, along a road covered in ice. They made us go into a little café, a bistro, in which a lot of French people were waiting. They had cleared some tables to make a space in the corner and we were all squashed in there with the little ones in front. And the French people were staring at us like people do when they are going to buy a horse, as if they were sizing us up to make a choice. There was an old Basque woman with us who could speak French and she offered to act as interpreter. An official from the town hall said, 'Well these people want to take in a Spanish woman; they will sleep and eat in their house and be like one of the family.' Then we were each asked a lot of questions, how old we were, if we had any illnesses and so on. I asked the interpreter, 'But what is this all about?' She said, 'It's so that you and this other girl can go to the house of the gentleman over there; he's a butcher and his wife's just had a baby and needs somebody to help out.'[1]

I and the other girl, who was about my age, sixteen or seventeen, were taken to the butcher's. They gave us some soup and we went to bed: that was the first time I had slept in a bed for ten days. Very early next morning the butcher's wife woke us up and made a sign to

1. The village school at Paladin c. 1925. David Granda second row from back, far right.

2. Republican militiamen laying siege to the Nationalist forces inside Oviedo during the early months of the Civil War. *Hulton-Deutsch Collection.*

3. David Granda in Gijón, Christmas 1936, on two-day leave from the Anti-Fascist Regiment, the 'Maxim Gorky'. Note the typical *mono* or boiler-suit 'uniform' of the rank-and-file Republican soldier.

4. Consuelo Granda, aged thirteen, just prior to the outbreak of the Civil War.

5. Consuelo's mother, Maria Contreras-Gutierrez, c. 1935–36.

6. Spanish refugees, flanked by French mobile guards, crossing the border at Le Perthus, January 1939. *Hulton-Deutsch Collection.*

7. The rearguard of the Spanish Republican army crossing the frontier at Bourg Madame, February 1939. *Hulton-Deutsch Collection.*

8. Wounded soldiers and civilian refugees in a compound prior to their dispersal to the concentration camps. *Hulton-Deutsch Collection.*

9. David Granda in the concentration camp of Septfonds, 1939. In this photograph, posed to send to his parents in Spain, he has placed a shoe on his empty left trouser leg to conceal his amputation.

10. Consuelo Granda (*far right*) with a group of Spanish refugee workers on a farm at Lus-la-Croix-Haute in the Spring of 1939.

11. Consuelo Granda in Marseille, December 1945, shortly after the Liberation.

12. David Granda (*far right*) outside his parents' house at Paladin on his first return to Spain, August 1957. (His father is seated, his mother front row second from left and his three daughters Ethel, Marilda and Nadia front row to the right).

come downstairs and we were given two buckets of water and a broom. Well we didn't know what we were going to be asked to do and we were laughing to ourselves, 'Are they taking us on a picnic or what?' It was freezing cold and we were led outside, through a tunnel cut out in the snow because it was so deep, and into a slaughterhouse next door. There was animal blood and skins and offal and we were told to wash down the floor and I was barefoot, standing in the freezing water.

About ten o'clock we were given breakfast in the kitchen, black coffee and paté or *saucisson*, but we didn't eat very much because we were used to only a little food. And it was only then that the woman went up into the attic to look for some shoes for me. She came down with some canvas shoes with a thick rubber sole. The husband said something to her and I understood him to say that they were not warm enough and that my feet would get wet, so she went to get some shoe polish to put on the canvas so I could wear them like that, without any socks. After breakfast we washed vegetables and cut up meat to make sausages and *charcuterie*. I was taken into a bedroom and shown the baby so I could look after it while the woman went to do some shopping. We worked all day long like slaves and both of us had colds and were coughing. When we went to bed about midnight we were exhausted from scrubbing the floors and cleaning everywhere. The next day I was told that I was being kept on but that the other Spanish girl was to leave; she was the lucky one, she was taken on by the deputy mayor to work in his general store and some time later she returned to Spain. But I had to stay there working for no pay, from four in the morning through to late at night, without a rest. Whenever someone came to the butcher's shop and asked the woman if I was happy she would say, 'Oh, yes, yes, she's happy.' But nobody ever asked me if I was happy or not. And the three hundred francs a month that the woman received from the authorities for my pay she kept for herself instead of giving it to me, as was the case with the other Spanish women who were servants with French families.

In that region they wash the bed linen twice a year, in spring and at the beginning of the winter, and the first week I was there I had the pleasure of that experience. We took four or five big wash tubs full of sheets in a cart to the washing place, the public fountain, and we had to make a hole through the ice with a pickaxe because it was frozen over. The water which fell on the ground froze and I was wearing only canvas shoes. That day I washed thirty sheets, although I had never washed one in my life before. I was crying with rage; I would have preferred to have died like a dog in Spain. At that time my mother was living in an old house where they put all the old people that nobody wanted to employ. I said to her, 'I'm going back to Spain.' But she refused, she said that I was a minor and couldn't go without her consent. She was frightened to go back to Spain.

I didn't speak a word to the butcher and his wife. I was so angry that I refused to talk although I could read the newspaper and understood everything. The woman said to her husband, 'She understands, you know; she doesn't speak but she understands. She reads the newspapers.' When Madrid fell in March and was taken by the fascists I had already been there a month and on the first of April I read the newspaper and saw that Madrid had fallen. Among the refugees we always had the hope that Madrid would hold out and that the situation would change. Vain hopes. When we met other Spaniards we were always saying, 'Ah, the war is not over yet, Madrid is hanging on. Things will change; perhaps the other countries, England and France, are going to do something.' I read the newspaper headline: 'Madrid Has Fallen'. I threw the paper on the kitchen table in anger. The woman said, 'Oh là là, what's the matter?', and she picked up the paper and saw what it was. So when her husband arrived she said, 'Consuelo understands French, she understands all right because she was looking at the newspaper. She refuses to talk; she's a sneaky one.' She asked me why I didn't want to speak when I knew how to.

There was an old French woman called Dora who looked after the house where my mother and the other refugees were living and she was very kind and helpful to the Spanish. She said to me, 'You must leave where you are because they are exploiting you. Go and explain to the mayor why you can't stay and that they won't clothe you properly.' I had only one lot of clothes; if I wanted to wash them I had to do it at night before going to bed and put them to dry on the stove and in the morning get up and dress before the others. I was like a tramp. Also the butcher's wife was always trying to frighten me: it was like blackmail. She said, 'Oh, but if you are not happy you can catch the train and go back to Franco.' So I went to see the mayor and took a little Spanish boy with me who could already speak French. When he found out that I was not being paid the three hundred francs he said, 'Right, you collect your things together today and you can stay with the old folk.'

When I told the butcher that I was going he said, 'You can't go, you haven't the right; we need you – there's the baby.' His wife sat in the kitchen crying, not because I was leaving but because she was losing a free domestic. She was moaning, 'Who's going to do all the work in the house?' And the butcher was shouting at her in an angry voice, 'Yes, if you had been kinder she wouldn't be going.'

From that moment I lived in the 'Refuge' with the old people and the women and children that nobody wanted to employ. But I still had to look for work because the little that my mother and I were given for food was not enough to keep us. During the summer I went with another Spanish woman to look for work on the farms and in one place we went to turn the hay in the fields at around eleven o'clock in the morning, just as it was getting hot, and after that, while the hay dried, we went back to the farm to wash sheep's wool which had been soaked in alkali and the liquid really stung your eyes. The other women of the farm, the French women, would take a siesta but we worked on without a break, back into the fields in the afternoon to turn the hay again and it was so hot up there in the mountains. The sun really burns. We then had to help the men load the hay on wagons and take it to be forked into the bailer. It was really men's work and for that we were paid ten francs a day and fed.

In winter things were very difficult for us because there was little work and it was not easy to leave the house because of all the snow. People went about on skis. But I had to work because I didn't earn enough through the summer to tide us over the following winter and my mother was not working, except once when she went to clear snow from the road for the town hall. I went to work on farms from seven o'clock in the morning and it would take an hour to go a mile because the snow was up to your thighs and I had no winter boots, just ordinary shoes and trousers. I would take a broom to clear a way through the banks of snow.

The people of the village showed little respect for the Spaniards. For example, I went to do sewing in one house during the winter and when I was owed a lot, the husband or the wife said, 'Oh, give her just half the money, she's a refugee, Spanish. If she's not happy she can go back to where she came from.' So I knew that if I worked one week I would get paid, but if they owed me for two or three weeks they wouldn't pay. 'That's too much money, give her just half and that's enough; these Spanish people come here to take the bread from the mouths of the French.'[2] I was often treated like that and generally the people in that village couldn't stand us.

One day a woman from the Red Cross came to the 'Refuge' and said, 'Right, I'm going to give you a sheet of paper and I want each of you to write a list of all the things that you need and when I come back in a month's time I'll bring whatever you want.' We were really happy; we put down that we needed winter shoes, slippers, underwear, dresses and someone even included a swimming costume. There was an old Catalan woman there of eighty-seven who couldn't speak a word of Spanish; she swore like a trooper and was quite bald. We said, 'Antoinette, why don't you order a wig?' And she was waiting for one, she really believed that it would come. We would say, 'Antoinette, you're going to be so happy when you get your wig.' A month later we were each given a parcel with our name marked on it but inside there were only tablets of writing paper, kilos of it, and sanitary towels. But no envelopes, no stamps, nothing. They must have been having a joke at our expense. And the same day they came with a lorry to disinfect us, to kill the lice if we had any, which we didn't. They disinfected us and we were able to have a bath, but as for any clothing or food, nothing; nothing at all.

Fortunately we were in good spirits. In the evening we would eat before it got dark and then go into the yard near to the road to sing. There were women from Madrid, Catalonia, Andalusia, Santander, Asturias and each would sing songs from her region. And the French people going by would look and say, 'Oh, they are full of high spirits; how can it be that they feel like singing? Here we are with a war on our hands and they feel like singing.' We couldn't care less about the war with Germany, not a damn. We would say, 'Well we've had our war now they can have theirs and good luck to them.'

During the summer of 1939 a lot of the people who were living in the 'Refuge' returned to Spain and in the winter of '39–40 the French wanted to make us go back. They said to us, 'Here there is a war going on. Franco has promised that everyone can go back in safety, nothing will happen to them.'[3] But my mother had received letters from Spain, from my Aunt Enriqueta, saying not to go back because she ran the risk of being killed and that I might be in trouble too, they might put me in prison. They shoved no matter who into prison, even very young people. And Enriqueta wrote, 'Your uncle is living opposite where you used to live', and opposite the infirmary was the prison of Infiesto. She dare not say openly that he was in prison but we understood from the letter that he had been there two years. My uncle had never fought in the war, he had done nothing, and yet he was arrested. By 1939 he had been in prison for two years and they had not even asked him his name. My mother was frightened to go back and even if she had not been charged and brought to trial she would have been killed by murder squads. All the fascists were against her because she had requisitioned things from them for the hospital. Years later I was told in Infiesto, 'If your mother had come back, even in 1960, she would have been killed.'

The French told us that we could either stay in France, in which case the daily subsidy of ten francs would be stopped, or we could return to Spain. Those of us who decided to stay had to go to the town hall and sign a paper stating that we were staying in France but that we had no claim on the government. All those of us who were living in the 'Refuge' had to leave because the town hall could no longer subsidise our accommodation and we looked for a room to rent. But because there was so much snow it was difficult for me to get out of the village to find work and we couldn't afford to pay a rent. The town hall told us that we could live in the cellar below; at the back was a door and it was there that they stored the coal and wood. There was one light, a tiny window about a foot square and a stove. We shared the cellar with a woman called Maria who had a boy aged ten, Ramiro, and a little sister of seven or eight who had the face of an old woman, all wrinkled, because she had suffered so much from hunger and deprivation. Maria and I went out to work together, if we could get through the snow or if there were any jobs to be found, while my mother looked after the children. We passed the whole winter of 1939–40 in that cellar. We had no blankets, no linen, nothing; we covered ourselves with straw. I slept in a wooden trough that they used to kill pigs in and the children and my mother slept on planks raised on trestles because there were rats.

I remember the Christmas of 1939 particularly well. The children had seen that there were Christmas trees in the village so my mother asked me to get one when I went out to work; there were plenty of them growing around. My mother wrapped chestnuts in silver chocolate paper to hang on the tree and we lit some candles and turned out the light and the silver paper glittered. It was to make the children believe that it was a festival; they were overjoyed and clapped their hands. But there were no presents; it was just to give the illusion of a special occasion. I worked sometimes for a French woman called Paulette whose son was a butcher and she asked him to put aside scraps of meat for us that the customers didn't want, pieces of liver and fat. My mother fried it up and then added bread and water and a bit of garlic and that's what we had for our Christmas dinner, bread soup. There was a Spanish refugee called Ramón who had been taken out from a concentration camp to work on a farm and he asked if he could spend Christmas with us. When we had eaten we began to talk about Spain and Ramón suddenly burst into tears, he was crying like a baby. He said, 'I was so unhappy last Christmas all alone and now I've got someone to talk to.'

For a long while we had lost all trace of my sister. After crossing the frontier she had been taken to the department of the Gard. Angelina wrote everywhere to try and find us, to the Red Cross, everywhere, but it was rare that people refound each other through the Red Cross. We were trying to find her too, but without any luck. Finally my sister wrote to my Aunt Enriqueta to say that she was in the Gard and through her we were able to make contact again. But when we made an application to the Prefecture of the Drôme so that she could come and join us there it was refused; the Prefect would not accept any more refugees in the department and the Prefect of the Gard likewise would not accept us down there.[4] We were told that we could only be reunited if we all agreed to return to Spain. Well the authorities down in the south decided to send all the lost refugee children and the orphans back to Spain by train – there were so many children like that who didn't know where their parents were. Angelina was put on the train and sent to the orphanage in Oviedo and it was my Aunt Enriqueta who went to take her from there.

Since Catalonia I had lost touch with David and besides he had decided to end things because he said, 'We can't get married; there's no future for us.' When we crossed the frontier he hadn't come to join us so we had lost touch and I didn't know the address of his family in Spain. But at Lus-la-Croix-Haute my mother wanted me to get married. I went to work for one family in the village and they proposed that I should marry a nephew, the only son of a big farmer. He was very shy – not stupid, but shy – but I had never spoken with him. People said to my mother, 'You know the way out of your problems is for Consuelo to get married; you'll be out of that miserable life and things will be easy.' My mother wanted me to marry. 'Things will be better, you won't have to go to work through the snow.' But I didn't want to marry anyone. I wanted to know where David was, but there was no word and it was nearly two years since I had last seen him.

Then I met a Spanish refugee and had two children. I loved to go dancing in the village. I remember that in 1939 another Spanish girl said, 'Shall we go to the dance on 14th July?' (Bastille Day). I made myself a white dress from a sheet and off we all went, the young and the old. The boys and girls of the village were looking at us as if we were strange animals, 'Look, there's the Spanish!' As if we were savages. Well some boys came to dance with us for a joke; I think that they thought that we could not dance and that they would have fun at our expense. But we could all dance well and after that all the boys wanted to dance with us; the French girls were jealous and angry with the boys.

Well in the spring of 1941 I went by train each day to work in the village of St Julien, which is close by, and at the station I met a group of Spanish men who were in a foreign worker brigade: they were wood cutters.[5] We got talking and that is where I met the father of my two oldest sons, José and Paquito. They asked if there were any dances around there. At that time Pétain had banned all dances but the young people would organise a clandestine dance in a barn or garage with an accordion or gramophone music. The police had orders to arrest anyone going to those secret dances; it was quite a serious matter. Well I told the Spanish workers that there were clandestine dances and they came to Lus-la-Croix-Haute and that's when I began to go out with one of them. And then we got married, not because I really liked him, but because I was so fed up with my mother always nagging me. She said that two women alone were unprotected and at that time there was something in that – people would make you work and then refuse to pay you; you were badly treated and robbed. My mother thought that the families where there was a man were better respected because they were protected by him. My mother said, 'Listen, you get married.' I said, 'Well all right. I'm fed up with you going on about it.' But he never came to live with us because he could not leave the foreign worker brigade.

Then, in April 1942, just before my twentieth birthday, we were sent to a concentration camp.

11 The Concentration Camp of Septfonds – David

From La Tour de Carol we were taken by train to Septfonds, but when we arrived at the station it was a long way from the camp and we were all lined up between ranks of Senegalese soldiers to make our way there on foot. I don't know whether you can imagine what it was like, that enormous file of refugees, crippled soldiers, wounded men, all sorts, all strung out in a huge column. The French guards were shouting, '*Allez! Allez!* Everyone to the camp.' There was a song that all the Spaniards began to sing at that time, '*Y critan los soldados, Allez! Allez!*', because when we first arrived that was the constant call, the gendarmes shouting, 'Move! Move!'

When we got to Septfonds camp and saw the lines of huts people began to say, 'What the hell are these sheds?', because they only had a roof and two walls, those facing north and west. And most of the huts had no floors. That place is called Septfonds because it's like a marsh – *fond* meaning a low lying, boggy place – and the soil is very wet and soft. They spread straw on the ground but even with that you would still sink into the mud. The reason why the huts had only two sides was that they were still being built by a team of workmen. A lot of them were Italian and one day one of them took out his trade union card to show me, 'Look, you see, I'm in the Confédération Générale du Travail.' 'Ah, so you are left wing?' 'Yes, yes, I'm a Communist.' But there he was helping to build a concentration camp for Spanish Republicans. But soon after we arrived they organised groups of Spanish carpenters from among us to finish the barracks.[1]

The day after we arrived the police began to issue us with identity cards; they took our photographs and fingerprints just as if we were convicts. Most of us has no passport or other Spanish papers or if we had they had generally been thrown into the sea or destroyed. Waiting in the line with me was an Asturian with a wooden leg who was as deaf as a door post; we called him *El Sordo*. When the police asked him for his card he couldn't hear, let alone understand, and he just grinned and 'Bang!', one of them smashed him a terrible blow in the face. *El Sordo* was in such a rage that he had diarrhoea and he kept on saying, 'I'm going back to Spain. I'm going back to Spain.' Years later I came across him in the street in Oviedo and I said, 'Do you remember that policeman who gave you a punch? Have you still got diarrhoea?' '*Me cago en dios!*' Before the Civil War he had owned a carpentry shop in Mieres and now he was reduced to being a shoeshine; he hadn't got two pennies to rub together. Anyway when I was issued with an identity card I noticed that my date of birth was one year out, but I thought if I say something perhaps they are going to give me a hiding too. Ever since then I've been officially one year younger than I really am.

When we arrived in the camp we were the victims of a propaganda campaign which really put us down. The French people, both inside and outside the camp, had an extremely low opinion of us. They were influenced by the propaganda coming out of Franco's Spain and by the newspapers and radio which carried out a vicious smear campaign. They thought we were a wild, uncontrollable lot; that we were ignorant, without any intelligent ideas of our own; that we were taken with the idea of revolution but were not truly revolutionaries. There was a French deputy from the Basque region, Ybarnegaray, who said, 'Our army is poorly equipped and our own soldiers are short of blankets while the Spanish refugees, this band of terrorists (because we were seen as church incendiaries; the butchers of priests and nuns), while these terrorists have plenty.'[2] But that was not true because we were not given any blankets and for a long while I slept with cement bags over me. The left-wing deputies said, 'It is not true because the last thing which a soldier abandons when he retreats is his blanket. Those who have blankets brought them with them, and the refugees make a sorry sight; it is shameful to see how they are being treated in the camps.' And there were even some politicians who proposed that we be taken to French Guiana, which was a penal colony, while others said, 'The best thing we could do is to put them all in a ship and sink it in the deepest well of the Pacific.' Yes, I don't think you could say that the French people were ignorant of how we were being treated in the camps.

Perhaps those Spaniards who were lucky enough to get to an industrial region were better treated, because the people were more progressive, but in the agricultural regions, especially in the south where most of us were, we were seen in a very bad light. I was told, for example, by the former Mayor of Villaviciosa in Asturias, a man who had left a considerable fortune in Spain, that he was sent with two or three refugees to work in the fields of a French peasant, to hoe the maize. Another peasant came past and remarked, 'I say, I see you've got some Spanish hands; do they know how to work?' The other replied, 'But yes, they are quite civilised and they are good workers.' You see we were not considered as normal human beings, we were inferior and they were surprised to find that we were capable of doing anything. It took a long while to convince the French that we were decent human beings.

Some of the most humiliating treatment was received at the hands of the camp commander, a French colonel who was, I think, of Russian origin. Within the camp was a separate compound called the *camp de triage* where they would take the inmates of the barracks, a hut at a time, to count them and to try and persuade us to go back to Spain. The colonel would say, 'Listen you lot, you say you have fought for a workers' Republic but are you aware that you are here taking food from out of the mouths of French workers? You must choose where you want to go because we can't keep you in France.' I thought, 'Bloody hell! It's unbelievable that he can say things like that.' And he would say, 'If you want to go back to Spain, Franco won't hurt you; if you are afraid you only have to come and see me and I'll give you a letter for Franco so that everything will be all right.'[3] He must have thought we were idiots. For some time French police came to each hut every day to persuade us to leave for Spain or other places; some refugees opted for Mexico or other Latin American countries, and a few went to Russia. When they asked me, 'Well and you, do you want to go? Don't you want to return to Spain?', I would say, 'No, I've opted for France.' 'But why do you want to stay in France? What is this country to you?' 'For the moment I'm choosing France. It's said that France is the Mother of Liberty, the Rights of Man and all those things; don't they still count for something?' 'But France can't carry on with this burden; you are like parasites, you are destroying the French economy.' Other refugees would say, 'Me? I held an important position over there; you know what happens to the likes of me.' And every day they came round like that to put pressure on us and some men got so exasperated, their pride was so wounded, that they would say in a moment of anger and desperation, 'All right, I'll go back to Spain.'

Every day when we went to the *camp de triage* to be counted the usual question was popped, 'OK, all those who want to return to Spain cross over to this side.' And every day there were one or two who went. Straight away those people were removed to another camp where they were given better food and clothing – I think it was the

Red Cross which took charge of them – and then they were sent back to Spain. Almost certainly a lot of them ended up in prison or being shot. Sometimes those who stepped aside to return to Spain were attacked by the other refugees. They would say, 'You bastard, you're not taking back anything with you that doesn't belong to you', and they stripped them naked. The gendarmes would have to intervene.

But gradually we began to impose ourselves on the French and they came to give us some respect. For example, when Septfonds was packed full there were some 23 000 Spanish people and the police just could not control that number. Each day we were taken, hut by hut, into the *camp de triage*, to be counted and sorted, but at the end of the day they could never manage to get us correctly numbered. And that went on day after day, for months, and still they couldn't succeed. In the end the camp commander gave up. He obviously knew that we had our own leaders and our own organisation because we were soldiers and had fought a war and, damn it, there just had to be a leadership. So he appealed to the Spanish commanders and gave them a degree of authority and allowed them to use the loudspeakers which could be heard all over the camp. And immediately the problem was resolved and the complete chaos which reigned was reduced to order.

There was a kind of exchange mart on the camp called the *Barrio Chino* after the red-light district of Barcelona. You could go there and barter anything, a shirt for a packet of cigarettes, a watch for tins of condensed milk; if you needed a postage stamp or anything that's where you went. You could also find every kind of game going on, cards, lotteries, skittles, you name it. Well the camp commander wanted that to end; he didn't want any gambling or market because he thought that con men or criminal types were cheating the other refugees or running a black market. But the colonel in charge was a really nasty piece of work and he ordered the police to go in heavy. The *Barrio Chino* was out in the open and the police charged into the crowd on horseback, swinging their long truncheons. It was like a riot and the police were driven back under a hail of stones. One police lieutenant got hit on the head by half a brick and fell from his horse as if he were dead. So the commander had to call one of the Spanish leaders to the microphone and he said, 'OK, here we are taken for savages; everyday we hear the propaganda in France denigrating us. They think that the Republicans are animals, people without any civilisation. We're going to prove to them that we are not what they think.' So he gave the word and all bartering, the *Barrio Chino*, disappeared overnight. Well the French police were flabbergasted; they said, 'But their own leaders have got more authority than us.' After that the bartering went on just the same, but it was carried on in concealment inside the huts. There were men who would come round the huts asking, 'Anyone want some coffee?', and they would bring you a little packet; or it might be cigarettes or soap. The police couldn't see what was going on and there was no sign of what they called 'the system of extortion' which we practised among ourselves.

But I think that what really shook the French and their low esteem for us was Bastille Day of 1939. The 14th July that year was the 150th Anniversary and, as the national day in France, it meant something special to the French people, but for us Spanish Republicans perhaps it carried an even greater meaning. Well the whole camp mobilised itself to prepare for the 14th of July and all the Spanish artists set to work. Since they had no paints all the charcoal from the wood-burning stoves in the canteens was put aside and they asked all the disabled soldiers in our hut to go round and collect all the stones we could find of different colours and to grind them down to make a powder for painting. Others dug for clay to make sculptures. The taking of the Bastille was drawn in charcoal and paints across the front of several huts; the whole storming was there, from beginning to end. When the French saw that, they were almost struck dumb, they could not believe that there were such good artists among us. A team of metalworkers designed the insignia of their union, a huge cogwheel which must have been thirty feet in diameter, with a compass and hammer. The detail was perfect. Then the sculptors made a reproduction of the famous painting of a reclining nude by Goya, the *Maja Desnuda*; it was the exact image, worked in clay. In the middle of the main street of the camp there was a map in relief of Spain with the insignia of all the crafts and unions. There were other maps too; one showed Spain grasped by the tentacles of an octopus representing fascism crushing Spain. In another relief Spain was behind the bars of a prison and bound about with chains and to one side stood a woman, all in black, crying into a white handkerchief. Some refugees took pieces of barbed wire – there was plenty of that to hand – removed the barbs and made little saws by cutting teeth in the wire. With those they worked bone or wood and made some fine things, rings, draughts sets, little crucifixes in bottles.

And in among all the drama and tragedy, the Fall of the Bastille and the enslavement of Spain, there was a hut covered in cartoons. For example, we would always be asking ourselves in the camp,

'When will we be getting out of here?' Someone would reply, 'Oh but it seems that people are saying that we are going to leave soon.' 'Yes, that's what they say.' And painted on one hut wall was a scene showing two young Spanish soldiers carrying a big latrine bucket on two poles on their way to empty it and the one in front was saying, 'They say we are leaving soon', and the other, 'Yes, that's what they say.' And they were both big strapping fellows, all muscles, and the huts behind them were new. Then further along you could see two little old men, all wizened, almost falling over with the weight of the latrine bucket, and they were still asking the same question, 'So, it seems we're leaving?', and the other, 'Yes, yes, that's what they say.' But the huts were in ruins, they had no roof and planks were missing. And the men were old, with white beards. Another cartoon showed a birdcage and inside, in place of a bird, was a rope sandal and below it a lettuce leaf, and one refugee is asking the other, 'Blow me, when are we going to get out of here?' 'When this canary sings.'

There were things that were so well done that the camp commander saw there was something worth showing to people from outside. So all the French people in the town nearby were told and a lot came, the priest and all. And when they came into the camp and saw our work they were bowled over, 'I say, there are people in here who are really something!' Everything which could be carried, all the little things we had made, like the crucifixes in bottles, they took away with them and to pay us back they sent us presents of cigarettes. The French had to recognise our skill and they came to realise that the Spanish were not as barbaric as they had thought. We were pleased to have countered some of the fascist propaganda which showed us in such a bad light.[4]

The refugees at Septfonds were pretty skilled when it came to inventing things or improvising. Our hut, the one in which all the disabled soldiers lived, was the only one with a plank floor – all the rest had only dirt – so it was there that we put on all the plays and shows. For a long while there was no electricity so some craftsmen, with tools they had made themselves, constructed candelabra cut out of tin cans. They made candles with grease from the kitchens and cotton wicks and some nights they put on a really spectacular show. There were men who played the part of women; some danced really well and they were so well made up you would think that they were real tarts. But there were a lot of homosexuals in the camp; bouahh! Something terrible.

There was a lot of political activity at Septfonds. The political commissars from the Spanish battalions, along with some intellectuals, the college teachers for example, were in charge of our own organisations within the camp. If, for example, a particular hut needed extra help because there were lots of old or disabled, they would send a team of helpers. In our hut, Number 55, all the disabled soldiers were put together and a team of school teachers came regularly to help us wash clothes because there was an epidemic of lice. Or when the mud was so deep outside that we couldn't get through they would go and fetch our food from the canteen. And one day they stopped coming and we began to wonder what on earth had happened to them and it turned out that the police had come in the night and taken them from the camp. They were put in work gangs to maintain railway tracks and we were left without any helpers.

Strictly speaking, of course, that was not political organisation, it was a form of self-help and solidarity among ourselves, but the authorities suspected that there was a clandestine political organisation, and they were not wrong. Of course it could be partly seen in the way in which our leaders could so quickly impose discipline by a word over the loudspeakers, as happened in the disturbances over the *Barrio Chino*. So they began to identify and isolate the leaders. I don't know how they managed to find out who they were, perhaps there were informers, but find out they did, in spite of the pretty rigorous secrecy of the Communist Party. When we first arrived the police began to keep records on each of us, with photographs and everything, just like common criminals. Perhaps they began to piece the information together; if one let slip that he was an army captain or a commissar in Spain they kept a note. We saw the leaders gradually being weeded out.[5]

There were tremendous political rows inside the camp between one political faction and another. I suppose that always happens after a country has lost a war and people begin to talk about who was responsible for the defeat. The political parties were at each other's throat; the Socialists said that the Communists were intransigent; the PCE said that the PSOE, the Socialists, were gutless; and both united in agreeing that the Anarchists had grabbed too much power in Barcelona, that they collectivised the factories and public transport and controlled everything, causing an adverse reaction abroad among those who might have supported the Republic. Everyone blamed everyone else: it was incredible the political battles that took place in the huts; it was like a poison at work.

The Communist Party, which is a party which gets quickly organised under the worst conditions, even like those in the camps, began to hold meetings. At the back of the camp was a sports field and we would be told to go there at a certain time; we would wander over in small groups, a few at a time, and sit down. A lot of the Communist leaders were foreign and I belonged to a group under a German. Well he would explain the situation to us, 'Yes, here there's a kind of poison being spread around to embitter the relations between different tendencies; we must avoid this poison because if not there's going to be a lot of angry fights and things will be unliveable.' Then he talked about our situation on losing the war, 'If there's a battle going on in a ditch you have to go down to the bottom and then climb up the other side and perhaps we tried to jump straight over and fell down in the middle. And now we are stuck in the ditch and the enemy is trying to stop us from getting out. But we must try by every means to climb out, in spite of all the poison which the agents of fascism are trying to spread between the political parties. We must try to cross to the other side.'

Well about that time the Treaty of Berlin was made between Hitler and Stalin and that was just about the last straw.[6] I think that if there had been guns to hand there would have been a shoot-out right in the camp. The Socialists and Anarchists said, 'There you are, just see what the Communists are like. You are the same as Hitler.' Well there is no doubt that for some while the Communist Party in the camp did not have the information to explain the reasons for the pact, because the diplomacy of the whole business was very complicated. The people who arranged that knew why they had made such an agreement, but it took some time to get through to us. A lot of people were really shaken: 'Jesus Christ, are they in the right or not?' Afterwards came the explanation; they said that all Western Europe, the capitalists of the West, were trying to engineer a conflict between Hitler and Stalin. But Stalin saw what was going on. 'OK, if you want to play games like that then I'm going to ally myself with Hitler for a while.' Because Russia was not well enough armed at the time to go to war. Before this explanation came, the camp passed through a really difficult period, because we had just been through three years of war and we thought we were politically educated, but faced with the pact we were really lost, in the dark. 'For Christ's sake why has Stalin allied with Hitler? It's not possible.' But in the end there was a clear enough logic to it. However, the PSOE would never accept the argument; they said that even if Russia had done that to have the time to arm, Poland was sacrificed. Things were really tough.

Among us disabled soldiers in Hut 55 there was intense political discussion all the time. We had a kind of news sheet called *El Periodico Mural*. It was really a noticeboard and anybody who had something to say could write it down, a little political article or whatever, and give it to the secretary for propaganda. If it was interesting it was pinned up. I wrote some things like that, what I thought of the situation, how we were badly treated by the French and so on. Everybody had a go at that.

However, a lot of the day-to-day tensions in the camp had less to do with politics than disputes between men from different regions, especially between Asturians and Catalans. A fight might blow up for any number of reasons. Refugees from different regions tended to hang together and if an Asturian was threatened by a Catalan or anyone else, there would be trouble. One of my best friends at Septfonds was Paulino Alvarez; I first met him during the Civil War in the barracks for disabled soldiers at Vich. He had been badly wounded in the head; half his skull had been shot away and he had lost his memory and could not speak properly. After a while he began to regain his memory and it turned out that he came from Pola de Lena in Asturias and had been the leader of the miners' union there. During the early months of the war he had fought right near Paladin and it was he who mined and blew up the bridge in the pass at Peñaflor between Paladin and Grado, to stop the Galician column from advancing.

Well Paulino may have lost his memory but he was absolutely unbeatable at dominoes. One day he was playing in our hut against a Catalan, a little ruffian type, and he beat him. I think there was a little bet at stake; an argument broke out and they both went outside to have a fight. Well Paulino was a big fellow, in spite of being badly crippled, but I knew that if he got a blow on the head it would kill him because on one side he had no skull. The Catalan drew a knife and put himself on guard all ready to fight. I was standing close by and thought, 'Well this little game has gone too far, it's got to be stopped.' I always carried a walking-stick, a fine one of bamboo, and I gave the Catalan a blow with the handle behind the head, on the nape of the neck, and he fell like a log on the ground. Another Asturian said, 'That's done it, you've killed him', and as I stood there I heard a noise – 'phhissss' – my bamboo stick had broken in two and sand was pouring out of the end. It had been packed full of sand to give it weight. Someone fetched water in his cap and threw it in the Catalan's face and he came round. We took the knife, which had a

The Concentration Camp of Septfonds – David

really magnificent engraved blade, and snapped it in half and gave him the handle back. 'OK, the next time we see you pull a knife round here we'll kill you.' Well he was pretty scared and after that he kept on trying to get transferred to another hut.

In spite of the right-wing propaganda saying that we were taking food from the mouths of French workers, the Spanish Republicans were paying their own way. The French government had taken over quite a lot, all the lorries and material that the Spanish army had brought across the frontier. But later the French said that it had all been returned to Franco. Perhaps that is true because in 1931 the Republic had signed a treaty with France by which it was agreed that if the Spanish Republican government needed arms it would buy them by preference from France, and Spain had even deposited gold reserves in French banks for that purpose. Well all that gold, the guarantee deposit, was given to Franco. But in addition to that the Republicans had other reserves abroad and we were told that the French were being paid ten francs a day to maintain each refugee. During the first two or three months all the army officers in the camps received money from the Republic and us disabled soldiers were paid too. But later the Germans managed to freeze the funds and the Spanish government in exile was in danger and its members had to leave for South America and London or go underground. Some, like Largo Caballero, were taken prisoner and ended up in German concentration camps, while Companys, the head of the Catalan government, was returned to Spain and shot. Well at that moment everything fell apart and there was no more economic aid.

After the subsistence allowance stopped everyone at Septfonds tried to contact people whom they knew abroad to try and get money or food parcels sent to them. You could buy almost anything you liked in the way of food in a shop on the camp, if you had the means. But what we were given to eat was pretty awful. I remember that we were given beef which must have been from a stockpile from army deep freezes because the carcasses were stamped '1928'. Perhaps meat like that is all right from the fridge, but when it was brought in by lorry and then kept in the kitchens, unfrozen, for two or three days, it was very bad. It might have been one cause of the dysentery which raged in the camp.

Anyway us Asturians began to write everywhere for help. There was one old sailor from Gijón who had the address of the Asturian Center in New York; he said it was a really wealthy organisation. So the twenty-two of us Asturians who were in Hut 55 wrote to the

Center and they sent back quite a tidy sum of money. But the French authorities intercepted it and wanted to know where it came from; they said we were getting help from outside political organisations. Then they said, 'All your comrades here are in need. When you draw the money it's got to be shared by the whole hut.' We complained, 'But no, it was an Asturian group who arranged this, if the Basques or Catalans want the same they should get together and write to their own centres.' We wrote back to the Asturian Center and told them not to send any more money and instead they made arrangements through their contacts in Paris to have food parcels sent to us. But this time the food was retained in the centre where all incoming aid from the relief organisations was collected and they said the food had to be shared by the whole camp. In the end I didn't get anything at all.

Eventually I managed to get in touch with my own family at Paladin. When I reached Barcelona during the Civil War I had gone to the Red Cross because through them you could contact relatives who were in the zone occupied by Franco. I filled in a form, but nothing ever reached them. Another time at Vich there was a friend of mine, Benancio – he was a sailor from Bermeo and we had been together in the hospital at Infiesto – and he was moved to a rest home for the disabled in Biarritz, run by the Basque government. I asked him to post a letter for me in France, but that never got through either. Well the first thing I did on reaching Septfonds was to send a letter to Spain. I didn't have a stamp so I just put it in the post like that. That time it reached them and it was the first news that my parents received of me since I left Asturias nearly a year and a half before. My mother thought that I was dead because there was no sign of my being alive and she had promised to some saint or Virgin that if I lived she would go on her knees from Paladin right up to the little chapel near the Palacio at Volgues. I'm told that when she got my letter from Septfonds she tied rags round her knees and set off and that she climbed right up the hill from Paladin to Volgues on her knees.

My father often exchanged letters with his brother in Cuba, at Cieglo de Avila; he was an estate agent and quite wealthy. That uncle was also my godfather, although he wasn't present at my baptism. When he heard that I was at Septfonds he wrote to a friend or business associate at Biarritz so that he would send me money in the concentration camp. Just as things were going badly for me a letter arrived from this man in Biarritz with some money and lots of stamps and a note saying that he would be sending me ten dollars every month. But several days later I got a letter from my uncle in Cuba. He wanted to know what had happened during the war in the region where he was born, at Aguera. But what annoyed me was the political position that he showed; he gave me a whole lot of advice as to what I should do, that I should go back to Spain, that the Civil War had been a mad venture. It was the advice of a priest. He ended the letter, 'Don't think that I am against the Republic.' But everything that he had said before revealed that he was.

Well I was not pleased and I wrote back to say that I had never asked anything from anybody, that I took full responsibility for my actions, that I had not asked for his charity and that there was no point in him telling his friend to concern himself about me. He was quite wounded by my letter and his contact in Biarritz wrote again saying that my uncle was a fine man, that he would still be glad to help me and so on. But I told him there was no need to put himself out on my behalf, that I didn't need anything. So I managed to cut the connection. Some while after he died Castro came to power in Cuba and my uncle's daughter, who was in the property business too, became a refugee in Miami. Well it speaks for itself what kind of people they were.

Given the conditions in the camp I suppose it was not surprising that a lot of people cracked up. The better educated or more cultured the refugees were the sooner they went round the twist. In general they were lawyers, teachers or professional people; perhaps they felt the enormity of the injustices which we were suffering more deeply. When we first arrived at Septfonds the latrines were really primitive; there was a kind of log platform raised high off the ground and you had to climb up there and shit in buckets underneath. It really stank. And then it was completely exposed with no protection and during the months of February and March the weather was terrible, it rained and snowed all the time, and for us disabled it was dangerous to climb up on the slippery logs. But later, in the summer, they made concrete trenches and the latrines were at ground level above big tanks which were emptied from time to time by peasants with a pump, to put on their fields. One day they had removed the concrete covers to suck out the sewage when a man, all dressed up in a black coat and a black hat, leaped in. He walked around inside the tank with the shit right up to his armpits. People shouted, 'There's a madman who has jumped in the shit.' The police came and managed to get him out and his pockets and his boots were full of shit. In the centre of the camp, running between the huts, was one of the major alleyways which we called 'Liberty Avenue' and he was taken down there towards the showers. There were crowds of refugees but they all stood right back because he stank so badly and on top of that it was a very hot day, around the month of June. The man walked down the middle of the avenue, dripping with shit, mad as a hatter. I don't know what happened to him after that but almost certainly he was taken to Montauban because all those who went crazy were taken there.

One day one of the disabled Asturians I knew, a car mechanic called Ordás, was taken away to the madhouse at Montauban. I met him years later in the street in Gijón and it turned out that he had not been mad at all. He said that from the very moment he arrived at Septfonds he could not stand being locked up there; it just was not possible for him to stay in the camp. He noticed how the mad people were taken to the hospital at Montauban so he pretended to be crazy. He attacked the guards, simulated idiocy. When he got to hospital life was nice and easy but after a while he began to see that he couldn't trick the doctors for much longer and they were beginning to suspect that he was trying to evade the camp. But the amputation he had of the leg was a bit like mine, badly done, and there was a pointed bone just under the skin which grated. So when they told him that he was cured and was to return to Septfonds he said that he couldn't because the stump of his leg was hurting so badly. He was so insistent that in the end a doctor said, 'All right, do you want us to operate on the bone?' 'Yes, yes.' He knew that like that he could stay in the hospital for another month, so you can see how badly he wanted to keep out of the camp. But one of the nurses, a nun, told him, 'All those Spanish refugees who come under the scalpel of that surgeon die.' Did she say that to frighten him so that he would return to the camp or was there some truth in it? I don't know.

Anyway Ordás changed his mind about the operation and he knew that he could be sent back to the camp at any moment. He couldn't escape because his clothes had been locked away and all he had on was a hospital gown. He said to the nun, 'All right, since I'm going back to the camp bring me my clothes so that I can walk around a bit, see if there's anyone I know in the other wards.' She said it wasn't allowed, but in the end he buttered her up a little and she brought him his uniform – he had been a lieutenant in the Republican army. He went for a walk round the grounds, and at the gates, which gave onto the main Bordeaux–Montauban road, was a guard. Ordás strolled over and said, 'Where can you buy cigarettes round here?'

'Oh', he said, 'just opposite; you cross the road and you'll find it easy enough.' So out went Ordás, all dressed up in army uniform and perhaps the guard mistook him for a French officer. His idea was to try and get to his wife who he knew was in the department of the Lot-et-Garonne and Ordás was just on the bridge which crosses the River Tarn when two policemen came along from the opposite direction and when they drew level they saluted him! He asked where the station was. 'You can see it just over there. But where are you going?' 'To the Lot' 'Well there isn't a train just yet, but take a seat over there and we'll be coming back in a while, we'll show you which train to catch.' They turned out to be the police who patrolled the station. Well Ordás told me, 'Jesus Christ, I got my ticket, found a bench and along came the policemen.' They said, 'Ah, it's you again; you take that train, the one that's coming in just now.' So in he got and away to Villeneuve-sur-Lot where he found his wife.

At Villeneuve Ordás got a job as a panel beater in a garage and he got on well with the boss because he was very skilled and hardworking. Later he joined the Resistance and acted as a courier between the Lot and Toulouse. Sometimes he would leave on a Saturday and not get home until early on Monday morning and at work he could hardly stay awake. The owner would say, 'What's the matter with you that you're so tired? Don't you get enough sleep?' 'Oh it's OK, don't worry.' But somehow his boss found out that he was in the Resistance because he said one day, 'Well now, you're in the Resistance aren't you?' 'No, no.' 'You can tell me because I'm in it too and I happen to know that you're in it.' And it was true, the owner was in the Resistance. Well after that Ordás couldn't put a foot wrong; he was being paid a good wage and he rented a smallholding and raised geese. He and his wife didn't spend a penny on food.

After we had been at Septfonds about seven months the war between France and Germany broke out. When the Germans began to attack, the government wanted the Spanish soldiers in the camps to join the French army. Well the same colonel, the camp commander who had been telling us for months that we were eating the food of the French workers and that we should go back to Spain with his letter for Franco, now said, 'You who have seen fascism face to face, you who have witnessed Guernica: those who destroyed Guernica are now attacking us. You cannot then be insensible to the nature of the enemy which threatens France. You must join the ranks of the French army, you must help France to defend itself, France which welcomed and sustained you like brothers.' Well we all thought, what a stupid bugger! First he tells us we are scum eating their bread and now this. But we were also told that those who joined the Foreign Legion would be reunited with any wives or mothers who were in the other camps. Because when the Republicans crossed the Pyrenees all the women and children were almost immediately separated from the men, and because of that a lot of refugee families were split up. But any volunteers, we were told, would automatically become French soldiers and their relatives could leave the camps and be given the same rights as French citizens. Quite a few did go into the army and it seems that some were reunited with their families, but a lot of those who engaged found that their wives were still kept in the camps.[7]

After a while the French authorities began to empty the camp and all the Spaniards who were capable of working were organised into labour gangs and taken off to work. The only ones left at Septfonds were the old men and the disabled soldiers. They said, 'We are going to arrange something for you too.' They asked what kinds of jobs we were capable of doing. I said that I would like to work as a mechanic and I was given an aptitude test to see if I could go and work in Toulouse for the aeroplane company Breguet. There was a French engineer and a Spanish interpreter at the test: I was given two pieces of metal, a hacksaw and a file and told to make a dovetail. When I had finished the engineer said, 'All right, that's fine; return to your hut and in a little while you'll be leaving here to go and work at Breguet's.' But at that time the French thought that the Germans were going to be held by the defences right up in the north, but in less than two months they shattered the French army and there was just nothing they could do about it. By then there were not many of us left at Septfonds and they decided to evacuate the camp. We were sent to the chateau of an old and very rich French woman called Mademoiselle de Vals.

12 Aspres Concentration Camp – Consuelo

In April 1942 the police came to round up all the Spanish refugees and we were sent to a concentration camp. An order had gone out from the French government that all the Spaniards who had no fixed work should be interned. We were put on a train and taken only seven or eight miles to the south of Lus-la-Croix-Haute to a camp in the department of the Hautes Alpes. It was next to the main Grenoble–Marseille road, about a mile from the village of Aspres. There were 260 to 290 of us there and we were put into four big buildings which had been a cement works: the cement, which was manufactured in a quarry up in the mountains was brought down there to be put in sacks. The shed we lived in was built of stone, had a concrete floor and was about thirty yards long. Inside it had been divided up with wooden planking into little rooms and there was another floor built above all in wood. But there were gaps between the boards so that you could hear everything going on and when people swept upstairs all the dirt fell down through the cracks. My mother and I had a little cubicle with two iron beds and mattresses of straw or leaves and a sleeping bag and army blankets for cover.

All the doors of the sheds opened opposite the building where the guards and the head of the camp lived; you couldn't make any move in and out without being seen. The head was in the militia, the Croix du Fer, as were the few guards. They were fascist types and it seemed to us that the camp was not under any proper government control. In one building there was a room with a sign 'Surgery', but it was empty and there was no doctor, no nurse, no medicine, nothing.

At that time I was pregnant with José, but all the children who were born in the camp became ill and died. They might live for three months and then they died. Many of the older children, aged from three to five, had tuberculosis and the babies which were about a year old when they arrived in the camp were very thin with skinny legs. There was only one refugee, a young woman from Gijón, who had a healthy baby and that was because her husband was working on a farm nearby and could bring her food from outside. She said to me, 'When your baby is born try and get out of here, because otherwise it won't live.'

All they gave us to eat was spinach or carrot soup but there were hardly any vegetables in it and it was far too thin and liquid, just green or yellow water. Sometimes you might find a little bit of cabbage, but nothing substantial. It gave you diarrhoea and we were running for the toilet non-stop. We were starving. When my mother arrived in the camp she had a coat which someone in Lus-la-Croix-Haute had given to her; she could just button it up. But a year later we were both able to get into that coat together.[1]

On Sundays people would come from the nearby village and look round the camp. One very hot day in the summer of 1942 I noticed a big, dark-skinned man with a woman and someone said, 'That's the doctor of Aspres with his wife.' He saw that I was pregnant and he said to me, 'Have you got any outside help?' 'No.' 'Well my little one that's not jolly, it's not jolly at all. What do you have to eat?' 'What they give me in the camp.' 'And don't you have diarrhoea?' 'Yes.' He looked me over, he tugged at my hair and looked in my mouth and then said, 'Listen, I'm going to give you some advice. Eat no matter what! Anything! Too bad if it's dirty, you've got to eat. Go where they dump the waste from the kitchen and eat anything you can find, potato peels, bits of carrot, anything; or go down by the river and pick dandelion leaves.'

You can't imagine what the hunger was like, a hunger so bad that you couldn't sleep and in the morning you would get up hungry and at mid-day and evening always the same. They gave us just a few grammes of bread and it was so hard that if you tried to cut it with a knife it flew into bits. My mother and I decided to take turns to fetch the bread and to eat each other's ration on alternate days, one day her, next day me, and before you got back to the shed it was swallowed. Once a month we were given two bars of chocolate and a kilo of lump sugar but in two days the sugar would be gone because when you are hungry you will eat anything. You've got just one idea in your head, to eat and eat.

There were some people in the camp who had relatives outside who would sometimes come and bring them food, but my mother and I knew nobody. But I began to go out of the camp at night with some other Spanish women to look for food. The camp was surrounded with barbed wire, but along one side was a river. You couldn't get through in the spring because it was full of meltwater from the snow in the mountains and there were blocks of ice floating down, but in summer you could wade through. Once we went to exchange with peasants our chocolate rations for wheat and we ground the corn up in a coffee grinder, husks and all. It was forbidden to make fires in the camp and cook, either inside or outside the sheds, but we would place lookouts and we cooked up the flour in water to make a porridge. But later we decided that perhaps the chocolate was more nourishing than the grain; the only thing was the porridge would fill you up more and stave off the hunger for a while. Another time, when I was already eight months pregnant, I went with some others in the night to steal pears and we brought back a sackful. That was a real feast.

During the summer, for the fourteenth of July celebrations, the director of the camp asked us to put on a show for the people of Aspres who would pay to get in. He wanted to give the impression to the local people that things were fine in the camp, that we were happy and all in good health and that we were not mistreated. The refugees began to rehearse a typical Spanish operetta, Tarthuella's *La Vervena de la Paloma* which is the story of an old pharmacist who wants to court a young girl, one of two sisters, but there is always an old woman keeping watch. One of the sisters was played by Esther, a very striking woman from Llanes in Asturias who later married a member of the Resistance; the other by a young woman whose husband had disappeared during the war; and the old woman was played by my mother. A stage was set up in the washroom; planks were laid over the big washing tubs and rows of benches and chairs set up in front. On the fourteenth of July there was a heatwave and it was decided to have the show in the cool of the evening. All day I was lying on my bed, too tired and hot to move, but when I heard that there was going to be a film show too that was not to be missed. The washroom was full of people and they began to show a documentary film about a school for chefs; it showed them preparing meat, sauces, cream cake, pheasants, mountains of chips with sausages and sauerkraut; how to set a table. There we were close to starvation and we were going crazy watching all that food, but instead of getting angry all the refugees began to laugh fit to burst, you couldn't hear the commentary. The projectionist stopped the film and said, 'If you make all that noise we can't hear the words.' 'We don't care a damn about the words.' We were crying with laughter. And I think that made the French bosses angry because they wanted to make us upset, to see us complaining, but we laughed as if it was a Fernandel comedy.

The French guards always treated us in a harsh way. If a child broke a window pane or went to the toilet in the open because the latrines were half a mile away, they would punish all of us. Sometimes, when you had diarrhoea, you didn't have time to get right over there, unless you waited by the latrines all day. They punished everyone by stopping the chocolate or sugar rations for a month, the only things which were nourishing. Like that the guards built up the food stocks. The French had got the old men in the camp to build a cellar to keep the food safe; they said it was because they were afraid that members of the Resistance might come and attack the camp to get the stocks – as if they would take food from a concentration camp. That was not the reason why they were afraid. At night, after lights were out, we could hear lorries coming and we thought, 'That's it, they've come to take us away.' Later we found out that they were taking away the stocks to sell on the black market. All round that region was a big potato-growing country but we never got any potatoes to eat, except for a special treat on Bastille Day – exactly seven chips each.

To get our revenge on the guards we would sing. There was an old Catalan woman, a midwife, who said, 'We must not let them see that we are suffering from hunger, we must not show that we are dispirited.' So we made up groups to sing. At seven o'clock the lights were always turned out, although it was always dark in the sheds, so we would go outside on a kind of pavement and sit in circles to sing. There were women from every province in Spain; they would sing a *jota* or dance, the dances of Seville or Malaga, and we would clap the music with our hands. There was one old woman, a peasant from Malaga, who wore big skirts which almost touched the ground, like a gypsy, and she knew all the folk songs of Andalusia and Malaga.

Well just opposite was the building where the French director and the guards lived. We would spend an evening singing and dancing, although we were dying of hunger; you could not have been more hungry than we were. We did it to annoy them, because they would have liked to have seen us flattened, crushed down; but we knew how to get at them. There was an Asturian woman from Gijón, a fisherwoman from the 'Old Port', who had a terrific loud voice and we would say, 'Oliva, wake the boss.' The head of the camp was short but very thick-set, powerfully built and with no neck, so we called him *Toro*, the bull. Oliva would shout across, '*Hijo de puta! Jefe! Toro!*' 'Son of a whore! Boss! Bull!', and then she would sing traditional Asturian songs.

On Sundays people would come along the road which ran beside the camp to look at us: across the barbed wire you could see the cars stop, or they came on foot, to pass the afternoon to stare at us just as if we were in a circus. The old woman from Malaga had a daughter called Isabel who was about fourteen years old, with long blonde hair and blue eyes and as thin as a rake. She was a pitiful looking thing. Well when the French people came to stare the mother would call, '*Isabel, vete a la reja! Isabel vete a la reja, haber si encuentras mozo.*' To go and see if she could meet a boy. She was a pretty sight to find a boy! But the mother had just one thought, that her daughter would find a French boy, get married, and then get her mother and her brothers and sisters out of there. That poor kid Isabel was always hungry; she would have preferred a sandwich to meeting a boy.

The wife of the doctor of Aspres found out that I was able to do sewing and in August she said to me, 'Would you like to come to our house each morning to do some sewing? You can eat with us and return to the camp in the evening.' I was so pleased. They got the authorisation for me to leave the camp to work. The doctor told me, 'It's not that we really need anyone to work for us, but you need to eat something before you have your baby.' Since cloth was beginning to become scarce I made things for his wife from sheets, a beach dress, things like that. Well there I ate like a lumberjack, meat, everything, because they had all the food they could possibly want. At that time they were calling up all the Frenchmen to do forced labour in Germany and it was the doctor who had to give them a medical inspection to see if they were fit. When the peasants came to be inspected they would bring a bribe, a ham, sausages, eggs, butter or cheese, and the doctor would say, 'And here's another one who wants me to find him a severe illness so that he doesn't have to go to Germany'.[2]

The doctor told me that I should come into the hospital at Aspres to have the baby because there were no facilities in the camp. I went in on a Saturday and the hospital was full of wounded Germans from the Eastern front. In the evening at about nine o'clock a German soldier would come into the ward and thrust a bayonet under the beds; they were afraid that members of the Maquis would come disguised as visitors and murder the wounded soldiers during the night. The birth was very difficult; I was eight days in labour and had two haemorrhages. On the last day there was no doctor in the hospital and since it was after the 8.30 curfew nobody was allowed through the streets. But there was a Marseille dentist on holiday staying close by and he delivered José with forceps. He weighed five kilos and the woman on night duty said, 'I say, what have they been giving you to eat in the camp?' I said, 'Nothing, just dish water.' 'Well for someone living on dirty water your baby is huge.'

In November 1942 I got my first letter from David; he had written to a friend of mine in Spain and she had been able to find out my address from my Aunt Enriqueta. I've still got the letter and in it he says, 'I have received your address from your aunt, so like a good comrade I'm writing to know how you are getting on and whether you are in good health.' He sent me his address, he was in the concentration camp of Rivesaltes. I wrote to him, but said nothing about having a baby. I told him what it was like in the camp and that I was making plans to get out.

While I was in the maternity hospital a Spaniard had come asking for me; I had never seen him before in my life but it turned out that he had been in a labour gang with José's father. He was a very backward peasant, he could neither read nor write and he was very naive, but he was very warm-hearted and kind. When he found out that I was in hospital he brought me a big farm cheese, like a St Nectaire, and after the birth he came with another cheese and two or three litres of milk. He worked on a farm for a Frenchwoman and he talked to her about me, that I was in the camp with a baby and that I and my mother were suffering from hunger. She sent me her address and said that I should write to her and she would try and get us released. If a French person was willing to accept responsibility for a refugee, to assure their being housed and fed, they could make a request to the authorities to have them freed from the camp.

Well all through the winter of 1942–3 the woman tried to get us released, but she wrote to say that it was very difficult. She had tried every channel but they would not release us. However, she said that if we could manage to escape she would find a place for us to live, give us directions how to get there and send some money for the train. Eventually she sent us a letter with a fifty-franc note inside and an address in the village of St Eusebe which was very high up in the mountains above Gap, near to the Bayard Pass. At three o'clock in the morning in the month of May we escaped from the camp. We had to wade in the river a long way downstream, perhaps five hundred yards, before we could cross over and the river was full of chunks of ice coming down from the mountains. I carried José, and my mother a little packet of clothing, and that's all we had.

13 The Camps of the Holocaust – David

From Septfonds all the disabled soldiers were moved to a castle on the River Tarn near Montauban and in charge of us was a former Spanish university rector called Martin. He tried to impose a strict discipline on us and threatened to send us back to the camps if we got out of line. But one day Antonio, the former commander of the disabled soldiers at Vich, turned up. He was in charge of a small villa for severely disabled soldiers, all those who really could not look after themselves because they had lost both legs, both arms, were blind or paraplegic. He was a good friend of mine and he said, 'I know what, why don't you come to the "Residence for the Disabled" and work as my secretary?' Antonio had lost one hand in the war and on the other he only had two fingers so he couldn't do the paperwork. Martin was glad to see the back of me because I had gone off to Montauban when it was out of bounds. So off I went with Antonio to the villa in a village called Albe Feuille la Garde near Montauban. There life was really cosy and the League for the Disabled supplied the residence with some 60 000 francs a month to pay for rent, food and staff.

But some time later the funds were stopped. I think that the Spanish Republican government had deposited a sum of money in Switzerland to aid the disabled and others in need, but the Germans had blocked the fund and the money stopped coming through. One day we were told, 'Well there's no more money, everyone will have to fend for himself from now on.' But just then another incident put paid to my good time in the residence. Since I worked in the office I sometimes came down to eat later than the others and one day, when they had already finished, I went to the kitchen and said, 'Oh, excuse me, I'm late to eat.' The woman I spoke to belonged to the Juventudes Libertaria Party which is even more extreme than the Anarchists. Her husband was there, a former Catalan boxer who had lost an arm in the war, and be began to pick a quarrel. He said, 'What do you think you are up to coming here asking to be served at this time? Who do you think you are?' 'I don't think I'm anyone; if she wants to she can bring me my food to the refectory, if not I'll help myself.' He began to shout a load of political rubbish. He said, 'I know you are in league with the boss and that you're trying to organise a Communist cell to get away to Mexico.' In the end things began to get heated and I said, 'Now you really are getting up my nose.' The Catalan came for me with a kitchen knife and at that time I went around on a crutch and a thick walking-stick so I belted him on the head with the stick and he went down, with a big wound on the head. The cook, a sailor from Valencia, grabbed me from behind so I couldn't move my arms but I had a little knife and I said, 'Let me go or I'll cut your hand', so he freed me.

But the funniest thing was that an Asturian called Paulo, who was nearly blind, came to my defence. In his time Paulo had been a bodyguard to the Socialist leader Gonzalez Peña and he had a reputation as a militant who always went armed. During the 1934 October Revolution in Asturias he was being chased by the civil guard and he got hit by a bullet near the base of his spine, just as he was crossing a railway line. He was lying there between the tracks, unable to move, as they closed in and he took a big revolver and shot himself through the temple. He survived, but he was nearly blind and you could see the scar where the bullet had gone in and come out the other side. But he would never admit that he had tried to commit suicide, he said it was the police who shot him. When he was at Septfonds with me he had this enormous 9mm army revolver; I don't know how he had managed to get it into the camp because we were all closely searched for weapons. Well when the Catalan boxer came for me with a knife Paulo drew out this gun and he said, 'What's going on here, who's against Asturians, against the Communists?' He was pointing the gun in all directions: 'Just tell me where the target is.' He couldn't see well and he wanted to take aim, but I said, 'No! No! No!'

Well Antonio, the director, said, 'Jesus Christ, you've really set the cat among the pigeons; you can't stay here any longer otherwise we're going to be in the shit here; there's going to be mayhem.' So I agreed to leave and another disabled soldier came along with me. We took a little boat, rigged up with a sail, and went up the River Tarn to Montauban. We went to a refugee hideout which we called the 'Haunted House': it was a flat that was very difficult to find, even when you managed to get into the right courtyard. The police often came there to search the buildings but they never found it. A number of Spaniards were hiding there but the leading figures were a political commissar from an Anarchist division and a very famous Asturian journalist, Jesús Ibanez, who wrote for the Socialist *Avance* and was a close friend of the editor, Javier Bueno.[1] He said to me, 'All right, you know that I've got only a little place here. I've been expelled from France, I've been expelled from Italy, Argentina, Germany, everywhere.' He was talking about the period before the Civil War. 'But you can come in with us.' Ibanez had been in Russia for some while and he said, 'The "Little Chinese" sent you packing from over there, eh?' He called the Communists the 'Chinese'. 'You see, the "Little Chinese", that's what they're like.' I said, 'But no, it's nothing to do with the "Little Chinese", it's because I got involved in a fight.' He said that he would go to the League for the Disabled in Montauban to see if they would give some food or money to support me and when he returned he said, 'I've been over there; you "Little Chinese", you don't help each other. They're bastards. You should leave the Party because they're worthless bastards. Do you know what they want to do? To send you back to the concentration camp.' 'Oh.' 'But as long as we've got a penny to share you can stay with us.' We slept on the floor and to eat we would go to the market and get a sheep's head and boil it up to make a gruel and we would eat the brains and all.

In Montauban I came across my old friend Benavides who had been in hospital with me at Aviles, with gangrene. Since he knew French and had worked in a bank he had managed to get a job with the American Quaker relief organisation. He said he would find a way to get some food to me, but in the meantime a few of us in the 'Haunted House' decided to leave; we were fed up with the bad atmosphere in that little nest of refugees where everyone was always spying on the politics of others.

Several of us went to see if we could find a place in the countryside and we managed to rent a house with a bit of land for seventy francs. There was me and two other Asturians who had been with me at Septfonds, José Garcia and Paulo, and also 'Paxaro' or 'the Bird', and Prieto, both from Estramadura, and one or two others, in all about six or seven. We dug the garden and planted vegetables and when we had a little money we bought some hens and rabbits. During the day we would look to see where the fruit was growing and then go back at night to steal it. We also took ears of wheat from the fields to feed our chickens. We passed the whole of 1940 there. We were still given a bit of help by the League for the Disabled at Montauban and I would go with another Spaniard by tandem into town to collect our money. I had lost my left leg and him the right and to dismount at Montauban we would pull alongside a wall and lean on it. But coming back there was no convenient wall so we would go along until we found a soft landing spot, where the grass was deep alongside the road, and let ourselves fall off.

Our little group of refugees was quite content in the countryside; we even set up our own cottage industry making rope sandals which we sold. A man from Nice would bring us enormous bails of raffia which we braided into cords for hat-making and each time he came to pick it up he would bring more raffia and pay us. There was also a shortage of the twine which farmers used in their machines to tie up the straw bails so we made raffia cord for them. All in all we had enough to get by on.

Then one day at dawn, around four o'clock in the morning, the police arrived in a lorry and came into the house. They were shouting, '*Allez! Allez! Allez!* Come on, get your things, we're going.' 'But where are we going?' 'We don't know yet, We're going to the Prefecture and perhaps from there you'll be sent somewhere else.' 'But we've got hens and rabbits and our vegetables outside.' 'Oh, there's no time for all that; go on, move!' So we grabbed the few belongings we had and, at top speed, we were hustled into the lorry. We drove around for quite a while, picking up other Spaniards here and there. I already understood French and I heard one policeman saying to another, 'Why are we picking up all these people who don't ask a thing from anyone and have got the means to keep themselves here?' The other one said, 'Search me; it's the Prefecture that decided on all this.' All the Spaniards in the region were rounded up and taken to Montauban. It turned out that there was a tribunal at work in Toulouse, aimed at suppressing so-called 'Communist subversives', and it ordered that all the refugees who were living free in the towns or countryside should be returned to the concentration camps.[2] We were only a short while at Montauban and then we were taken back to Septfonds. Only this time things were very different because conditions were very bad and it was now what they called a 'camp de répression'.[3]

When we arrived at the camp it was almost completely empty; there were only two huts in use, one for the Jews and the other for Spaniards, and they were both surrounded by barbed wire, completely caged in. There were some people already there when we arrived and they were very thin and didn't smile or laugh. We asked them what was going on and they said that conditions were very bad. The superintendent in charge of the camp was a nasty piece of work. When we first arrived, for example, we had to hand over all our belongings at the control point and one Spaniard managed to smuggle past a cut-throat razor. One day a guard came into the hut while he was shaving another man. He said, 'How did you get that razor in here? Right, come. You and the one you're shaving are going to pick all the weeds growing between the huts. I want it completely cleared.' Well the one who owned the razor had lost one leg and the knee cap of the other and he could only stand up with crutches: the one being shaved had lost a leg too. They were both given a pickaxe but they couldn't even lift it or they would have fallen over. The superintendent told one of the policemen, a man called Mouton, to stand guard over them and to make sure that the weeding was done thoroughly, but he refused. He said, 'I'm not going to watch over disabled men in that situation; I won't do it', and there was a confrontation. But the two men still spent a whole day on the task.

Every morning they blew a bugle and we all had to go outside and form up in lines while the *Tricolore* was raised on the flagpole. And at midday and in the evening it was the same show again. And sometimes the rain came down in buckets and we still had to go out. But what was worst was the food; what we were given for a day wasn't enough for one hour. We ate very, very badly. They gave us a soup made with Jerusalem artichokes, which look like dahlia tubers. When they are fresh they are edible, but if they are stored like they were at Septfonds they become spongy. When you were given the gruel they would float on top and when you bit into one all the water squirted out because they were empty inside. We were given the same kind of bread as in the prisons. When you picked up the loaf it made a knocking sound – 'clo, clo, clo' – because the soft inner part had separated away from the crust and formed a ball inside. The bread was very difficult to cut and to divide fairly so we would choose the oldest from among us to do the cutting. We had a plank with a nail on one side with a string tied to it; the string was drawn across the loaf to mark where to slice. After the whole thing was divided up one man would place himself before the bread and say, 'Who is this piece for?' and another, with his back turned, would reply, 'That one is for Rodriguez', and so on down all the list of names. Like that there were no arguments and each day all the crumbs left over were gathered into a little pile and that was given to a different person in turn. We were also given small pieces of pâté and that was distributed in the same way. Once we were given some cherries and when they had been shared out there were eight each, five good ones and three rotten. We ate them all, rotten or not.

When I first returned to Septfonds I had a tin of sardines, the kind which are very salty, and I began to clean off the scales and encrusted salt when an Asturian miner called Seraphin said, 'But what are you doing?' 'I'm cleaning this off.' 'But that's not for throwing away.' 'Why not, it's only salt and scales.' 'Ah my poor lad, put it in a piece of paper for me; when you have been here for a week you'll see what it means to eat here.' It was terrible: the hunger was unbearable. Even the Jews in the other hut got parcels sent to them and one day I saw something coming out of one of their little windows. When I went to look it was the stones from olives which someone had been eating inside. I gathered up a handful and smashed them with a stone to extract the kernel, but there is nothing more bitter than that, really nasty and sharp.

Every Thursday trestles were put up outside and we were told to take out all our bed linen to be aired in the sun. There was a very thick, green grass there and one day some Andalusians said, 'Christ, that grass is good to eat.' 'It's good?' 'Yes, sure it's good.' We were on it in a flash. As we collected the bedding we pulled up armfuls of grass and washed it at a tap outside the hut. We all began to chew away just like cows and a kind of green saliva was dribbling from our mouths. There was also a Catalan opera singer with us, a big burly man like a lot of opera singers, and he would say, 'You must not fight, quarrelling is bad, you should sing.' Then he would start singing a piece from an opera or a Spanish operetta and when he had got through it he would be completely exhausted. 'Blimey, I can talk; I can't go on.'

Before we returned to Septfonds some of the disabled refugees had been measured up by the American Quakers at Montauban for artificial limbs. They had a workshop where they were made. One day the Americans asked for permission to come into the camp to see some of us to take further measurements. When we had first come into Septfonds we had stumps which were quite thick and fleshy, but when the Quakers came they were really thin, like sticks, and all the previous measurements were out. When they saw that they left in a real hurry, 'My God, what's going on here? They are being exterminated.' I don't know what kind of strings they pulled but soon after we were told, 'OK, it's the American Quakers who have got you out of here, you're leaving for another camp.' We said, 'Fine. No matter if it's another camp, even if it's bad it can't be worse than here.' So one morning we were all taken by lorry to Caussade, a really terrible journey, and from there by train to the camp of Rivesaltes in the Pyrénées-Orientales.

At Caussade we were kept in the courtyard of the police station before going on by train. The Jews who were with us thought they were already on their way to the extermination camps in Germany. They were not completely certain, but they had information about what was taking place there. It was terrible for them. Well while we were waiting there to go onto the station someone said to a guard, 'Hey, can't we go and have a piss here?' 'Yes, just over there.' 'But we can't get into the toilet, its locked.' 'How can it be locked?' So the policeman went to check and it was locked from inside. They had to get some tools to take the door off and inside was a Jew who had cut his throat: it was a man who had a bed just next to mine at Septfonds. 'Jesus', a Spaniard said, 'why did he do that?' The other Jews said, 'Because we are going to the extermination camps.' But us, pah!, we didn't believe it.[4]

For the journey to Rivesaltes we had been given a litre of wine and three artichokes between two people. Artichokes are all very tasty with a vinegar sauce, but there's almost nothing in them. So when we got to the station we telephoned ahead to the Quakers at Montauban saying that we were coming through on a train and that we were starving. When we arrived there they were waiting on the platform. The only food they could get together in the time was a lot of potatoes boiled in their skins – there were bucketsful. When they came onto the train, blow me we went crazy to see all those spuds and we really filled our bellies. With the Quakers was my friend Benavides and he told me to write to him from Rivesaltes so that he could send me something.

Rivesaltes was enormous; it was a former training camp for the French army and must have been eight miles round the perimeter. There were people of every race. All of us from Septfonds were put in Block H and we were all like skeletons and some half-blind. As soon as it began to get a bit dark I could only see the shape of the other people moving between the beds. 'I must be seeing things', I thought, I asked the others, 'Can you see all right?' 'Yes.' 'Well by Christ I can't see properly.' We had to have a medical inspection; I weighed forty-six kilos. The doctor said, 'Yes, you are very weak, you are going to go and eat a supplement with the little children.' There were lots of children in the camp, Spanish, gypsies, every possible race, and they went to eat in a canteen run by the Swiss. I had to go there every afternoon and was given a kind of thick soup with grated cheese which was very good.

When you first arrive in a new camp it always takes a little while to find your way around, how you can get a bit more food, what kind of things you can make and sell. But with experience you begin to learn how to survive. I decided to make *espadrilles*, rope sandals, but I didn't have any canvas or cord. I knew an Asturian woman who worked in the camp post office and asked her if she could steal me some strong canvas mailbags in exchange for *espadrilles* for her children. She managed to get hold of some and I and two others, an Asturian and a Galician, unravelled the sacks to plait ropes for the soles and the uppers were of canvas, although we had to turn it inside out because the sacks were stamped with big letters. A Portuguese man had found a way to sell the *espadrilles* outside the camp so we did business with him. But conditions were still bad in the camp and, as always, there wasn't enough to eat.

But there was an Asturian woman from Pola de Siera called Rosa and one day she asked me if I wanted a job. I said of course, if there was something in it for me. She did the domestic work for the head of the camp, a former officer in the French airforce, and she said that she could take me to see him. The next day we went along. Rosa said, 'Here he is, a countryman of mine who wants to work to get a little extra bread.' The officer had been smashed up in an aeroplane crash and all his teeth were gold. He asked me, 'Can you type?' I said no, I could only write longhand. He had a job to type the record cards of the Jews, they had names which he couldn't work out. But instead he offered me a place as head of a barrack. In return there were some privileges, an extra portion of bread, seven centimes a day, and the right to go out of camp to the local town, a fine place called Salses, every fortnight. I accepted and he went to see where there was a free place he said I could start straight away. I was to be in charge of a hut of gypsies.

When I got to the hut it was full of gypsy women and children from Holland, Belgium, Alsace and Hungary and almost every other country, although there were no Spaniards because they were in another hut. The poor things had no electric light and they had refused to give them any bulbs; at night-time, since they had kids with them, the place was a real shambles. So I went to the man in charge of the stores, an Asturian from Aviles called Daniel. He was supposed to supply any bulbs needed, but he said, 'Oh the gypsy women, they can do without.' 'What do you mean, that gypsies don't need any light?' So we had a bit of an argument and afterwards he gave me some bulbs. The women were really pleased, they said, 'Hey chief, you are a good chief.' They told me that they didn't have many blankets and since they had big families they preferred to sleep together on the floor and to share the blankets to keep warm. I said it was all right by me, as long as they put the beds back in place with the blankets folded on each to give the impression to the guards when they came round to inspect that all was in order.

There were a lot of huts with women where there was a man in charge but there was some skirt trouble and the authorities decided to put all the women in one block under the charge of women and separated from the men. I was removed but since I was already acting as head of a hut I was transferred to look after another one, Hut Number 30 or 31 in Block G. The barrack was a big, solid building of concrete with four bedrooms near the entrance and a long, open dormitory. When I first arrived the place was completely empty, the only things to keep me company were the bedbugs. The place was swarming with them and at night-time, as soon as you put out the light, they would drop from the ceiling and you could feel them running about on your arms and legs.

One day a new group of internees arrived; they were all Jews and the hut was filled up. I had to make a list of all their names, have the beds properly installed, issue blankets and look after the general running of the barrack and every day at ten o'clock I had to report to the camp headquarters if there were any problems and so on. Each time I reported I received a small piece of bread and there was one other perk for those in charge of the huts, we could fetch our meals ourselves from the kitchen and they served us a little extra.

The Jews knew that the authorities were preparing to take them away. Often they would say to me, '*España*, Spanish; you David, you Jew too?' They thought I was a Jew because of my first name. 'No, no, I'm not Jewish; but what do you want?' Then one would say, 'Look, we're going to escape. There's my father, my mother and brother and I've got to get them over the Pyrenees. It's very cold so I'm going to take some blankets.' 'All right, take what you need.' Well there were others who went off like that and every time I gave them a blanket each. But the problem was that every week or fortnight the man in charge of the stores would come round and check everything; he counted the number of beds, the blankets, everything. The blankets were locked up each day in a store in the hut. They were all folded and stacked in a big pile and the guard would just count each fold. So each time we were a blanket less I could cut one in half and fold up the two pieces to make them look like separate blankets.

Rivesaltes was a bad enough place, but in one respect it was all right, until the moment when the Jews were deported security was not very strict. The Jews didn't find it difficult to escape and some of them made it through to Spain. Those who were caught were transferred to other camps which were more secure. Then came a time when they began to separate out all the Jews. Several times over our hut was gradually filled with new arrivals and when there was no more space we were all ordered outside and a list of names was read out. All the Spaniards had to go to one side and the Jews to the other. Us Spaniards then returned to the hut while the Jews were put inside a smaller compound inside the camp which was very heavily guarded by special security police. Several days later you would see a train come into the camp and the Jews were put into wagons – not ordinary passenger trains, but cattle trucks. Then as more Jews began to arrive and build up in the camp another lot would be separated.[5]

We would say to the Jews, 'Oh, perhaps they are just going to take you to another camp.' They said, 'No, no, they are going to take us to Poland, to Maidanek.' All of them spoke of that place Maidanek. There were some in our hut who committed suicide at night; they cut their arteries, they stabbed themselves, it was terrible. There was an organisation at work in Rivesaltes to get Jews out of the security compound. There was a group of workers who would drive into the camp to empty the latrines; they loaded big containers of sewage onto the lorry and took them away to empty in the fields. There were some Spaniards who did that job and sometimes, instead of taking out a container full of muck, they would hide a Jew inside and smuggle him out of the camp. A few got out that way, but it was said that the Spaniards were asking for large sums of money to do it – 46 000 francs – and it was a real racket. However, the network was uncovered and some Spaniards were tried in the central court at Riom and imprisoned. They freed the Jews only for money, because there were all sorts in the camp, good and bad.

In November 1942, when the allies landed in North Africa, the Germans came down and occupied all the south and they ordered all the refugees to be cleared out of Rivesaltes so they could make use of the camp. The French got in a panic; they didn't know where to put us and they brought in some goods-wagons in a hurry to take us away. A while later some high-ranking German officers arrived and when they saw the wagons they asked the French what they thought they were doing. Human beings should be evacuated in passenger coaches not goods trains. The French said that there were no passenger trains available, but they were told to find some and when we eventually left Rivesaltes it was in high comfort, in first-class carriages.

We were all transferred to Gurs, a camp in the department of the

Basses Pyrénées; a very cold spot right up in the foothills of the high mountains.[6] There the huts were worse than at Rivesaltes, the surveillance by the guards much the same, while the food was very bad and steadily got worse from day to day. When winter came it was cold, so very cold, and although there was a stove in the middle of the hut we were not given any wood or coal. All us disabled soldiers were put into Hut Number 17; it was all in wood, the floor and the walls, and the roof was covered with tarred cardboard. The cold was quite unbearable and we began to think of a way to get hold of some wood for the stove. Well the whole place was prefabricated, bolted together, and there were twenty-two joists on each side supporting rafters which ran up to the central ridge beam and then the planking had been nailed or screwed onto the frame. I had managed to get hold of an adjustable spanner and we decided to unbolt every second support beam, eleven in all. It all had to be done in one night, because if the guards came and saw irregular spacing between the joists they would have noticed. So we took them all out in one go, sawed them up into pieces and hid them in our beds. I don't know how the poor old hut managed to stay up. That day we got a good fire going. In the evening, just before lights out, a French guard would come round to inspect. He said, 'I don't understand, we haven't given you any coal or wood and yet you can heat the place, the stove is always alight. How do you do it?' 'Oh, we've got friends who go with the lorry to bring in wood for the camp': there were some from the camp who worked as woodcutters to supply the guardhouse. When we had burned all the wood from the side wall and the roof we lifted the floor planks, which were nailed onto rafters, and set to work removing half of those too.

At Gurs we ate very badly. The bread they gave us was very hard and the quantity was tiny, just two mouthfuls weighing 175 grammes. We were given lots of turnips which had been stored for too long and were like sponge. As for fatty substances they were non-existent except for a little pâté; when it was divided the pieces were no bigger than dice and it would be polished off in one gulp. We were also given sixteen grammes of sugar which was handed out in a dessertspoon which was levelled off with a spatula. Often we would agree to give our sugar ration to another person, and the day after to another, and after three or four days you could claim your sugar back all in one go. In that way you would have several spoons of sugar and if you did the same with your bread rations you could then mix it all up with water and have a real feast.

We would dream of eating all the time, day in day out; we would imagine ourselves having a big blow-out. When Gurs was first set up as a camp in 1939 there were lots of men from the International Brigades who kept gardens and planted potatoes and vegetables between the huts. When the spring came there were several old potatoes left in the ground which began to sprout and you would see refugees beginning to dig for potatoes. In the end there were deep holes and ditches everywhere; it looked like they were digging for gold. Another time the place was infested with rats and poisoned meat was put under the huts to kill them off. We were warned not to touch it, but an Italian and a Spaniard scoffed it nonetheless and the first died and the other only just pulled through. When people are hungry like we were they will eat anything. There was a Jew who went to work in the kitchens to clean vegetables and although there were guards he still managed to stuff himself with raw potatoes and raw Jerusalem artichokes. He ate so much that he collapsed and died.

One evening about nine-thirty or ten o'clock a cat came wandering into the hut, a fine black cat which must have belonged to the policemen. It walked down the middle of the barrack, cool as you please. People began shouting, 'There's a cat! A cat!', and everyone was trying to grab hold of it. It was speeding around and a bloke walloped it right on the nose with his crutch and laid it out stiff. A man from Madrid said, 'Right, we'll eat it', and almost without anything to see by he skinned it, cleaned out the guts and boiled it up just by itself, without garlic, salt or anything. By eleven o'clock at night we were sitting round eating cat. I've never seen anything so off-putting; the meat still had bits of fur sticking to it, but everyone ate his share.

A French priest set up a chapel in one of the huts and those who went were given a scoop of boiled carrot. There was a big cauldron near the door and as they went out they held out a hand and got a dollop in the palm. It was a way of profiting from the hunger so that people would go to mass; they enticed them with food. There were some who went and didn't care a damn about religion, 'What I want is food; I don't care a bugger about the priest.' One day I came across the opera singer from Barcelona. I said, 'How's things, happy as always?' 'Oh', he said, 'I've found the connection; when I go to the church they give me a ladle of carrot after mass. Why don't you come?' 'No, I don't want to go.' I never went; it was too degrading.

We got help from various relief organisations. Once the *Secours Populaire Français* gave us all a medical inspection. A doctor weighed and examined us and those who were feeble were given extra food in their centre. The doctors had a chart and worked out what you should weigh in proportion to your height. I was told, 'Yes, you don't weigh much, but if you had your leg you would weigh enough, so you can't claim an extra ration.' They subtracted what my missing leg would weigh! But nearly everyone else in our hut went to their centre in the afternoons to get a little supplement. However, I had contacted my friend Benavides who worked for the Quakers at Montauban, as he had told me to do, and one day there was a call over the loudspeaker for a 'Daniel Granda'. I knew that it could only be for me and I was sent to the hut of the American Quakers. They said that they had received instructions from Montauban that they were to give me a bowl of soup in their refectory every afternoon. So every day I went along and got a plate of soup and sometimes a kind of cornflakes or maize flour with beans. Well that began to give me more strength and to lift my morale. Towards the end of my time at Gurs I ate better than at Septfonds or Rivesaltes. But in spite of that you could see people beginning to go crazy because they had been in the camps too long.

One day we were all woken up at about four o'clock in the morning; the camp was surrounded by German soldiers. They said, 'Come on, everyone outside; all those born between 1910 and 1930, outside.' We said, 'But there are only disabled people in this hut.' 'The disabled too.' There were quite a few disabled who had been given artificial limbs but they didn't wear them yet, or very little, because they hurt and as we went out you would see some on crutches with a leg strapped on their back. We were taken away to a heavily guarded compound and were held there for a week. There was seaweed on the floor of the hut to sleep on. All the male refugees in the camp who were fit were taken away by the Todt organisation to work on the heavy fortifications the Germans were building along the Atlantic coast, the 'Atlantic Wall'. Those who were disabled were only taken if they volunteered. I remember a Jew saying to me, 'Be careful because if you say yes they'll take you away.' 'But I'm disabled.' 'Yes, but they'll ask you to go anyway as a volunteer and I've seen some of your comrades going away before.' 'Oh, don't worry,' I said, 'there's no way that I'm going to work for the Germans.' Well there were quite a lot who went, including some disabled men who had lost an arm. They were formed into groups to move off and when we asked them why they were going they said they had nothing to lose, at least they were getting out of the camp and perhaps they would be able to escape. The Germans made all kinds of promises, that they would get a wage and so on.[7]

It took the Germans a week to sort out the recruits for the Todt organisation and during that time we never ate so much. I don't know why exactly. Perhaps because so many were going off to do forced labour, so many Jews being taken away, that all the relief organisations, the Red Cross, the *Secours Populaire*, the American Quakers, the different church organisations, came running to give us food. Normally they gave priority to children and very old people, it was very rarely that their aid reached us, but during that week we ate very well. They even gave us salami and bread; it was a feast.

After that I think that the French government must have decided to close the camps and each day the authorities would call us all together in a hut to read out a list of the names of those who were to leave for the labour battalions, to work as lumberjacks, in the mines or on farms and so on. But us disabled were left behind. It was always the same problem, what kind of work could we do outside? One day we came across a Spanish captain called Vigile, a Catalan who had been living a long while in Paris before the Civil War but who had returned to Spain to fight. He was the commander of a group of foreign workers in the Puy-de-Dôme and also acted as the chief interpreter. We told him that we were capable of organising to do various little tasks, that we could do the chores in the barracks where most of the work force lived. He said, 'Perhaps. We'll see what can be done.' Then one day, out of the blue, we were told, 'All right, all the disabled come and report to leave the camp.' We could hardly believe it, but blow me if it wasn't true. It was about May 1943 and we were put on a train at Santa Maria de Oloran, near the Spanish frontier, and taken right up into the mountains of the centre, the Massif Central.

14 The Coming of the Liberation – Consuelo

After we had escaped from the camp through the river we made our way to the station at Aspres and it was already getting light when we reached it. We climbed into the last wagon of a very long goods train without knowing if it was going to take us in the direction we wanted to go, but we were in luck because it headed for Gap. We got off all right without being seen and from there we followed the directions we had received from the woman. We had to get a lift with the lorry driver who went up to the Bayard Pass to collect milk from the farms. My mother went in the cab in front with the baby while I climbed up on the back where there were milk-churns and already seven or eight other people who were going to try and buy food from the peasants because there was nothing left in the towns. It was bitterly cold as we went up into the Alps and it was difficult to hold on in the bends because the churns were moving about.

When we got to the village of St Eusebe the countryside was beautiful, with little neat meadows and my mother said, 'Oh, là, là, it's like paradise here; it's lovely and the sun is warm.' And we felt for the first time for a long while as if we were free. It was early in the morning when we arrived, about five or six o'clock, and there was no one in the streets. We were afraid to meet anyone because we thought they would see easily enough that we had escaped from somewhere, especially since we were so thin. My mother looked like a skeleton while she said that she couldn't bear to look at me when I got undressed at night because I was so thin.

The woman had given us instructions how to find the house which she had rented for us: there was a tiny path like a sheep track which went down between two houses towards the *lavoire*, the fountain where people washed their clothes. From the village you couldn't see the place at all because it was down the side of a ravine which went down to the River Drac and the pine forest on the other side seemed so close it was as if you could almost touch it with your hand and you could see little white farmhouses in the meadows.

When we reached the house the door was unlocked and inside there was a big kitchen with a wood-burning stove and a bedroom with two beds and straw mattresses. We stayed closed up in the house all day and didn't go out at all except to wash in the spring, but someone had seen us because next morning we found in front of the door a dozen eggs, a big loaf, milk, potatoes, cheese, two cooking pots, blankets and sheets. We got the stove going and had a real feast and in the evening the Spanish refugee who had visited me in hospital and had arranged all that came to see us. He said that in a few days time I could start work for his employer and for her sister and that they had already asked other people in the village and there would be no lack of work. They could pay me in money or kind, as I liked. One woman in the village lent me a sewing machine, another person a pram for José; the people were very, very kind. A woman came and said that she could deliver us two litres of milk every evening and that we could pay her later in money or by working. Well there we were happy. My mother couldn't believe our good luck after what we had been through in the camp.

There was a Spanish woman living in a little village near by. She was not a Republican refugee but had lived in Marseille for years and had come up into the mountains with her two babies because of the allied bombing. She said that if I could buy food locally, lard, ham, butter, cheese and so on, we could take it in a suitcase to Marseille and get a good price because there was a great shortage in the city. I soon got to know the people in St Eusebe so it was easy. On our first trip down to Marseille I bought an old radio for two kilos of butter and from then on we could listen to Radio London and we knew everything that was going on in the war.

One day I went down to Gap and by chance managed to find Esther, the very beautiful Spanish girl who had been in the camp with me at Aspres. Her parents had managed to get out and had rented a little flat and Esther was living with them. We got talking and Esther asked, 'Do you know Marseille?' I said yes and she invited me to go with her one day to buy art materials for a painter that she knew. So some while later I returned to Gap and stayed overnight with her parents who were Asturian. We talked about things back home, but they didn't have any idea that their daughter was in the Resistance.

Next day we set off for Marseille with two enormous suitcases which we could hardly lift. I said, 'But what on earth have you got in them?' 'Oh, there are potatoes for the friends we're going to stay with.' We caught the train from Gap to Vienne and there we had to change but when the Paris–Marseille train came in it was packed full, except for some carriages reserved for the Germans, which were nearly empty. Esther said, 'Right, we've got no time to wait, we'll get in with the Germans.' 'Well you've got a nerve.' But we couldn't lift the suitcases up into the train and two Germans got out and carried them in for us. The soldiers were very polite. They were reading newspapers and Esther said, 'Speak in French not Spanish.' If the Germans knew you were Spanish or saw your identity card which was marked, 'Spanish Refugee', they would say, 'Spanish refugee? Communist and terrorist.' And that was it, you were in trouble. So we spoke the bit of French that we knew because since the Germans didn't know much French either they couldn't tell if you spoke it well or not.

When we arrived at Marseille we couldn't get the suitcases down and again the Germans offered to carry them. They were so heavy they asked, 'What have you got in the cases?' Esther said they were potatoes for her family who lived in Marseille. The soldiers carried the cases down onto the platform and then right through the two checkpoints where people were usually searched. At the French control the soldiers were let through without a word and the same at the German checkpoint and they came with us right out to the taxi ranks in front of the St Charles station. As we got into the taxi Esther said, 'Don't let them know where we are going; any address will do.' The Germans were standing at the door of the taxi and when they asked where we were going I said Ste Marthe which is right on the other side of town. But as soon as we drove off Esther told the driver to go to the Rue de la Madeleine. We went into a house where there were two men and a woman and when they opened the suitcases there were just a few pounds of potatoes and underneath they were packed with dismantled arms and ammunition. I said, 'Jesus Christ!', and we began to laugh. Esther said, 'Yes, I would have told you but I was frightened that you might be nervous.' It turned out that Esther's fiancé was in the Resistance up near Gap and the weapons had been parachuted in for the movement in Marseille.

At the end of June 1944 German soldiers came and rounded up all the young men in St Eusebe and in two other villages close by. There were a lot who had hidden away in the mountains to avoid forced labour in Germany; they would come back in the evening to pick up food and then go back into hiding. There was a young woman called Jeanne who had come to live in one of the villages and she invited all the young men to a birthday party on her saint's day, the feast of St Jean. But it was a trap because in the night the Germans came and surrounded the place and arrested them all. Then they went from house to house to pick up other men and they knew exactly where to look because they would call from outside, for example, 'François Durand, come on, come out', and they were all taken away by lorry. The same night they went to the house of a family of Spanish Anarchists from Catalonia; they turned the place upside down but because it was dark they missed the fourteen-year-old daughter who was sleeping in a kind of recess behind the bed. They tied the mother to the bed and beat her, although she was pregnant. They smashed everything up and took the husband and a lodger away in a lorry to Gap and it seems that they were very badly beaten up too. The people in the village were too scared to go and see the Spanish woman and to give her help and when my mother and I went two days later she had gone mad. A few days later she gave birth to a baby boy, but she was so scared she wouldn't go to the maternity hospital in case she was arrested.

From her or someone else the Germans had found out that there were some other Spanish refugees in the village of St Eusebe – that was us – and during the night they came and arrested some old men and searched for us, although they couldn't find the house because it was so well concealed down the ravine. The next day when I went to the fountain for water there were some women there who were crying and when I asked them what was the matter, whether someone had died, they looked at me as if I had come back from the dead. They thought the Germans had come and taken us away. When I told my mother that the Germans had come and that they were looking for us she was angry. She was not crying, but really angry and she said, 'Oh we can never be left in peace; what do these bastards want? Perhaps they will come back and get us?'

Hidden in the forest close by were two old German Jews from near the French border in Alsace. They lived in a hole in the ground which was covered with a black umbrella and branches to keep the rain out. They passed through the whole of the winter and spring concealed there. One day the man had come to our house, perhaps because it was the first in the village, and asked where they could buy food in safety. At first I would buy him things and he would come and fetch them; like that he could come through the forest to our house without being seen. And every morning he came to get the latest news because we had a radio. When I told him that the Germans had come in the night, searched everywhere and taken away the men, he nearly fainted. He slumped down on the ground, 'Is it true? Perhaps they were looking for us?' 'I don't know, but what ever the reason they searched for us but couldn't find the house.' After that the Jews must have gone off because we never saw them again. They had twin boys and twin girls and the boys were hidden by some Jesuits near Aix-en-Provence and the girls were in a convent at Marseille.

About 15 August the American army landed in the south and moved up really fast towards Grenoble and the Alps because the Germans didn't put up much of a resistance. From St Eusebe we could see the German army retreating along the main Gap to Grenoble road: they had no lorries or cars because they were out of petrol and they looked like tramps, on foot and pushing carts. And behind, fifteen or twenty kilometres away, was Patton's army.[1] The Germans were pushing wounded soldiers along in carts, just like us when we had to cross the Pyrenees. They had no more weapons, no more ammunition, nothing; all shabby and without vehicles – an army in full rout. But as they retreated they mined bridges and houses to slow down the Americans and we could see little villages along the road in flames. There were two men from the village who went down to have a closer look and they didn't come back for three or four days. People were saying, 'That's it, they've been killed.' But they returned, barefoot and in their underpants, because the Germans had beaten them and taken their clothes so that they could disguise themselves as civilians and get away.

In October 1944, after the Liberation, we decided to move down to Marseille. We didn't want to pass another winter at St Eusebe because the snow is very deep and the people have to stay closed up in their houses. If you had the means to lay in stocks of food and everything you needed for the winter it was all right, but I didn't earn enough in the summer months to pay the rent and food through the winter. In Marseille we found a little unfurnished apartment and rented two beds and I found work in a shoe factory machine-sewing the uppers.

While we were still in St Eusebe José's father came to see us two or three times; he was still in a company of workers. I knew by then that I couldn't continue with him. My mother said, 'We made a mistake . . .' I wanted to get rid of him as soon as possible. I said, 'It's finished; I don't want to have any more to do with him.' Then Paquito was born in March 1944. When Llamas was in the company of workers he didn't live with us and he didn't help us at all – he had that excuse – but after the Liberation he carried on the same. It was as if there was just him and he had no children. And in Marseille I told him that I didn't want to see him again. 'Leave me alone; I don't want to see you again and don't come here ever. Forget me, as if we had never known each other.' He went away and we never spoke again.

And about that time I received letters from David and since he didn't know anything about what had happened to me I decided to write and tell him. I didn't have the courage to tell him before, even though he told me that he didn't love me any more and that I should find somebody else, somebody with two legs who could work and provide for a comfortable life. But since I didn't want to know about anybody else but him I said to myself, 'Right, I'm going to explain, I'm going to tell him everything.' I took my courage in both hands and wrote a letter. He replied that it hurt him to hear all the troubles that I had had, but there was no point in regretting what was now past. It was a consoling letter, but he didn't say that he still loved me, nothing at all. I said to myself, 'Good, that's over; now I've told him I can have a clear conscience and there's no more equivocation.' Then some while later he wrote to ask if we could still write as friends: I said good.

After the Liberation there were a lot of Spaniards in Marseille. During the occupation I think that they had been in hiding or isolated up in the mountains, but with the Liberation they all came down to the city, to Marseille, to find the others. Even if we didn't know each other, we were so glad to meet in the street and to talk: 'Me, I'm from Bilbao; and you?' 'I'm from Gijón.' It was as if we were all related, like brothers and sisters; we would hug each other when we met, even if we didn't know each other. 'And where were you during the last four years. . . ?' If you saw a circle of people talking in the street it would be a group of Spaniards. There were two cafés near the Canabière, the *Grand Cardinal* and the *Alsace* which were always packed with Spaniards. If a Frenchman came in he would hear everyone talking Spanish and then go out again. The waiters were French but they had to pick up some Spanish to do their job. We were at home there; you could go, talk with the others at all hours. It was like a non-stop talking session in those two cafés. If you were looking for someone and couldn't find them in the *Grand Cardinal*, you would be sure to find them in the other.

The Italian consulate had been closed down and it was taken over to serve as a Spanish information centre. All the refugees would go there when they first arrived. And sometimes there were concerts there to keep the people's spirits up and political meetings. On one occasion Federica Montseny the Anarchist, who had been Minister of Health, made a speech lasting four or five hours, like Fidel Castro; there was no way that she was going to be stopped. The others, Álvarez del Vayo and Prieto, couldn't get in a word edgeways. The demonstrations were quite extraordinary; the whole of the Canabière would be jammed full and all the people there would be Spaniards, thousands of them. We were so happy to be all together and to meet each other.

Some days there would be a call to go to the Spanish consulate to take down the Nationalist flag. Somebody would say, 'Shall we go and take down Franco's flag?' 'Yes, come on, let's go and pull it down.' We would all go off through the streets demonstrating and at the consulate the most agile would climb up to the balcony and pull down the flag. It was burned and the Republican flag flown instead. The police didn't say anything because after the Liberation it was a bit like a big holiday, a time of freedom. Moreover the Spaniards were in good standing because of their role in the Resistance and the liberation of Marseille. When the Americans landed the Spanish Republicans had already retaken all the towns in the south, Nimes, Marseille and elsewhere.[2] The Americans just walked through because the main fighting was over. So the police had a lot of regard for the Spaniards during two or three years because of the Resistance. They didn't say anything when we hauled down Franco's flag at the consulate.

While we were still in St Eusebe, Pablo, the man who had managed to get us out of the camp, was working on a farm near by. But in May or June 1944 he was called up to go and do obligatory labour in Germany and he escaped into the mountains to join the Maquis. He came one night to our house and said, 'I'm off, I'm going to join the Maquis in the Savoie region.' I said, 'But why don't you stay in the mountains round here?' 'Oh, because a friend has written to say that I'm needed down there and, if I can, to take a supply of cigarettes.' It seems that was the one thing they were short of in the Maquis. He bought tobacco on the black market and sent me round to buy up cigarettes wherever I could find them. He filled up a suitcase and off he went. But he was naive because at that time the Savoie Maquis was surrounded by the Germans. He told me later, when he came back from Germany, that when he got off the bus he was well dressed in a suit, like a traveller, and carrying his suitcase full of tobacco. But he was followed by the Germans; they picked him up and he was beaten so badly he couldn't stand up. They asked him where he was going, but he didn't say a word, and afterwards they sent him to a concentration camp in Germany – I think it was Belsen. There he was held for three months in a kind of pillory and beaten.

In April or May 1945 I was waiting at a bus stop in Marseille and just as I got onto the bus I heard someone shouting, 'Consuelo!

Consuelo!', and I could see a small man trying to run after the bus. I got off at the next stop and walked back and it was Pablo. He was just like a skeleton. Before he had been a big strong man but he must have lost at least eighty pounds in weight. His neck was a scraggy thing and thin like that of a baby, his head was covered in lumps and his eyes were sunk so deep into their sockets and he was still wearing the striped prison uniform of the camps because he had just arrived the day before. Every day people were arriving like that from the concentration camps. In the evening people would go to the station to welcome back the deported people as they got off the Paris train; some could just walk, others were carried on stretchers, and they were still wearing the striped clothing of the camps. Pablo could walk, but his legs were all wobbly like someone who was drunk.

Pablo told me that he had starved for three months; the only food he had eaten was a thin cabbage soup. And for all that time he couldn't sit because he was locked up with his ankles and wrists in iron rings held by chains and his head stuck through a wooden board like a pillory. When he was released by the English he fell in a heap on the ground; he said just like an umbrella without any ribs in it: if you put it on the ground it would just collapse. The English had filled bowls with dry milk powder and before they could mix it up with water the starving prisoners threw themselves on all fours and began to eat like pigs from a trough. 'We fought', he said, 'to get to the bowls.' But he nearly choked to death on the dry powder and had to be taken to a first aid post. He survived because he was very strong, but a lot of the others died from suffocation. He said, 'I saw them dropping like flies.' You could see the wood burns round his neck where it had been in the plank for three months and the marks of the chains on his ankles.

I wrote to David to ask him if he wanted to come to Marseille; I had even found work for him. I knew a Basque doctor who worked in an American dining room and she said that she would be able to get him a place handing out meal tickets at a counter. It paid quite well and, most important, you got fed. But David didn't want to come because he had already found a job in an aluminium factory in Riom. So I said to my mother, 'Right, I'm going to see David.' 'What for?' 'Just to see him.' He had asked me to go and visit him and all the things we had to say to each other couldn't be said by letter, we had to talk. I went to Riom and we talked non-stop for three days and then we agreed that I should come back in a month's time and that we would live together.

15 The Coming of the Liberation – David

When we left the camp at Gurs we were taken by train to St Gervais d'Auvergne up in the mountains of the Puy-de-Dôme. While we were waiting at the station for the lorries to come and take us down to the headquarters of the foreign workers group at Manzat we met some Spanish woodcutters. There were a lot of them working in the forests around there and they were free to move about as they pleased. When they saw us they made a collection among themselves and the money was handed over to a man called Espinosa. There was a fair amount but there was some trouble a few days later when he gave us a packet of cigarettes each as our share. Everyone said, 'That bastard is trying to buy us off with a packet, but he's kept half the money for himself.' They wanted to punch his face in. Eventually we were taken down to Manzat by lorry – it's just a little town with a few shops and bars – and it was already dark when we arrived and the other Spaniards had been waiting for us since late afternoon with a cauldron full of lentils and peas. They gave us so much to eat that most of us were ill during the night.

Next day we were free to go out and walk around just as we liked. Those who had a little money bought things while those of us who had nothing just wandered about and watched the people. It was the first time for a long while that we felt free. Near to Manzat there was a dairy where they made cheese and we heard that there was whey to be had, the part of the milk which is separated out in cheesemaking and which is usually given to the pigs. Quite a number of us disabled went and when we got there we found Jesús Travieso, from Gurs, and another Spaniard who had been in the secret police before the Civil War. They said that it was true that there was whey for sale and they had drunk so much they couldn't get up. Well, both of them were lying on the ground unable to move.

The labour barracks at Manzat worked in the following way: if a peasant or small employer in the region was in need of a worker he could come along to the barracks. The work centre was responsible for finding us clothes and boots and the peasant would lodge and feed the worker and pay a really small amount directly to the barracks. We were told that the whole system was to provide help to the peasants, but it was a wholly exploitative arrangement. The peasant got a worker for almost nothing and of the money he paid to the work group very little reached us; most ended up in the hands of the government. What was also absurd was that in an agricultural region like that there was no work suited to many of the refugees who had never touched a pick or fork in their life. Yet you would see a teacher or professor working in a quarry or trying to cut hay. However, most of the Spaniards at Manzat were found work of one kind or another and in the barracks they set up a cartwright's shop, because at that time everything was carried in carts, and there was also a big stable of mules. But when most people had been found a job there was still the problem of finding something for us disabled to do. We had begun to make *espadrilles*, by unravelling blankets or sacks to twist ropes for the soles, as well as other small articles. We would go round the farms and barter a pair of *espadrilles* for a cheese or a piece of bread, or if we made a bit of money we would buy tobacco.

But in time the French directors of the group began to see that they couldn't find us proper jobs so we were sent elsewhere. I and a few others were sent a few miles away to a little spa town called Chateauneuf-les-Bains where there was an hotel full of refugees. Most of them were Jewish women from Belgium, Holland and Germany, although there were also a few men lying low there who had the private means to do so.[1] When we arrived several of us disabled worked as a team to cut wood for the kitchen or we swept the courtyard and did other jobs. The hotel was full of women who spent the entire day playing bridge and other card games and amusing themselves. Every day we cut wood and when we had finished our duties we would go off for a walk. One day I was with another Asturian, José Garcia – he had lost a leg too in the war – and we saw that our names were down for peeling potatoes, on the work list pinned up on the wall. All those Jewish women were sitting around doing nothing and we were put down for spud bashing. We said to the French boss, 'We will cut wood, we'll sweep the yard if you like, we'll do the man's work, but we're not going to peel potatoes.' A bit of that famous Spanish pride was coming out, 'If you don't peel the potatoes I've got the power to have you sent back to the concentration camps, only this time it will be Vernet. That's not like the camps you were in before; that was like a holiday compared to Vernet.'[2] 'It doesn't make any difference; we are not going to peel potatoes.' A Spaniard, a former engineer, who worked in the office said, 'You're both mad. You must peel the potatoes because the boss doesn't mince his words. He really will send you to a concentration camp.' We said, 'He can send us where he likes; we've said once that we won't peel potatoes so the matter is closed. We are not peeling potatoes. Up to now we've cut the wood, if they want the potatoes peeled all they have to do is organise a few of those women.' 'If that's how you feel about it. But it's rank disobedience and he's going to send you to a camp.'

José and I decided we would make a break for it, but the silly buggers in charge had our ration books locked up in the office and if we cleared off without them we wouldn't be able to buy any food. There was no way we could get in there unseen to steal them. The cook in the hotel and her husband were Spaniards and we knew that we could trust them. We told them that the director was intending to send us to Vernet and that to make a trip that long they would have to prepare three or four days' rations. The cook promised to let us know if she was asked to make food parcels ready. The day before José and I had been up to a water-mill in the mountains above Chateauneuf, on the road to St Georges d'Auvergne, and the miller had given us some flour in exchange for *espadrilles*. We asked the cook to bake us some bread in readiness for our escape. A little while later she came to look for us: the boss had told her to prepare cold rations for two people, two days supply each. From these preparations we knew that the police would have been informed and that they would be there in the morning to take us away. So at three o'clock in the morning we took our supply of bread which the cook had baked, got our crutches and made off across country through the fields, which were deep in snow. We came to a road and when a bus came past early in the morning we stopped it and went down from the mountains to the plain, to the town of Riom.

Right next to Riom is a village called Mozac where there were the barracks of another foreign worker group, so we went along there. The Spaniards lived in wooden huts and most of them went out to work in factories. They did their cooking there and ran a '*popote*', a system by which they shared all the food expenses and ate together. When we showed up the man in charge said we could stay there while things were sorted out and that we would need to see the commander in charge of all the foreign workers in the Puy-de-Dôme. The commander, a Frenchman, was a really decent type. He telephoned straight away to the director of Chateauneuf-les-Bains and spoke in our presence: 'I've got two badly disabled workers here in my office; they quitted your place because they say you wanted to send them to a concentration camp?' The other said it was open rebellion; that we refused to do the things which he ordered. The commander replied, 'Our job is to get these people out of the camps, not to send them back inside.' He asked us if we had any kind of identity card. The first time we had been freed from Septfonds to go to Montauban the police had issued us with a little paper, a pass card, but they were still locked up at Chateauneuf. The commander said he would try and get them back so we wouldn't get into difficulties moving about and several days later he managed to get them returned.

However, that wasn't the end of our troubles because the director at Chateauneuf had informed the police that we were on the run and they were still searching for us to take us back. We knew what was going on because some police telephoned the Spanish barracks at Mozac and said, 'Have you got two disabled men there? Tell them to clear off because we're coming soon to pick them up.' That was in 1944 and was a sign of the way in which people were going over to the Resistance, as soon as they saw that it was finished for the Germans. At that moment I was helping to load a lorry with hay to take up to Manzat for the mules and the cart-horses of the worker group. A bloke called Minguillon said, 'I'll leave a hole in the hay so you can hide, but we can't take you back to Manzat. We'll leave you in Combronde.' Sure enough, just after we had left in the lorry of hay, the police arrived at Manzat to carry out their orders, although they were not keen to arrest us at all. In Combronde, a small town a few miles from Riom, there was a centre for Spanish women and children and there we were hidden in an attic where we slept on piles of seaweed. After a while we had to move on again because somebody was going to inform on us and our friends came in a lorry to take us back up to Manzat.

At Manzat the men in the Spanish labour battalion were already a little more free in their movements and they had formed a *popote* to share the food expenses. But us disabled were always having to depend on the others because we couldn't find work. We were like pennyless guests, always being kept at the others' expense. There were some who would have given you the shirt off their back, but there were others who complained. There was a man called Andreo who came from Carthagena who, when he had drunk a bit, would say, 'There are too many guests here. We pay, but a lot of others don't fork out anything.' Things couldn't go on like that, hearing such words when you were eating. We were always on edge and it was demoralising. José and I went to see the captain, Vigile: he said,

'Pah! That bunch of silly bastards', and he told the complainers to go to hell. He said, 'What kind of men are you? Why were you fighting in Spain? What kind of Republicans are you and where is your solidarity?'

But he saw that there was a real problem as far as the work was concerned and there was only one job available that we could do. At that time the lorries worked with charcoal burners because there was no petrol or diesel and when they came back from a trip they had to have all the dust cleaned out and the charcoal was riddled. It was a very dirty job and whoever did it was soon black from head to toe. Well it was José who was given the job and I said to the captain, 'And me, what am I going to do? I'll have to go somewhere else.' Vigile said, 'Do you want to go with a work group who are living up in the mountains?' I said, 'Yes, but what do they do?' 'Oh, nothing much. Before they were woodcutters but at the moment they are on a little farm up there. To a certain extent they come under the orders of our battalion.' The worker group at Manzat was the '262'. He said, 'You understand French already, you can be useful to the group.' I was taken by a driver called Martin up to a little isolated house in the mountains above Manzat; it was tucked away in some trees near the foot of a little volcano. There were a few Spaniards living there, the former mayor of Villaviciosa in Asturias, another man called Novara, who had been a mechanic in the navy, and Juan Rueda, and they constituted a Resistance group.

The group were under the orders of the French Resistance movement at St Georges-de-Mons. Most of the time we worked the smallholding – we kept chickens, grew potatoes and had two or three mules – but when the others began to trust me Novara said, 'I'm the leader of the Spanish Resistance here and I receive written orders from the French at St Georges.' But he couldn't read French so he asked me to act as interpreter. The messages which came in would keep us informed of police movements or what the LVF (the *Légion des Volontaires Français*) or the Germans were up to. The St Georges group seemed to know everything that was going on and they would bring clandestine news-sheets which we would then take to St Hypolite, a village on the edge of the mountains, for distribution.[3]

Members of the Resistance group at St Georges came quite often to the farm. A lot of them were Poles who had worked before the war in the steelworks at Les Ancizes, not far from Manzat, or in the coal mines at St Eloy. They learned what had happened to me at Chateauneuf-les-Bains, that the director had tried to send me to a concentration camp and that I had never recovered my ration book, so they decided to go after it, because even up there in the mountains someone would go down to the town with the ration cards to get supplies. The men from the St Georges group went down to Chateauneuf and got hold of the director. They told me afterwards that he was shitting himself because they were carrying guns and one Pole said, 'Shall we shoot him straight away or not?' The very next day the director, a Norman called Pomard or Pomier, and another man, the storekeeper who was called Castagnier, fled. They were absolutely terrified. The group returned all my ration vouchers for sugar, milk, bread and clothing.

One day German soldiers came to the farm and we thought our number was up. There were three or four officers and the same number of soldiers. They drove up and came into the house and one of them said, 'Who are you; what are you doing here?' 'Us? We're farm workers.' At that moment they caught sight of a lot of eggs that we had: 'Oh, you've got eggs', and they took the whole lot and cleared off. The whole area was crawling with Germans and several days later there was one hell of a fight all around Manzat and right in the streets of the town itself. There was one man that I knew at Manzat and he got under a van and began firing while the other members of the Resistance made their escape. But he got wounded in the hip and couldn't get away and he was kicked to death by the Germans or the LVF. The *Légion*, the fascist militia, were much more savage than the Germans. There were a lot of battles like that towards the end, just before the Liberation. When you come down from the farm in the mountains where our group was towards the plain the first village you come to is St Hypolite where we used to take the newspapers printed by the Resistance. One day some men were surrounded in a house there by the Germans and the LVF and they set the place alight. Only Peyrol from Riom managed to escape.

One day I went with our chief, Novara, in a little horse-buggy which we called the '*Cibeles*' after a statue in Madrid which has a chariot drawn by lions. We had heard that at Charbonière-les-Vieilles, a village not far from Manzat, beyond the Lake of Tazenat, there was a baker who would sell bread without a ration book. The track was incredibly rough but we did manage to get some bread and when we got back to the house the others said, all excited, 'Come on, quick! We've got to get down to Riom.' 'Why, what's up?' 'The Liberation has come.' We went straight down to the plain and when we came into Mozac there was a little bar where the village begins

The Coming of the Liberation – David

and people were singing. The cars of the FFI, the *Force Française de l'Interieur*, were coming down from the mountains into Riom. That's how the Liberation came, in a flash.

One day in November 1944, not long after the Liberation, I went with my friend Pastor to fetch wood in the mountains and when we got back to the barracks of the Spanish workers in Mozac there was a bloke there who said, 'All the others have gone off in lorries and Bretones (a Communist Party member from Madrid) wanted you to go with them. They waited a while but you were too long coming down, so they went.' The Spanish Communist Party was organising a big guerrilla operation to cross the Pyrenees into Spain in order to try and trigger of a liberation movement in the interior. I said, 'Well, it doesn't matter anyway. What the hell am I supposed to do on crutches, up in a front line?'

They took as many men as they could round up and almost the entire group of Spanish workers from Riom went. But the whole expedition was a catastrophe; the whole thing couldn't have lasted for more than a week or so. Some of those who went from Riom, Fernandez, the Fernandez sons, 'Chuleta', and so on, were there and back inside twenty-five days. A lot of the guerrillas managed to cross the frontier but it was right in the middle of winter, high up in the Pyrenees, and of course the whole frontier on the Spanish side, up to twenty kilometres into the interior, was completely swamped by the police and army of Franco. After the first skirmishes most of them retreated, although some managed to infiltrate and to reach the interior. But they had no Spanish identity cards and the peasants in the frontier zone were afraid to give them any help and wouldn't conceal them. They were expecting to trigger off a big reaction, to put the match to the powder keg, but there was no support. A lot of those who crossed over were arrested and shot or put in prison. So apart from blowing up a few bridges they achieved nothing. The whole thing was a farce, something the political leaders cooked up.

There was one Asturian in Riom called Ramón who was sent into Spain and he managed to get all the way back to his home village, Travia, and afterwards he was picked up by the police and thrown into prison. He was held a long while and during all that time his mother, his wife and a small baby were left behind in Riom and, since the Spanish organisation in France was weak in supporting the families of those who had gone back into Spain, his wife and child were completely abandoned. In the end his wife gave him up for lost. She thought that he would be in prison for ever and she took off with a man who had an hotel in Nice. But Ramón did eventually get out of prison and he returned to France, but his wife just didn't want to have anything to do with him and there was one hell of a row about it because Ramón wanted to kill those who had sent him to Spain. 'Bunch of bastards', he said, 'my wife's left me because she had nothing to live on. Nobody helped her when I was in prison and my mother was treated the same.' He was broken-hearted and that finished him off because he began to drink and he died an alcoholic at Riom. But others, like the men of the Fernandez family and 'Chuleta', when they got up in the snow of the mountains just made an about-turn and headed straight back home. 'Chuleta' said, 'It really froze your arse.' There were men who were completely demoralised on that operation; afterwards they just didn't want to have anything to do with politics, while a lot of others ended up in Franco's gaols and we didn't hear from them again, we lost all contact. It just wasn't on to go into Spain like that with a force that was armed with only a few rifles and machine guns. What was necessary was some kind of explosion inside Spain, among the Spanish people inside the country.

On a wider front the period after the Liberation was a great deception for the Spanish Republicans. De Gaulle owed quite a debt to the Spanish because of their part in the liberation of France, but when it came to the guerrilla operation I don't think he liked it and was quite happy to see the thing collapse. Perhaps the left in France said to themselves, 'If Spain catches fire we'll begin to give support.' But when nothing happened they kept quiet. We also expected big things from the Allies. Right through the war a constant subject of conversation was how, when Hitler and Mussolini had been defeated, the Allies would tell Franco he would have to go and a new government would be brought in. It was that which kept up our morale through all the time we were in the camps and after. We were all waiting for the day when Spain would be liberated. But while Franco was, at one time, squarely on Hitler's side I think that gradually he began to break away from the Germans; for example, he wouldn't let them come through Spain to take Gibraltar. Perhaps the Allies didn't overturn Franco after the war because of that, because Spain moved over a little towards the Allied camp. Also the Americans, the French and the English, towards the end of the war, began to move away from Russia and each side began to take as many countries as they could. While the Russians had Central Europe, Romania, Czechoslovakia, Hungary and Poland in their camp, the

The Coming of the Liberation – David

others began to support the capitalist governments on what they called the 'democratic' side. That's why Franco was saved; as soon as the war was over the English and French recognised him.[4] That was a great wrong done to us; it was we who ended up paying for everything. We lost the war; but truly lost. There were countries which were under the German boot and the Allies liberated them, but no one liberated our country. It was said that Franco was a child of Hitler, but as such he was left in power.

After the Liberation I never went back into the mountains but stayed in the barracks of the Spanish workers at Mozac. I was told where to go and find odd jobs. The first time it was at a lawyer's in the Rue Marivaux where I worked in the cellar breaking up big hard lumps of coal with a hammer. His wife promised me ten francs a day and a pint of wine and the first day that's what I got and in the evening I walked all the way back to the huts. But the next day she gave me a pint of lemonade and said that she hadn't got any wine left, so I was already the loser. After that I cleared out a loft for a butcher; there was a huge pile of wood to saw up and they gave me plenty to eat. At that time people would make soap from animal fat to sell on the black market because there was a huge demand for that. So I asked the butcher if he could give or sell me a bit of grease from the carcasses. He said, 'Ah, sorry mate, but the cows are so thin right now that they haven't got any fat left on them.'

At that time I already had an artificial leg but I never used it and went about on crutches. One evening in the barracks the stove was alight and I decided to saw my crutches up into pieces and to burn them. An old Spaniard who was watching came over and grabbed the saw. He said, 'Why are you sawing your crutches up?' 'Because I'm going to put on the leg.' 'But listen you madman, what will you do if you can't walk with it?' 'Well that's hard luck, I've got to walk.' So I sawed up the crutches and burned them and put on the leg and it really hurt like hell. But after a while I got used to it and could get about.

Later we were told by the leaders of the Spanish worker-battalions that the organisation was to be wound up. We were each given a paper, a demobilisation certificate, and told to go to the police station to be issued with an identity card and to get other instructions. Well the French police issued all the Spaniards with work cards which only allowed them to do certain categories of heavy manual labour, on the land, in the mines or as woodcutters. They didn't want to put us in the better-paid factory jobs. The police said to me, 'Right, we're going to put you down as a landworker.' 'But I can't work in agriculture.' 'Why not?' 'Because of this', and I tapped my leg which made a hollow sound on the wood. So they didn't put down any category on my work card. When I got back to the barracks I thought, 'Shit, what am I going to do now?' Now we all had to fend for ourselves and I didn't know how I was going to be able to find any work. 'Bloody hell', I thought, 'if I don't find something I'm going to starve to death.'

I heard from some other Spaniards that there were a lot of jobs going at Aulnat airfield near Clermont-Ferrand and I managed to get taken on by concealing the fact that I had only one leg. Aulnat had been a German base and after the Americans bombed it they were trying to clear away all the damaged hangars and other debris. There were also a lot of big bomb craters, some of them fifteen feet deep and full of water, and we had to cut trenches to drain them. I could work very well in a trench wielding a pick because I could lean on the side. But I had to give that up because it was just impossible to cope with the long journey to work. I went to see the owner of a small aluminium factory in Riom which made pots and pans. He said, 'All right, I've got some other countrymen of yours working here and I'm very pleased with them. In your condition I don't know how you are going to make out, but I'll take you on for a two-week trial and if it works out I'll keep you on.' All the sitting jobs, like packing, were taken by women and the only work going was standing up, so I was taken on as a polisher, the dirtiest work of all. The owner said, 'If you can manage to work standing up you'll do fine.' And that's the job I did for the next twenty-eight years.

When I started to work in the factory I left the work-brigade barracks at Mozac and rented a room for three or four hundred francs a month in a small hotel opposite the hospital. After I had paid the rent and my meals in a café – because I couldn't do my own cooking there – I had just enough left for a newspaper and cigarettes. But later I was able to rent a small room with a kitchen in the rue Gomot and after that things began to get better and I could buy my own food. I knew a Spaniard called Martin who had been in the work battalion with me; he went by lorry to pick up milk from the farms in the mountains and he was able to buy food from the peasants. Everything was still rationed and in short supply but whenever I needed a dozen eggs or some vegetables he would get them for me. I had a little chest of drawers in my room and there I kept beans and potatoes, a plate which had travelled everywhere with me and a

The Coming of the Liberation – David

spoon and fork. That's how I was living when Consuelo turned up.

While I was still in the camps I had written to a friend of Consuelo's, Suceso, who lives in her home village at Cardes and she went to see Consuelo's aunt who then sent me her address in the south of France. We began to write to each other. Late one evening, about eleven o'clock, the old woman from the hotel where I had stayed before came knocking at my door. She said, 'My husband's thrown me out and I've come to sleep with you.' I said, 'But you must be mad. You can't sleep with me; I'll go and stay with a friend and I'll leave you the room.' She had already done something like that before when I was in the hotel. Her husband would get drunk and beat her and one night she came in her nightgown and nightcap saying that her husband wanted to kill her. It was true: I could hear him bellowing downstairs. So the second time I thought it was true and that the old bird wanted to hide in my room again. But it was just a trick because suddenly Consuelo jumped out from a corner in the staircase. She came in and we got to know each other after all that time. Consuelo didn't know that I had moved to the rue Gomot and she had turned up at the hotel where I was staying before. Then the old woman said, 'Well, I'm taking her back with me now. I can find a bed for her.' I said, 'But I've got a bed here, that will do for the two of us.' 'Ah, she's going to sleep here?' 'Yes, and what about it?' So she went off.

I didn't go to work for three days and after that time a bloke from the factory came knocking at the door. He said, 'We thought you had been asphyxiated by gas or something.' 'No, you can see I've a woman in bed.' 'Ah well, that's already better.' Later the boss gave me a bit of a ticking off, that I could at least have given him some warning. 'Well', I said, 'that doesn't happen to me every day.' A few days later Consuelo went back to Marseille and we agreed that in about a month's time she would move up to Riom with her mother and the children.

16 Life in Exile – Consuelo

I came back to Riom a month later and we began to look about for a place to live, which was none too easy because the rents were so high or people would refuse to let because we were Spanish refugees. They would say, 'Ah, no, no, we won't take any foreigners here, only French.' So we had to stay in David's tiny place at Number 2 in the rue Gomot, a narrow street in the old town. The children slept downstairs with my mother and we were in an attic which was full of the bric-à-brac of the neighbours who lived in the other apartments, old cooking pots, suitcases, chamber pots. We slept on a single bed and in winter we froze while in the summer it was so stifling under the roof that I became ill. When it rained we had to go to bed with an umbrella. But after a year we had the good luck to find a bigger place at Number 9 in the same street and it was much better for Ethel who had just been born.

And there we were in luck and things worked out well for us, because when you are down in the mud like we were, without a penny, it's really hard to fight your way up again and to find enough money for furniture and clothes and to build a decent life. I began to make dresses for a woman who had a ready-made clothes shop in the rue Gomot. She would give me enough material, buttons, zips and cotton to make, for example, ten dresses and she paid me three francs the piece and if there was enough material left over I would make another one and sell it for myself and it was there that I could make the most profit. I had so much work. Every day I would get up at the same time as David, at four o'clock in the morning, and work right through the day so that I always kept up with the orders. There was money coming in all the time and there were some months when we didn't even need to touch David's pay. I was happy and the woman of the shop was happy; it went well. The first things we bought when we had a little money were four chairs because we had absolutely no furniture. They looked so beautiful to us and we would admire them as we ate, but they were really ugly, really cheap and flimsy things made during the war. But to us they seemed special because we had bought them with our own money and they were our first possessions.

We had been living together for a year and we weren't counting on getting married, nor did we have the necessary papers to do it because, apart from the identity cards, we had nothing. Copies of our

Life in Exile – Consuelo

birth certificates and other documents could only be had in Spain or Mexico. But my mother said, 'Ah, the other Spaniards are all talking about you living together and not being married.' I was seven months pregnant with Ethelvina and then at that time you didn't have the same rights as you do now if you have children when you're not married, for the family allowance and other benefits. So we decided to get married.

There were four of us at the wedding, including two Spaniards who acted as our witnesses, Saturnino Olmeda and Pastor. And Olmeda's wife told me later that she didn't even know that he had been to a wedding that day so you can imagine how well dressed we were. David had on some trousers that I had taken in and resewn and a blue workman's shirt and I had a pair of new shoes. At the town hall the official looked at us as if we were the most poverty-stricken creatures. Olmeda had a sheepskin jacket tied round the waist with a woman's stocking. Pastor was more presentable in a suit which had almost certainly seen the Spanish Civil War but which was clean and neat. We were a sorry sight. After leaving the town hall we had just got to the market place – it was March and there was still snow on the ground – when we met Favard, the Communist, who worked with David. He said, 'Where have you been like that?' David said, 'We've just got married.' Favard burst out laughing; he looked at us and he just laughed and laughed. 'Is it true Granda you've just got married?' 'Yes, yes, we've just married.'

At that time I had plenty of work coming in all the time from the dressmaking. It was the period when we had the most money and lived the best. Ethel was born in 1947, and then Marilda in 1948, and she could not yet walk when Nadia arrived; every fifteen months another one was born. People would open their eyes wide; they must have been thinking, 'What's the matter with these two?' and my mother said, 'But you are mad. What are you thinking of? You've got to put a stop to it.' David would laugh and say, 'What must people be saying? That we are crazy to have so many children at a time like this?' Because we had nothing at all, only hope. I don't think there was any family in Riom as poor as we were, but David said, 'I'm happy with the children.' And that's the period when things were best, when we had hope.

At that time David was in the Spanish Communist Party and whenever there was a problem to sort out somehow it always seemed to end up on our doorstep. There were a number of Communists who had been in the underground inside Spain after the Civil War and who, for one reason or another, crossed into France and came to Riom. In 1949 there was a big police operation in Asturias to round up the Communist underground, but some of them escaped and two, Justo and his wife, came to live in Riom. About a year or two later they received a telegram from two of their friends, Theodoro and Pilar, who had just escaped into France and were stuck in Bordeaux without any money.

This couple became very good friends of ours. Theodoro was a Cuban who had moved to Spain when he was young. He was only sixteen when the Civil War started but he later fought at Teruel and was a commissar for culture. After the war he married Pilar and they both became involved in a Communist underground in Asturias and were arrested in the big political sweep of 1949. Pilar spent nine months in prison and him too and they were both tortured. They did something really bad to Theodoro with injections: I think it was zinc, and he was held in a lunatic asylum in Oviedo. When he got out he was always being followed by the police and he couldn't carry a package in the street without being stopped and made to open it. At that time people were starving in Spain and Theodoro was so feeble when he left prison that he would go to the abattoir and collect blood in a bottle when the animals were slaughtered.

They eventually decided to go to France and after working for a while in Bilbao to get some money they found a professional smuggler, a *'passeur'*, to take them through the Pyrenees at night. They got to Pau in southern France where they had a contact but the comrades there had been on strike for a month and could only give them enough money to get to Bordeaux. There they went to the Cuban consulate, because Theodoro still had Cuban nationality, and it was then they sent a telegram to their friend Justo in Riom.

Justo came to see David because he said that he didn't know how to find the money to send to Theodoro for the fare up to Riom, but he and his wife were just mean because they had sold their business in Oviedo and did have the money. David went with another Spaniard, Belarmina, and collected a little money from each refugee in Riom and when he went to pay for the money order there still wasn't enough and he made up the rest from his own pocket. Pilar and Theodoro eventually arrived and they would come and visit us quite often in the rue Gomot. However, they were not happy staying with Justo and his wife so David said that they could stay in the attic at Number 2 in the rue Gomot where we had slept before, because we still rented the room below for my mother. They hadn't got a penny.

Life in Exile – Consuelo

Somebody told them they should go through the dustbins for wastepaper to sell but after four nights they gave up because the bins were already cleaned out. After that they both worked hoeing sugarbeet, or Theodoro dug trenches to lay electric cables. Theodoro was a teacher, an intellectual, and he had never done heavy manual work; his hands were in a terrible mess, covered in blood after a day's work. When he first tried to find a job people would ask to see his hands and they would turn him away.

After they had first arrived we had to accompany them to the police station because as foreigners they couldn't stay in France or work unless someone was willing to declare that they accepted responsibility for them. The policeman filled in a form for Theodoro. He asked, 'What is his profession?' 'Professor of mathematics.' 'Good, God, and he finds himself in this situation? Can't he find suitable work here?' David said, 'But how is he going to do that, you need to have a French degree to be able to teach here.' That really shook the policeman. He said, 'My God, to be on hard times like that!'

And then Justo came to the house with another Communist called Angel Gallego who had escaped from Madrid where he had been in a clandestine organisation. The other Communists at Riom were always depending on us like that. Justo said that it was better that we went to the police station with Gallego because we spoke better French. So I went along with this man and the police must have seen that I didn't even know him because each time they asked him a question, his name, if he was married and so on, I had to ask him in Spanish. The policeman gave me a funny look because that was not long after taking responsibility for Theodoro and Pilar.

For a while we moved out to a house in the countryside, to Cerret just outside Riom. We had had to give up the apartment at Number 9 and Marilda had got rickets because it was so dark in the rue Gomot and the doctor said that she needed to be in the sunlight. We didn't pay any rent at Cerret in return for doing all the work on the smallholding of the owner. It was a kind of share-cropper deal. We had to work really hard and we grew over two tonnes of potatoes and two tonnes of beet, half for us and half for the owner. But there were always rows with those people because they didn't want the children playing near their house or there were disputes over the crops, so we left and went back to live in the rue Gomot at Number 30, where we stayed for the next seventeen years. It was there that the last two children, Mimi and Mallory, were born so there were seven children in all. We were really crowded there because there was just a small bedroom which looked onto the street, a big kitchen which David separated into two rooms with a plank partition, and another bedroom at the back. The sun never came in at all and it was so dark that you had to keep the light on all day. And it was also very damp because the Volvic stone used in the old buildings is porous: the wallpaper would peel off and the lino rotted even after a year. The house was very old and aristocratic and in the bedroom at the back, in a kind of separate pavilion, there was very fine wooden panelling and a parquet floor. When the doctor came to visit somebody who was ill he would say, 'How beautiful this room is, with all this panelling.' But we would have preferred two extra bedrooms and a bathroom in place of the finery. Behind the panelling you could hear a whole regiment of rats scuttling about because down below there was a real warren of deep cellars.

17 Life in Exile – David

When I first started to work at the *Menagère Aluminium* factory in 1945 my pay was 18 francs the hour for a working day which began at five o'clock and went on to one fifteen with a quarter hour break at nine o'clock for a snack. It was very difficult to get any increase in pay from the boss. My job was to polish the pots after they were shaped. They were held on a kind of lathe which spun round very fast and I would polish them with an abrasive using one hand which was wrapped in rags. They would come out all neat and shining, ready to have the handle fixed.

It was a very monotonous job, always the same and I had to stand at the machine right in front of a big window through which the sun shone very hot. It took a tremendous amount of time and pressure to get sunblinds put up; the boss continuously refused in spite of requests from our trade union. On top of that the job was absolutely filthy; it was dirty and tiring and it was nearly always the Spanish workers who were put to do it. It was rare to find a Frenchman polishing, although in a small factory like that we all tended to turn our hands to other kinds of work from time to time. At the end of the day I was always black like a coalminer and the only washing facility was a cold water tap in the yard with a stone trough like the ones horses drink from. Aluminium is very difficult to get off with cold water and the watchman who locked up the factory was always complaining that we polishers were stopping him from closing the gates because we took so long to wash. But although the factory was small the trade union, the CGT, was quite strong and we often managed to force the boss's hand. We managed to force him to install cloakrooms with hot showers, but he squealed for nearly a year afterwards: it really hurt him to spend a little money. Whenever we compelled him to do something like that he would say, 'OK, if that's how you want it, but I'll have to close the factory down; I can't afford to pay for this.'

When I first worked at the *Menagère* the boss, Poitevin, came to the factory by cycle like everyone else and his wife worked as a packer or in the office. Whenever the union made a demand he, like all the bosses, said that he was running at a loss. Yet Poitevin managed to buy a car and later on a mansion, the Chateau de Pertuis. There was one old worker in the factory, a mason and general repair man, who was sent by Poitevin to do some maintenance work in the chateau. He told us, 'Bloody hell, running at a loss is he? There are fifty-four radiatiors in his central heating system and there's a separate bathroom for him, his wife and his guests. Working at a loss? When he began he had nothing.' And we said, 'A bit of that belongs to us too.'

A little backward factory like the *Menagère* paid very badly and it was what the French call an *'usine de passage'*, a place where people would work just for a short while and then move on to something better. Over the years a lot of immigrant workers passed through, Spaniards, Poles, Africans. The French government ran a system of contract labour; all the foreign workers, like me, could only work for a particular employer if they had a contract. For the first six months they were tied to the same boss but after that they were free to seek work elsewhere, where the pay and conditions were better. A lot of Spanish Republicans and, later on, other Spaniards who had emigrated to France came to work at the factory and I was quite often able to find them a place there. But it wasn't easy for me because I saw people coming in for a while and they would say, 'Oh, I'm here because I'm waiting to go to another job', and then I would watch them leave and I couldn't. For someone with two good arms and legs it was easy at that time to find work, but for someone like me – ouff! And Poitevin would never give me a pay rise when I asked because he knew that I had a wooden leg and that I couldn't easily find work elsewhere. I worked at that factory, the *Menagère*, for twenty-eight years.

After the war there were a lot of Spanish political refugees in Riom and quite early on, from 1946, we began to divide up into political groups, the Communists on one side and the Anarchists on the other. There must have been at least fifty in the Spanish Communist Party at Riom, if not more, and apart from the closed meetings of the cell we would also get together every Sunday and sometimes organise big political or social events and go out into the countryside on excursions. But gradually I got really fed up with the Party and some of the silly buggers who were in it at Riom and eventually I gave it up. What I couldn't stomach was that we would be sent orders – we didn't know from where they were coming – and they had to be obeyed without question. I argued with the others that even when decisions came from the Party leadership we needed to discuss them for ourselves, to have the right to think a little bit for ourselves and not to be merely puppets on a string. But the others would say, 'No, this is the Party line and anyone who does not accept it is not a good Communist.'

Once there was a row because we were asked to make a collection for La Pasionaria.[1] Someone said in a cell meeting, 'They say that La Pasionaria has got a cold.' I said, 'In that case all she's got to do is cure herself, she's got the money to do it. If I get a cold I still have to go to work.' 'But you can't talk like that about our Secretary . . .' 'Oh go and screw yourself, you and your Secretary, she's doing all right for herself over there in the Soviet Union, but nobody cares a damn about us here.' Well I was called to order; it was treason, a breach of Party discipline to speak badly of a leader of the rank of Dolores Ibarruri. I said, 'It's not because Dolores Ibarruri says something that I'm automatically going to agree. If we discuss it among ourselves and afterwards I think that she's right, I'll go along with it. But just because an order comes from someone high up doesn't mean I'll accept it; we must discuss things first.' They were a bunch of idiots.

The cell meetings were almost always held at my house in the rue Gomot. All the pots and pans would have to be cleared out from the kitchen to make space for everyone. But the others, Tena, Gerardo, Fernandez and so on, always found excuses not to have the meeting in their place. For one it was because his wife was an Anarchist, for another because he was afraid the neighbours would find out. One day Felix turned up at our house with his fiancée and when I said that I'd got something to tell him he said, 'Come outside, don't breathe a word about the Party in front of my fiancée.' Shit, he couldn't even mention the Party to the woman he was going to marry in a week's time and, on top of that, he got married in church and tried to hush it up. The secretary of the district called Comarcal, a real rough diamond from Andalusia, would sometimes come to Riom from St Eloy-les-Mines. He would come to our house in the morning, take a look round the kitchen, and say, 'Right, I haven't had any breakfast today.' I was the poorest of any Communist in Riom, with a house full of kids and just my small wage, but nobody else would invite him to eat with them. Sometimes we would have just an egg in the place and Comarcal would eat it. Moreover, whenever any comrades got out of Spain through the clandestine network and ended up in Riom it was always Consuelo and me who would have to help them out, to sort out their papers with the police and so on. Yes, they were just useless.

But the worst thing of all was the way in which the Party treated those comrades who had escaped from Spain. There was the case of Ramón who had gone into Spain during the 1944 guerrilla operation and was arrested, tried in Madrid and put in prison for years. Somehow his mother, who lived in Riom, managed to get him sprung and he got over the frontier with a false passport and he returned to Riom. But in the meantime his wife had gone off with another man and was seeking a divorce. Well those in the Communist Party, even his best friends, just sent him to Coventry, they didn't want to have anything to do with him and treated him as a traitor. Someone said in a meeting, 'If he was a real Communist he would have stayed in Spain and not come back to France.' Well we had a meeting in a room above the municipal bath-house and there was one hell of a row because the others said that I should not give any help to Ramón, that I didn't know what I was doing, and they quoted the party line from *Nuestra Bandera* Number 4. I remember that *Bandera* Number 4 well because it stated the most abominable things imaginable against those Communists who crossed over into France: they were spies, fascist agents come to disrupt the Spanish Party.[2] There were spies everywhere and we had to be extra vigilant. Ramón wasn't the only one treated in that way. I brought up the case of a bloke working in Riom who had been in the Party for years but his wife was in Toledo and ill and literally starving. He decided that he would have to try and get back to help his family. I asked what would happen if he should later decide to return to France; would he be hounded from the Party too? They said, 'Yes, him too. It's *Nuestra Bandera* Number 4 which condemns him.' I couldn't agree with that.

Over the years my enthusiasm for the Spanish Communist Party began to wane and in the end I stopped taking the *Mundo Obrero*. Not that it was all that interesting to read in the first place because whether you read it today or in six months time it always said the same thing. It was like a record playing over and over. I told the others that I didn't want it any more, although they still brought it round to the house for a long while afterwards and tried to persuade me to come back.

There were also a lot of Anarchists in Riom and some of them were really fine people. The leader there, Rueda, would say, 'The only Communist I know in Riom is Granda', and that was true. Just after the Liberation, when there was still a lot of contact between Anarchists and Communists; we would often meet at the fountain opposite the hospital to hold discussions. The question of the death of Durruti came up, the Anarchist leader who died in mysterious circumstances with a bullet in his back. Some said that he had been killed by the Anarchists themselves or that it was done to put blame on the Communist Party. I said, 'I don't know any more than you

Anarchists do, but I think that if it was a Communist who killed Durutti that man is not, in my view, a true Communist and merits to be killed. But if it was one of your lot the same applies.' Rueda agreed with that. But others would insist, 'No, it is not possible that the Communist Party killed him', and the whole argument would take off again. It was impossible to reach any kind of agreement. Relations between the two sides were continuously poisoned.

There was one incident though which was quite funny. The Anarchists invited me, Consuelo, and Antonio, the secretary of the Communists, to go on a bus outing with them to the Lake of Montmazot. We thought it was just a social outing with a picnic. During the trip there was an Anarchist, a woman from Beriña in Asturias, who got up in the middle of the passage way of the bus and, fixing her eye on us, began to sing the Anarchist anthem. Antonio said, 'You're a sod, but we are well and truly caught.' When we arrived instead of just a picnic we found a big political rally of all the Anarchists from numerous departments. Us three Communists were stuck there like idiots in a sea of Anarchists.

Our relations with the French were very good in the early years but things began to change for the worse when there was a big influx of Spanish immigrant labour round about 1955–6. They were what we called the 'economic' Spanish, those who came in search of work, as opposed to us 'political' Spaniards who were refugees from the Civil War. Even the French neighbours saw the difference; they would say, 'But why is it that these Spaniards are not like you others? Why are they like that?' 'Ah', we would say, 'that's a different vintage altogether; they're not here for the same reason as us.' Most of the immigrants came from the poorest regions in Spain. Four out of five were from the south, from Andalusia or New Castile.

I remember having a conversation with one of them, Pedro Fernandez, who came from a little town called Turre. He said, 'Before, there were nine thousand inhabitants in Turre and today there's exactly three thousand. It's impossible to make a living down there; everyone will leave. The problem is there's plenty of sun, but no water.' In one region a Swiss company had come and bought up a huge area of land and brought in irrigation and the land produced lorry loads of oranges and vegetables. Pedro said, 'If only the Spaniards had done the same thing where I lived.' I said, 'Yes, because afterwards you have to work for the Swiss and they take all the profits.' He replied, 'But it was them who brought the water in from miles away.' 'That's what the Spanish government should have done before the Swiss.' And there were hundreds who said the same as Pedro, 'In my country there's nobody left, just old folk who can hardly walk.' The young people would emigrate to France and then begin to send for their families, their parents and relatives. In Riom they would move into one house and then gradually take over the whole street, like in the rue Soubrani. There was one family, the Joquina, which had seventy members but in the beginning there were only two of them. And the young, single workers would return home to Spain to get married and then come back with their wife or husband.

A lot of those immigrant workers were assisted by the Spanish government, by the Committee for Emigration, and each family was given a bed, a cupboard and so on. And they all had letters of introduction to the priest. When they first arrived the first thing they asked was where the church was and they would go and see the priest so he could help them find a flat and furniture. The Spanish consulate even arranged for them to have their own Spanish priests come over. Well those 'economic' Spaniards didn't mix too well with us; they had heard a lot of propaganda against us and they were afraid. We were the 'Reds' who had murdered priests and mayors, raped nuns and burned churches. But after they began to talk with us and to understand things for themselves they saw that they had been misled in Spain and they began to join trade unions and political parties. And when they first arrived the men had their hair cropped really short, like they do in Spain, but later they began to be integrated and to follow French ways and they let their hair grow longer or they grew beards.

But the first contacts between us and them were very difficult. They didn't have very much self-respect and they came to France with a completely different mentality, with the idea of making money and each was after his own interest and didn't care about anybody else. They had no political principles, no solidarity; their one purpose was to get money. I remember the stupid nephew of Rueda arriving from Spain and he said, 'Well if I don't find a job here I'm heading for Indo-China to fight with the Foreign Legion and then I'll be able to get the gold from the teeth of the dead enemy.' Those immigrants were different from us Republicans and I think that's when the attitude of the French began to change towards the Spaniards. In the fifties there was a great shortage of manual labour in France so I don't think we were disliked because we were competing for jobs with the French. But later, after the economic crisis of 1973, the situation began to change, unemployment increased and there were lots of other immigrants too, from Portugal or North Africa.

It was very rarely that I came across any direct racism. For example, during all my years in the factory nobody ever said anything wounding, except once towards the end of my time there when a young idiot called Goigout opened his mouth. For a while he came to work with me and another Spaniard on the polishing, a really dirty job which the French usually didn't do. He wanted to be paid at the same rate as he got on the presses and when the boss said no, that he would get the lower rate, the same as us, Goigout replied, 'But they are foreigners.' Nobody else in the factory would have been capable of making such a comment. But racism like that, when somebody insults you, is one thing, what is worse is the more subtle, half-concealed kind. For example, you might be walking along the street and meet one of your neighbours, a Frenchman. You stop, have a chat, perhaps go and have a drink with him because he's alone. But the next day you meet the same neighbour with someone else and this time he doesn't even want to know you. You have to ask yourself, 'Who is the racist?', and I think the answer is him, because he isn't frank and open. Or if a group of French are having a discussion among themselves and there is a Spaniard or foreigner listening in, even if they all work together, the foreigner is always an outsider and looked down on as inferior. Even if the Spaniard is intelligent enough to discuss things with them they won't take his opinion seriously. The French can come out with the most stupid bloody thing and it will be accepted, but if you say something to the point it's no good if you're not French. In my opinion that's what racism is. What wounds me most is the racism with a fine nuance, which puts you down, the kind which is a bit more subtle. That hurts more than the blunt kind.

The children experienced racism too at school. One day Ethel told me that she'd had a fight with a boy who called her 'Espagnolette'. I said, 'But give him a smack with your slate, break his head'. She said, 'But I did.' I said, 'If you break your slate on the head of a type like that I'll buy you a new one.' Another time, because we were living out of town at Cerret, José went as a boarder to the Sacred Heart school in Riom. Once he told me that he had to chose a theme for a drawing and then take it to school. At that time Picasso's 'Dove of Peace' had just come out and everyone was talking about it so I said, 'Why don't you try your hand at that?' So he did and when he handed the drawing to the teacher, an Alsatian fascist and of course, being in that school, a Catholic, he said, 'But what's this?', and he screwed it up in front of the whole class and threw it on the floor. Well after that José wasn't too happy and we took him away from that school.

18 Homecoming – Consuelo

I first went back to Spain on holiday in 1954. I had always wanted to return to live there. In Marseille after the Liberation it was in my mind all the time but my mother said, 'You're not going back, you're staying with me.' She was frightened to return to Spain because they would have killed her. Then in 1954 I went to the Spanish consulate at Lyon and was able to get a passport for myself and my three little girls. I didn't have Spanish nationality, I was Mexican, but my identity card was marked, 'Refugee from the Spanish War' and with that I was able to get a pass. Some of the Spanish refugees in Riom criticised me for going back, even on holiday, but that didn't bother me too much. One of the families who spoke out against me themselves returned to Barcelona for good in 1966.

I went by train with the three children and when we got to Venta de Baños we had to change for Valduno. We had to wait for some while and lying on the platform were sleeping harvesters wrapped up in blankets, with their scythes by their side. They were going to hire themselves as labourers for the corn harvest. When the train arrived it was packed and a priest said, 'You won't be able to get into the train with the children, it's too full.' But some young tourists from South America gave me a hand and they passed the girls and the suitcases in through a window.

The whole journey took two days and two nights and when we finally got to Valduno somebody who got off the train went ahead and told the family in Paladin that David's wife and three children were coming. As we went along the track towards the village we saw Valentina, David's sister, coming along with a donkey and she sat the three girls up on its back and held up a big umbrella to keep off the sun because it was very hot. And a bit further on we met Enrique, and then the grandfather, and the whole family like that coming to greet us and strung out along the road. At Paladin they seated the girls on a big log under the chestnut tree and the whole village was there to welcome us because it was the first of August, the parish festival of Valduno.

We stayed at Paladin for a week and just before coming to Spain we had the girls baptised because David's mother was so Catholic. We told them that they were not to say anything about it, but the girls, Nadia, Ethel and Marilda, quickly picked up Spanish and

Marilda told her grandmother she could remember how she had been baptised with water and salt. David's mother was astonished because all the children in Spain were baptised a few weeks or months after birth. She said, 'That's not possible; it's incredible. Is it true you can remember?'

David's mother said that we should go and visit his Uncle Benjamin. His father told us not to bother, that it wasn't worth the trouble, but his mother insisted and we went to see the uncle whom David had often talked about, that he was fat and rich and fascist. When we arrived at the farm my mother-in-law said, 'I introduce you to the wife of David.' He was a big, imposing man and said, 'Hum, if she's like he is! And you, what are you? Red or white?'. I said, 'Red.' 'Ah, what did I tell you, the same as him.' He was a very forceful and energetic man, but very coarse, a brute. We talked a while, although I didn't want to get into any discussion with him. He said, 'During the war my nephews (he meant Enrique and David) fired on me every day.' I said, 'What do you mean?' 'Yes, Enrique was over there', and he pointed towards the hills above Valduno where Enrique had been in command of a battery. 'Enrique fired on me with a field gun.' He really believed that, but the whole area had been shelled during the war. I said, 'But why didn't you evacuate?' 'No, no, no, I stayed in my place. I didn't want to go and it's not my nephews who are going to make me get out of my own house.'

He was not too complimentary about his nephews, especially Enrique. He said that the other people of Paladin had lost their head and fled in a panic when the firing started. 'Like her', he said, pointing to David's mother who stood there without saying a thing. 'Like her. As soon as the fighting started they were off and afterwards they came back crying because they had lost the cow or the pig. And their house was demolished by the soldiers, but they didn't touch my house because I stayed here. When you have a house you have to guard it. Why did they go?' Then he recounted the story of the whole village in the war, how they had all left, that such a person had lost a pig, that another had left a cow behind which then calved. It was incredible. And he felt angry towards the sons of his sister because they had fought in the war: they had volunteered just to be able to fire at him!

After staying a week at Paladin I went by train to Infiesto. When we arrived around half-past nine in the evening I was scared stiff because at that time the left was still being persecuted. On the train there were two civil guards because at that time at every station two guards would get off and another two would come on. Well the two police came on and sat just behind me and sitting in front I recognised the brother-in-law of the doctor who my mother had worked under in the infirmary and he was very right wing and couldn't stand me. I was scared stiff and I stared through the window hoping he wouldn't recognise me. When we got to Infiesto I waited a while until he and the civil guards had disappeared. Then as I was walking past the town hall I met a woman, a photographer, who recognised me. She said, 'How come you're here? We thought that you had been taken prisoner on the boat on which you left or that you were dead.' 'No, we were in France.' She didn't know what had become of us because my aunt wrote to us but she didn't tell anybody that she was in touch with us abroad.

When I got to Cardes with Ethel it was already dark. My aunt had a bistro up on the side of the hill and below was a skittle alley and from there I called up to the bar for my cousin Tino. But it was another Tino, Junco, who came out and I asked, 'Is Antonio there?' 'Yes, yes.' He called out, 'Hey, Antonio, there's a woman asking for you.' I heard my aunt say, 'Young or old?' He said, 'She's quite young.' Then my uncle Antonio came out; I went up the steps towards him; he didn't recognise me. I embraced him and he said, 'Who are you?' 'Don't you recognise me?' 'No.' 'It's Consuelo; don't you recognise me any more?' He began to cry; he embraced me and he took me into the house. My aunt Enriqueta was in the kitchen; she embraced me and cried a little and then we went into the bistro. My uncle said not to say anything, to see if the people there would recognise me. There were about fifteen people in the bar, some about my age and others older. I sat down next to my aunt: everyone was looking at me as if to say, 'Who's this one?' Then one, Piru, who worked in the cheese factory, got up from a table and came towards me, 'Meca! It's Consuelo!' He threw himself round my neck and then everyone was hugging and shaking me and we began to talk. It was very strange because I could recognise the older people but those who were younger I would mistake for the parents; the son would look just like the father at the same age.

I went to visit my relatives around Cardes and then one day I went to look for my sister Angelina. By then she was married and had two girls but we hadn't seen each other for sixteen years and she had been just a kid of fourteen when she got lost in the crossing of the Pyrenees. She was living in a mining town, Riosa, up in the mountains and when I got down from the bus the place was so ugly;

all the houses and roads were black from the coal dust. I didn't have her address and I was just asking a man in the street where I could find Angelina Contreras when I saw my sister at a window and the man said, 'Perhaps it's that woman over there. Yes, that's her.' Angelina came out to meet me and she was crying. It had been sixteen years and she was just fourteen and me sixteen when we got separated.

I stayed there three or four days and my sister was living in the most miserable conditions. She had nothing to sleep on except a sofa, there was no mattress, and her husband, who was a lorry driver, didn't earn enough for them to eat properly. When I arrived Angelina didn't have even ten centimes to buy a box of matches to light the fire. It was ten o'clock at night, the children were hungry, and she didn't like to tell me that she had no money. I could see that there was something wrong. I said, 'But why don't you give the children something to eat?' 'Oh, in a while, in a while.' But it was because she had no food and no money and couldn't even pay ten centimes for a box of matches, so I gave her some money and we went to the shops to buy something to eat. Afterwards she admitted, 'You know I didn't have a penny in the house.'

That's what things were like in Spain at that time, people were very poor and it wasn't pretty to see. And talking to people it was as if they had been in a prison for twenty years; they didn't know anything, they were cut off from what was going on in the world. Everything that they heard on the radio or from the priests they believed. Everything which reached them from outside sources was untrue. They would not believe anything you said. They were suspicious towards everyone and to a degree that it is hard to imagine. Today people are less like that, especially the young, but at that time those of my age wouldn't trust anyone. They were frightened of everything. You would ask them something and they would look around two or three times to see if anyone was listening and they lowered their voices. It was unbelievable.

The day after I arrived at Cardes I received an anonymous, threatening letter which had been typed. It said to make sure not to go on any lonely tracks; that there was somebody who wanted to do me harm and was determined to achieve their ends. That it was better that I left as soon as possible otherwise I would go through a bad time. I showed the letter to my uncle who said, 'Oh, you had better be careful, they are capable of giving you a fright one evening when you come up the road to the village alone.' The letter had been posted in Infiesto and my uncle tried to find out something by asking around, but we never found out who sent it.

At first people were afraid to talk about the Civil War or about the fascist repression after the fall of Asturias, but more recently, especially since the death of Franco, they have been more open. Every year that I go on holiday to Cardes I learn a bit more. There is a woman at Cardes called Maria the same age as me, and she told me how the Falangists had come and shot her whole family. Maria had gone to Oviedo to look after the baby of a relative so that the woman would be free to come and visit the family in Cardes. That's why Maria survived because she was at Oviedo the day the Falangists arrived. Maria had three brothers who had volunteered to fight on the Republican side during the Civil War and one of them, Fausto, who must have been about nineteen years old, saw the Falangists coming up the track. He hid in the stable under the grass they had cut for the cows, but they knew he was hiding there because a neighbour gave everything away. They lived in the last house in the village, up at the top of the hillside and surrounded by chestnut trees, and in broad daylight the Falangists – there were five or six of them – brought them out and shot them in front of the door. They killed the mother and the eldest brother, Pépé; they shot Raphael and Fausto and the woman, the cousin who had come from Oviedo. The cousin was right-wing and they shot her without even asking if she was left or right. The whole family was brought outside and shot right in front of the house.

When Maria, the daughter, came back from Oviedo by train she didn't know anything and it was the owner of the small cheese factory, at the bottom of the road coming up from Infiesto, who stopped her. He said, 'Don't go up to Cardes, come into the house', and he told her everything. She never went back to the house; she never returned home. The Falangists dug a hole in front of the house and put the bodies in and they were left like that for three or four days; nobody was allowed to touch them. Afterwards they asked permission to re-bury them properly, but not in the cemetery: right there beside the house. Maria was looked after by the family who had the cheese factory, she lived with them, and later she married a man who worked there called Pepin. Now Maria lives in Cardes and she knows who the men were who killed her family; she sees them walking about to this day.

The fascists also came to Cardes and put José, a relative of my mother's, in prison. He was the kindest, most gentle of men and had never harmed a person in his life. He had a shop and if there were poor people who couldn't afford to eat he would give them a kilo of rice, some bread or a litre of oil. His wife would say, 'We shall never be rich because we give away all we have.' It's incredible how generous that man was. But he was put in prison for years, for no apparent reason, and he was only released because he was ill and dying: so he would die at home instead of in prison. And my Uncle Antonio was also put in prison for several years. Sometimes people were denounced just so the fascists could get their hands on their property. A long while after Antonio came out of prison he was visited by a fascist who said, 'Right, Antonio, you're going to give me your winter boots, the ones in leather.' 'Why should I give them to you?' 'Because you have to, unless you want a bullet in the head', and he took out a revolver. My uncle went upstairs into the bedroom and came down with the boots; they were big thigh boots, lined inside and very fine. One day the head of the fascist group came into my aunt's bar and she asked him, 'Was it you who told that man to come and take Antonio's boots?' 'No, who came to take them?' She explained who it was and how he had threatened them with a gun. He said, 'Oh, we'll see about that', and the next day the man who had taken the boots brought them back and his face was a mass of bruises.

The chief of the fascist gang was a real brute; he was a law unto himself and he killed lots of people. He would ride down from Cardes to Infiesto on a white horse which was all finely decked out with little bells and trappings and if someone in a bar said something to displease him he'd threaten to take them outside and shoot them. He would boast that he had killed sixty people. One day he was coming up the road from Infiesto and a young man, just a lad of eighteen or nineteen, was waiting for him with a gun and he killed the fascist.

The fascists would come to people's houses and say, 'Right, you're going to give me the potatoes you've got in the attic', and they would load up a cart and take them away. They would go into the fields and help themselves to other people's crops. And nobody could do anything about it because if they complained they would be killed or put in prison.

When Asturias fell to Franco's army a lot of Republicans formed a guerrilla band up in the mountains behind Cardes. My best friend, Maruja, came from a large family and two of her brothers were taken and shot while another, Enrique, joined the guerrilla. The Falangists came to Cardes to get the mother and they took her to Infiesto, to an air raid shelter where they beat people and tortured them because the walls were thick and the screams could not be heard from outside. They tried to force her to say where her son was hiding in the mountains. They beat her so badly that her husband and daughters had to carry her home to Cardes in a blanket and when they got to the house and removed the blanket pieces of flesh from her back were sticking to it.

Originally there were thirty or so men in the group near Cardes, but they were all killed off one by one. The last two left were Enrique and a relative of my mother's, Manolo, who they called '*El Rubio*'. Eventually the Falangists surrounded the mountains where they were hiding and it appears that Enrique asked Manolo to shoot him in the head so that he would not be taken alive and afterwards Manolo hurled himself on the fascists. He had a grenade in his hand and he pulled the pin and blew himself up. All the people from the village went up to see and to bury the bodies and my cousin Tino, who was then just a kid of about twelve, told me, 'I went to see the bodies and '*El Rubio*' had two *chorizos* sticking from his mouth that the Falangists had put there.'[1] They wrapped the bodies in blankets and buried them there in front of the cave where they had been hiding.

In the year before I first returned to Spain, in 1953, there were still Republicans hiding up in the mountains. Once they came to the house of my grandmother, the mean one who my sister and I had lived with when we were small. Someone in the village must have kept the guerrillas informed because they knew everything that was going on. My grandmother had just killed a pig and prepared all the *chorizos* and hams when they turned up. They knew when to come. My aunt Rosario, the daughter of my grandmother, told me that her mother was so vexed and was crying so much that she couldn't fill the men's sacks with *chorizos* and they were in a hurry because they were frightened that they might have been seen by neighbours who would fetch the civil guards. They said, 'Quick, quick, grandma; fill the sack up fast.' She was crying her eyes out, 'Oh, oh, they are stealing everything.' They said, 'No, madam, it's not stealing. We're going to pay you; we're going to give you a receipt and the Republic will pay you.' They made out an IOU just as they had when requisitioning during the Civil War.[2] I wish I had been there to see that.

Maruja's youngest brother, who now works as a chef in London, was in touch with those hiding in the mountains, but they were a bit naive because they got him to take photographs of the group and when he took the film to be developed in Infiesto it was reported to the police. Somehow he managed to escape being arrested, but he had to go to Argentina using a false identity card.

I stayed on holiday all that summer with the children and the next year, in 1955, we came again. David couldn't go to Spain yet because he hadn't been granted a passport, but that year when we returned from our holiday he came down to the Spanish frontier at Hendaye to meet us and two of his brothers, Paco and Mario, came to see him at the border. But they hadn't got passports. We came to the Spanish customs post and then the bridge over the river which marks the frontier and on the other side was the French customs and we could see David waiting over on the other side. When I gave my passport to the Spanish police I said, 'These two gentlemen here are brothers of my husband. My husband is over the other side (we could see him across the bridge, waving). They haven't seen each other for eighteen years. Can you let them go just to the barrier?' He said, 'Ah, as far as we're concerned they can pass, but now it's up to the French.' Paco and Mario were really happy to go across the bridge and while I was trying to explain things to the French customs they had already crossed over into France and were hugging and talking with David: all three of them were crying their eyes out like big babies. The customs officer said that if David surrendered his identity card his brothers could go into France until nine o'clock in the evening. We spent the afternoon together in Hendaye and since Paco and Mario worked on the railway they were astonished to see the electric trains at the station. They had never seen anything like that because Spain was so behind the times. For them Hendaye station was just like paradise; they were very excited.

David applied for a passport at the same time as me, but it was two years before they would give it to him. In 1956 we were all set to go on holiday to Spain, the passports were ready, the suitcases packed, and David had bought a Citroën, but he didn't pass the driving test and we couldn't go. That was a great disappointment, but in 1957 everything worked out all right and David could hardly contain himself. Every time we talked about going to Spain he went white as a sheet, white from emotion. We set off in the old Citroën one evening at nine o'clock and we were really loaded up; there were five children in the back and Mimi, who was just a baby, on my lap in front. The car began to overheat. Next day in Perigeux the weather was very hot and when we stopped at a café in the countryside for a drink the water was boiling in the radiator. It was steaming and going, 'Ploff, ploff, ploff'. I thought, 'This car's going to blow up before we get down there.' Every hundred miles we had to stop and let the engine cool down. We got to the frontier at four o'clock in the morning in our second night on the road and David was apprehensive, especially when the Spanish police made him get out of the car and go to the office.

At that time Spain was very backward; there wasn't a single petrol station all the way from Bilbao to Santander and the roads were really bad: in places there had been landslides and there was just planks where the road had been washed away. As we got towards Asturias David was falling asleep at the wheel, but he was so pigheaded and just wouldn't stop. He said, 'No, no, my mother's expecting me; we've got to get there.' When we arrived on the road just above Paladin, David opened the door of the car and the three girls took a short cut and ran down the hill to the village through the 'Lower Meadow'. And everyone came up from the village and they were all trying to get into the car to embrace David. They hadn't seen each other for twenty years. And Mimi, who was just a year old, took fright to see all those strange people, David's mother all in black, throwing themselves on her father and she began to cry. We went down to Paladin and everyone was there because it was the festival of Valduno.

19 Homecoming – David

It must have been about 1953 that I first applied for a passport to visit Spain because there had been a political amnesty and I hadn't seen my parents for sixteen years. At the time there were some political exiles in Riom who were opposed to my going back; they said that anyone who applied to the consulate for entry was recognising Franco. But later most of the people who criticised us not only took out passports themselves but returned to live in Spain permanently, long before we did.

I applied to the consulate at Lyon for a passport and I asked if it could be guaranteed that I would not have any problems with the police or the authorities if I returned. I was told that if there was any question of that I would not be issued with a passport; if I was given one it was an indication that there was nothing against me. However, I would only be able to stay on Spanish soil for thirty days at a time during any visit. In the end it took three years to get the passport because the civil guard had to carry out investigations around Paladin to see whether I had done anything in the Civil War which might be punishable. That was quite a risky business because it was up to the local police to advise whether you were all right or not and neighbours could give information against you from sheer malice or spite.[1] If that happened bang went your chances of a passport and of returning to Spain. When Consuelo went back to Spain for the first time in 1954 she visited Paladin and one of my brothers told her that the civil guard had been making enquiries about me during that summer. After that there were further hold-ups with the bureaucracy in Madrid and in the end I didn't receive the passport until 1956.

I decided to buy a car to make my first return trip to Spain in 1956. At that time I earned 15 000 old francs a month and I managed to find an old Citroën '*traction*' for 85 000 at a garage on the Paris road. Mechanics has always been my passion so I was able to put the car in order, but the real problem was how to drive with one leg. I asked several garage mechanics for their advice and one said one thing and another something else, but one night lying in bed I thought of a solution. Between the brake and the clutch pedals there's a small space, a little play, and my idea was to weld a third pedal to the clutch so that when I put my foot on the brake it would disengage the clutch. I got a welder to do the job and it worked perfectly. After a few practice drives in the lanes around Riom I went for my driving test in Clermont, but I didn't get through and my hopes were really dashed because we were all prepared to go to Spain. When I went to find Consuelo in the Place Gaillard she could see by my face what had happened, 'Well that's that; you haven't got it?' We had the passports all ready to go. Consuelo went to Spain for three months with the children but I had to stay in Riom.

But in 1957 everything worked out and we loaded up the car and set off. There were all the children in the back, Ethel, Marilda, Nadia, Pépé, and of course we wanted to take lots of presents. Consuelo knew from her earlier trip to Spain that my family was really poor, that they hadn't got any cooking pots, so I was able to put aside lots of pots and pans from the factory, as well as other gifts. When we drove off all loaded up the car was almost scraping the ground. When you go from Riom to Volvic you begin to climb up through the chestnut forests into the mountains and already the car was banging and snorting – 'Pfou, pfou, pfou'. I had to pull up and carry out my first repairs and we were hardly out of Riom.

Eventually we got to the frontier at Hendaye at three o'clock in the morning and I was pretty frightened. The Spanish frontier police looked at my passport and said, 'Get out of the car.' They took me to an office and said, 'Wait here a moment.' I stood there wondering what was going to happen; they were going through the records to see if there was anything against me. Perhaps they were only a few minutes but to me it seemed like ages. After a while they wrote something in the passport and said that I could go on but that I would have to present myself at the local police station as soon as I reached my destination. 'Is that all?', I asked, 'Yes, yes, that's all. You can go.'

Eventually we arrived in Asturias and after Oviedo took the road for Grado and Paladin: I had been away for twenty years. I had written to say that we would be there for the festival of Valduno and everyone was waiting for me. I stopped on the road a few hundred yards above the village because there is a big, steep meadow with a short cut down to Paladin and I let all the kids out of the car so they could run down and all the family and people were shouting, 'It's him! It's him!' They couldn't wait for me to drive down. My father and mother came up the meadow to meet me and my mother got into the car behind and was hugging me so tight that I couldn't drive. 'Ah, my son', and so on and so forth. I said, 'Listen, let me drive or we'll never get there.' She said, 'But how can you drive a thing like this, you who never had a car. How do you manage?' 'Look, like this.' So we went down to Paladin and a big table had been set outside under the vine all ready for a feast and everyone was there, all my brothers, everyone. That was a good moment.

We spent a good month's holiday there. Of course lots of things were very strange after being away for so long. I would be introduced to a man aged twenty years, the same age at which I had last known his father, and I would mistake him for the elder. But the older people had changed less, they were more easily recognisable. And another thing which astonished me was that I would meet the relatives of someone who I knew had been shot by a firing squad after the Civil War, but when I mentioned his name they would say, 'He has disappeared' or 'He has gone.' They dare not speak about it and they lowered their voice in a whisper and turned their face aside.

I also found out all that had happened to my family, to my mother and father and brothers, during the fall of Asturias and after the end of the Civil War. When Franco's army, the Galician column, began to drive towards Grado and Paladin in late 1936 everyone in the village was afraid and moved out. People were afraid of the Arab soldiers and said, *'Que vienen los Moros!'*, the Moors are coming! In Spain there has always been this fear of the Arabs; they had the reputation of being men who killed with the knife and raped the women. Perhaps the brutality of the Arab soldiers during the repression of the 1934 Revolution had also left a bad memory in Asturias. The people of Paladin fled because they were afraid but also because, even if they didn't have a clear political position, most of them were not right-wing, they were Republicans, and they didn't want to see the arrival of Franco's forces. My parents piled everything they could on a cart and, since they only had one cow, they borrowed another from a neighbour to pull it. They moved out like gypsies, all their few possessions piled up on top along with the children, my younger brothers, Jesús, Mario and Luis, and my sister Valentina. They set out towards Aviles and stayed for a while on a farm of a peasant that my father knew. But later, as the battle front drew closer, they moved on again and that's where I last saw them, at Aguera, before I got out of Asturias by boat.

I think that the only person who stayed behind in Paladin was Zapatero. It's strange because all his family left but he remained. He had a relative who lived in the mountains on the Republican side of the front and he used to go back and forth between the Nationalist and the Republican lines. If he came across Republican soldiers he would shout, 'Long live the Republic!' and if they were fascists, the opposite. And one day he was coming down the hill when it seems that he saw some Moroccan soldiers and because they have red turbans he mistook them for Republicans. He shouted, 'Long live the Republic!', and bang! they began firing and he was wounded. And he began running and running and Zapatero already had a hernia before and when he got as far as Premoño he fell down dead. Zapatero was a rather peculiar type; he wanted to stay behind in our country while there was nobody else around. Alphonso of Paladin would always say to my father afterwards, 'It's a good job he died', because Zapatero was a really bad lot. 'If he wasn't dead he would have denounced us all and got us shot. He would have grabbed everyone else's property for himself, the whole village.'

Apart from him there was only one other person in the village during the war. Old man Ferro who was with the Republican army near Trubia and one day he was given an axe and told to go into the forest to cut some firewood. He crossed over the lines to Paladin and returned to his house and never went back. Apart from that the entire village moved out, into the Republican zone. Although I should add that my uncle Benjamin of Casuco, the one who was so right-wing and from whom we requisitioned the potatoes, did stay on his farm. He was rich and rented out land to other poor peasants and share-croppers and there was one of them who had fought alongside me during the war and when he came back afterwards to pick up the farming again my uncle refused to let him have his fields back. But my uncle had a son-in-law, an officer in the civil guard, who told him, 'But do you think we fought the war for this? No! These folks are landworkers and they must return to the soil. How else is the nation going to get back on its feet?' My uncle said, 'But this man is a Red; he's got the right to nothing.' 'Red or not Red he's going to get the land back.' But my uncle didn't like it at all. He was a real bastard.

After Asturias fell my parents returned to Paladin and found a whole infantry regiment with their artillery installed in the village. Since the soldiers had found all the houses deserted they must have thought they belonged to the 'Reds' and took everything they could lay their hands on. They ripped out everything, the furniture, the floor boards, the doors, and even the oven which was built into the wall. So when my parents returned they found the house with just the walls, the roof and the beams. The soldiers of Franco had taken everything else to burn or to protect themselves in the trenches from the rain. And the water-mill was full of shit because the Moroccans had used it as a latrine; it was really disgusting and my parents had to clear it all out to get it working again. There was nothing at all to eat and a captain in the infantry, encamped just in front of the house, saw they were starving and told the children, Mario, Luis and Jesús, that they could come and take any scraps of food left over by the soldiers. Gradually my parents began to scrape together a living.

But that wasn't the end of their worries because they had three sons who had fought on the Republican side, Enrique, Paco and me, and the fascist repression was beginning. A lot of the Republican soldiers who couldn't get out by boat went up into the mountains and formed guerrilla bands and they managed to survive for years, although most of them were eventually hunted down and killed. Others managed to reach France by walking through the mountains. Other soldiers tried to make for home and went into hiding, like the son of old Carola of Paladin and another relative of his who hid up in a small house just behind where my parents lived. Well the Falangists came – they were fascists from the area who knew what they were looking for, not the police – and they took them away a small distance and shot them both, in a small stream. There was another Republican who hid for a long time at Volgues and one day a girl died in the village, a cousin of mine, and he said that he was fed up being closed up all the time and that he was going to the funeral. The others said that he would be recognised and captured and sure enough he was taken and several days later they shot him. Yes, quite a number were wiped out like that. There was another man called Artir who had been to the front and he too was picked up and shot. When I first went back to Paladin I asked his father what had happened and he said, 'Oh, he's disappeared.' But everyone in the village knew that he had been shot by the Falangists. In the years just after the war there was no protection through the law. Those who were caught were not taken before the courts but were done away with by the fascists who were free to do whatever they liked. They shot whoever they pleased. There was no control, no guiding authority; it was like a country without any civilisation – terrible.[2]

Both Paco and Enrique were arrested and put in prison. There you could be in real danger because those held would be asked where they came from and then they would send for a Falangist from his village or area to see if he should be denounced and shot. And for the fascists just about anything was good enough reason to get you shot; accusations of being a 'Soviet' or 'Communist' or 'anti-clerical'. For them anybody who wasn't with them was a 'Red', a 'Communist';

there was no middle ground. Paco was held in a cell at Burgos for nine months and all the people who were crammed into it could be shot at any moment because they were all condemned men. None of them was tried, but at night-time the Falangists would drive up in their cars, pick out four or five at a time, and take them away to shoot them. And there were all kinds in the cell. One was a doctor who had been in a hospital where I was and he had gone completely mad and spent all his time praying non-stop.[3]

But after nine months Paco was taken away and put in a forced labour camp and for a long while he was just like a convict. But at least he got out alive and after two or three years he was able to return to Paladin. As for Enrique he was unlucky enough to have got wounded by shrapnel in the collar bone and the wrist on the very last day of the fighting. He was treated in hospital but when he had been patched up he was put in a forced labour camp near Madrid, at Guadalajara, where he worked in a joinery shop. That's what was called 'Reduction of sentence through labour'; for each day's labour in a work force a reduction was made in the length of the prison sentence. Enrique was there for five years.

But when Paco and Enrique finally returned home that wasn't the end of their troubles because they were labelled, *'Desafectos al regimen'*. They were classified as politically disaffected which meant that it was impossible to get a job with the state, on the railways, in the electricity industry or whatever. And even in private industry the owners asked for good conduct certificates which you had to get from the Falangists. Enrique in particular was badly affected. Things were very difficult for him. He couldn't find work anywhere except for a week here or a month there and that continued for a long while until he managed to get a permanent job as a carpenter with a big company. As for Paco he found work on the railway, not as a state employee but as a day-labourer, laying tracks and so on. But he had no job security; he would work for a while then be laid off. In order to work, Paco had to belong to the vertical trade union and to carry a Falange card,[4] but a time came when even the unions run by the government had to defend the interests of the workers. There was a law that anyone working for one complete year in a job could keep it permanently, but quite often someone might have a place for say eleven months and twenty-five days and then be kicked out. Paco managed to work on the railway for over one year when he was told, 'OK, you can take your cards and go, we don't need you any more.' But he went to the union office in Oviedo to complain and they said that he was in the right and the railway was forced to take him back. That's how he managed to get into the railway full time.[5]

But for the authorities or the Falange there was still the question of what had become of me and they made enquiries with my father. He told them that he had received a letter from me saying that I was in France. They said, 'But a letter's not enough; there's got to be a good explanation as to why he's over there otherwise it's you who'll be going to prison in his place'. So my father wrote to tell me the situation and I went to see the commander of the camp at Septfonds to get a certificate verifying that I really was in a concentration camp, and when he got that they left him alone. But all the people who had left the village and fled from Franco's army had to pay a fine when they came back. That was imposed by the right-wing people in the area. My father had to pay a very heavy fine and he just hadn't got the money; it was far too much. But one of the right-wing people, an old fellow called Juan de Valle, who was quite a likeable character in spite of everything, spoke out in my father's favour and said that he shouldn't be fined. During the Civil War a lot of right-wing men were put in prison next to the town hall at Valsera: you couldn't say that they were Falangists, they were people who were a little wealthier than the others, who had a conservative mentality and were against the Republic. Well one day my father was going past the prison when he learned that some men from Valduno were locked up and he asked permission to buy them a drink: he fetched them a beer or something. Juan de Valle was among them so when they were going to fine my father Juan said that he should be let off and he was.

Later, to give the impression that the people were in favour of Franco's regime, the right organised street demonstrations and big parades and people were forced to turn out. It was also a way of humiliating the Republicans. The Falangists came to my father's house and took away his ration book – without that you couldn't survive – and they said it would be handed back after the demonstration. If you didn't go you would have nothing to eat. All those who were forced to go along like that were given little flags to wave and told to shout the slogan, '*Viva Christo Rey!*' – 'Long Live Christ the King'. My father and Valentina and a lot of others from Paladin all had to turn up one weekend for the parade in Oviedo and my father had drunk a good skinful just on purpose and as soon as he got off the train, even before the demonstration had started, he began shouting like a madman, '*Viva Christo Rey! Viva Christo Rey!*', and waving his flag about. My sister Valentina says she felt embarrassed and told him to shut up. Everyone was looking and saying, 'Look at the old fellow, he must be a fanatic.' Valentina could hardly keep hold of him during the march because he was jumping up and down so wildly with his flag. And afterwards he began to drag it along the ground. Afterwards at the station, when the ration books were handed back, they said to Valentina, 'Listen you, take your old boy off and don't ever bring him back. We don't want to see him again.' That's just what my father wanted.

What struck me on returning to Paladin after so many years was the way in which everything was so backward and miserably poor and the people were as if they had been locked up for a long while without any contact with the outside world. We had already noticed the poverty on the road into Spain; between Santander and Bilbao – and that is a long way – there wasn't a single petrol pump. And we saw men working to repair the road, not with machines but pickaxes and stones and gravel which they carried in little baskets on their back. Later all that was to change with the economic boom around 1960–3, and we began to see new roads being opened up with American bulldozers and modern equipment. It was as if Spain went from the ass to the car overnight. But that first year, 1957, the standard of living in Paladin was very, very low; the wages were rock-bottom, the people were living in miserable conditions and everything was backward.[6] In my father's house there was no running water, no electricity, no comfort at all: everything was in the same position as it had been over twenty years before, if not worse. There was no longer a teacher in the village and the children had to go and be taught by someone who knew just enough to show them the rudiments. People were astonished to hear that the French workers didn't have to pay anything to send their children to school. Once I was discussing things with Enrique of Casuco who worked on the railway; he asked, 'But with so many children how do you manage to send them all to school?' 'But I don't have to pay for the school.' 'Well bugger that, I ought to move to France because here I have to pay everything, the lot.'

In 1957 you saw hardly any cars on the road; the only one in the area round Paladin with a car was an architect, a very wealthy bourgeois. Everyone thought that if you had a car you must be rich, with lots of money. During the month of August there are lots of festivals in all the villages round Paladin, at Valduno, Soto, Peñaflor, Santullano, and I would ferry everyone from Paladin in the Citroën, making two or three trips. And when I stopped in the field where the festival was being held all the people flocked round to look at the car, just as if it was a moon rocket. Jesus! All it was was an old banger: in France it was already fit for the scrapyard. And all my friends from the old days, when they first came up to me, said, 'I won't bother to ask you how you're doing because when you turn up in a car it can only mean that you're doing all right for yourself.' I tried to explain, 'You don't understand how things are. For me a car is the same as an ass to you; it's just the same. Perhaps your ass is worth more than my car. In France it's worth hardly anything.' But they didn't believe me and it really upset me to see how backward they were and that they thought I was bourgeois.

But there was also a funny side to things because of their naivety. They would ask me, 'But how did you manage to survive with all the bandits in the mountains in France; that must have been pretty tough?' They were talking about the Resistance; the Spanish press had reported that the mountains were swarming with '*bandoleros*'. I told them that there had been bishops up in the mountains too; did they consider them to be bandits? And my relatives were really astonished by some of the things we brought from France. When my sister Valentina went with Consuelo to do the washing in the fountain she was really puzzled by the girls' nylon socks. 'But what are they made from? Look, look how they stretch!' and she showed them to all the other women washing clothes. They had never seen nylon before. And my mother used to smoke all the time and when I brought her some filter cigarettes she lit the filter. 'Ah', she said, 'the French are very intelligent; with that thing they light much better.'

I think one could say that things were just as miserably poor as before the Civil War; the one difference was that there was no freedom. During the years of the Republic there may not have been much to go round, but at least there was freedom. But later on, in the 1960s, things began to change; that must be recognised. The country began to industrialise very fast and the tourists began to come and that not only brought in money, it also began to open people's eyes.

At the end of August my first holiday came to an end; it was time to return to France. When I was given my passport I was told that I could only stay in Spain for thirty days and that the authorities could ask me to leave the country at any moment, even before the month was up. The first day I arrived in Paladin I was afraid to report to the civil guard as I was supposed to because they might have sent me back to France and messed up my holiday. So I waited to the very last day of the holiday before reporting to the civil guard at Grado. The policeman at the station knew that I was a political refugee. He asked how things were in France. I said, 'Well if you want to know the truth, in contrast to how things are here, it's much better.' He said, 'Ah, it doesn't take much to be better than round here. Well have a good trip back. You don't need to worry about anything and if anyone tries to make any trouble for you come and let me know.' That sergeant was very likeable.

From 1957 onwards we made the trip to Spain almost every year; we would save up our money for months in advance. The owner of the factory where I worked, like the other bosses, would pay three-quarters of my holiday wages for the month of August in advance and I could always persuade him to give me the money for the whole month. Once we got down to Asturias we didn't have to spend very much but with the cost of the petrol and the passports we were usually down to our last penny by the time we returned and I was ashamed to ask my family for any money. You could never tell in advance what was going to happen on those journeys, if the car would break down or if we would run out of petrol, but somehow we always managed to get there and back. Sometimes we had no money left and Consuelo would have to leave a gold chain or a watch in hock to get a tank of petrol. Once, we were almost back to Riom, we had reached Pontgibaud and there was only thirty miles to home, when we pulled into a garage but the place was closed and we hadn't any money left. Parked just opposite was a petrol-driven lorry and I got underneath with a tin can and took out the screw in the bottom of the fuel tank. But the lorry was high off the ground and since I had a thick jersey on I let the petrol soak down my arm so that it dripped from my elbow into the can. And every trip to Spain was like that; we never knew whether we would make it there and back.

20 Uprooted – Consuelo

I had always wanted to return to Spain: ever since I first arrived in France it was an *idée fixe*. At first I couldn't go back because I was a minor and my mother was frightened to return. Later I didn't want to go back alone with two children and then I got married to David. After all that the French had done to us I had no wish to stay in France. When somebody treated us badly, when they did something dirty to us, I was pleased: I would say to myself, 'So much the better, like that I have even less wish to stay in France. I can go back to Spain even more happy.' Just before moving back to Spain it didn't bother us at all if people treated us badly. I was so firmly attached to the idea of going back to Spain that on thinking about all that had been done to me I was even more certain about the return. I detest the French; taking them en bloc I detest them, some for one thing, others for another, and above all for being cowardly and hypocritical and for the way they treated women. When they saw a woman all alone it was as if everything was permitted. As soon as I asked for work it was, 'Oh, but you are a good-looking girl, there's no need to work. There are many ways that you can earn a living.' How many times I've heard that!

We first moved to Spain in September 1973 and returned to France in 1974. We should never have come back to France that first time; we should have stayed down there. Mallory, the youngest, was then nine years old and he would have adapted to living in Spain. He might have had a difficult time for the first two years but afterwards he would have settled down. But everyone else in the family was pushing us all the time not to go, 'Oh, don't leave; stay here, it's much better.' But the others have never had to experience the things that we've been through.

I only have bad memories of life in France. There was a time perhaps when I was happy but that is greatly outweighed by the bad times. The bad memories efface the good, because all the things which I remember are bad, especially the way we were treated, always avoided, by those who lived near us in the rue Gomot. There were only two French people who spoke to us as if we were French because generally they speak in a different way to other French people than they do to the Spaniards. For example, in the rue Gomot there were some neighbours, an old woman and her daughter, who lived right opposite. The mother was a shop assistant in a milliners; they were not wealthy people, just ordinary folk. She had been living opposite our house for fifteen or sixteen years and we saw each other all the time, when we went to buy the milk, when we put out the dustbins or we leaned out of the window. If that had been in Spain we would have been friends, we would have spoken to each other. If I was French she would have talked to me.

One day during the summer I was on the boulevards with the children when there was a storm, a violent summer downpour. We were dressed in raincoats and had an umbrella and I saw the woman who had an allotment near by, sheltering under a tree. When I came up to her I said, 'Would you like to come under my umbrella as far as the house?' We lived just across the street from each other. She said in a feeble voice, 'Oh yes please.' I took her under the umbrella right to her front door. I said to myself, 'Right, now she's going to speak to me, she's going to say hello when we meet; she won't treat me like a dog and turn her head the other way.' The next day when I opened the window she was sweeping the doorstep; I looked to see if she would say good day. She looked across and when she saw that I was looking at her she turned her head away and pretended that she had not seen me. We met half an hour later going to fetch the milk and she turned her face the other way when we met. She behaved just as she had before. And they are nearly all like that.

When I go to Spain, as soon as I cross the frontier, it's as if I was forty years younger. I feel different, as if the sun was out. I am astonished when passing by a shop window to see my reflection, to see myself old – so very old – and yet I feel as if I'm fifteen or sixteen years. Sometimes when I'm in the street I sing and whistle and I say to myself, 'What's happening to me? Why am I singing? I've never sung like that before outside, in the street.' The streets in Spain may be dirty but the people you meet are friendly. In France it's cleaner, things are better organised if you like, but it's like death; you meet nobody, you speak to nobody. You are closed up like Napoleon on Saint Helena.

21 Uprooted – David

During the 1960s we made a lot of trips to Spain to spend our annual holiday. But in 1973 Consuelo and I decided we would go back to Spain for good. There were a lot of things that pushed us to take that decision. By then most of the children had grown up and married; there was only Mimi and Mallory left at home. And then came one or two rude shocks, the first being the closure of the factory where I had worked since 1945.

The *Menagère*, although it was a small concern, did have good potential but the owner was always afraid to take the initiative and to modernise. Just after the war when all the other factories were investing and increasing their personnel our boss Poitevin did nothing. When we heard that he was going to install some big presses and that the doors of the factory would have to be taken down to be able to get them in we thought that they were new machines. But they turned out to be very old presses which nobody else wanted and one, I think, was a German machine taken as war reparations. All the time mechanics were having to be called to repair the presses. Poitevin was afraid to try out something new and that's why, right to the very end, the concern remained a tiny affair, a worthless factory. And then the owner fell seriously ill and died of cancer and his family decided to close down.

I was given a severance payment of 400 or 450 000 old francs by the *Menagère* and went on the dole. In view of my age and condition it wasn't easy to find work. The mayor, who was trying to find jobs for those of us who were left unemployed, told me that the best thing to do was to go on retirement benefit; there would be no problem because I was disabled. But I couldn't live off a pension because I still had two children at home and a wife and it wouldn't be enough. I managed to find work as a car mechanic in a garage but it was very, very tiring having to stand in all kinds of positions, bending over or lying on your back under the car. I worked for ten months at that garage and it was terrible, exhausting and finally one day I said to myself, 'That's it, I'm stopping; I can't go on working like this.' I went to see an employee of the social security, an old Communist called Vialon, who advised me to register as disabled and after a while I was given my retirement and a pension.

All that was very unsettling and I suppose being on a pension first raised the possibility of being able to move to Spain. But what really decided us was something else. In 1968 we moved from the rue Gomot to a pleasant ground floor flat in a detached house in the rue de la Petite Provence. It was near the edge of town, surrounded by little vegetable gardens and fruit trees. One day the owner, Monsieur Le Noir, said, 'I shall not be renewing your lease when it expires.' There were still two years to run on the existing one. I said that there had to be a reason; were there complaints against me as a tenant? I had carried out lots of repairs on the flat at my own expense, completely repapered and redecorated it, fixed tiles in the bathroom and so on. 'No', he said, 'I don't have to give you any reasons, but I'm not renewing the lease.' I told him, 'You are not an honourable person. What you are doing is wrong; no decent person would do that.' And from then on he did not cease to harass me, to try and drive me out, and the reason for all that was that just behind the house lived a lawyer whose son was going to get married and the lawyer and the landlord were good friends and they were trying to put me out so that the son could move in. One day the landlord said there had been complaints from neighbours that I was doing car repairs, as if it was a garage, but no neighbour had ever complained about the few repairs I did for friends. Another time he came to look at the flats with someone he claimed was interested in buying the house and he just arrived without any warning and tried to push his way into the flat without asking permission or anything. I told him to get out and slammed the door in his face.

Then there was the time that Le Noir came into the yard with the lawyer and they called me outside. I went into the yard and said to the landlord, 'You are a bastard and, on top of that, a racist because if it was a French person in my place you couldn't do what you're trying to do because you know that the law is not on your side. So you're trying to mess us about because we're Spanish; you are a shit.' 'Eh', he said to the lawyer, 'write that down.' 'Yes, yes, write it down and also take note that I'm going to punch his face too.' Well the lawyer got in between us, 'Not that, not that; don't fight', and the landlord cleared off. I am almost certain that he wanted me to strike him; it was a provocation, so that he could take me to court.

After that Consuelo and I talked it over and almost the same day we decided that we would return to Spain. We were already fed up with how things were in France and thought that if we moved somewhere else locally we would have just the same kind of problems later. So we wrote to some friends in Gijón to look out for a small flat for us and eventually off we went in the summer of 1973. I got hold of an old Peugeot 403 pickup that somebody was going to dump in the breaker's; it was very rusty and the engine finished but I managed to patch it up so that it would get us to Spain. All the most necessary things like clothing and the sewing machine we loaded on the Peugeot and in the car of the father of my son-in-law Marcel. All the furniture and other possessions we left stored in a barn. The move down to Asturias wasn't all that easy because I had to return immediately to France to sort out all the papers for my retirement and, more important, Mimi had decided to stay on at school one more year to finish her baccalaureate. So the family was all split up with Consuelo and Mallory in Gijón and me and Mimi staying in Riom with either one of my daughters, Ethel or Nadia.

Towards the end of the year I bought an old Citroën DS to repair so I could drive down to Spain to rejoin Consuelo for Christmas and to carry down some more furniture. Mimi said to me, 'OK, I'll come with you and perhaps I'll stay down in Gijón with you for good.' It was almost Christmas Day when we set off in that old car, loaded up to the roof with our possessions. When we began to climb up from the plain into the mountains the snow was so deep that we could only get up by driving behind a snowplough. Then at Aigleton, what terrible luck, the car broke down right up there in the mountains, in the middle of all that snow. There was no way that I could get it going and Mimi and I went to a café to have a bite to eat and to fill a Thermos with hot chocolate. That night we slept in the car all wrapped up in blankets because of the cold and next day we telephoned Marcel and José who managed to come up behind a snowplough and they towed me into the forecourt of a garage close by. We went down to Riom for the night and next day I returned with Marcel. We worked on the engine all day and it was already getting dark when Marcel said, 'Let's try and drive it as it is.' But when we tried to start the car it moved very slowly; there was no power, so we decided it was better to stay where we were rather than risk breaking down out in the wilds, in the snow. We went back down to Riom again and next day I returned with Marcel and Alfred, who is keen on mechanics, and we said, 'Damn it, if we have to we'll take the whole engine to bits.' All day we worked on that car but we just couldn't get it going and we were completely worn out. We gave up and headed back down from the mountains from Riom and in the night we came across another car which had broken down. It belonged to a school teacher from a little village up near Rochefort Montagne and we managed to repair his car. He said, 'That's the first time that somebody's ever stopped like that to help me on the road; I invite you to come and eat at my place.' But we just had an aperitif and went home.

I was in complete despair. I said to Mimi, 'Well Mama is waiting for us in Gijón for Christmas and this car will never be repaired in time to get us there.' It was already 23 December, almost Christmas Eve, when Ethel and my son-in-law John-Paul offered to take me down in their Ford Escort. Jean-Paul said, 'If we take Mimi too there won't be room for all your things.' So Mimi said she would stay behind and after that she never moved to Spain.

Well from that moment all our troubles began because from then up to now we have moved from one place to another like vagabonds. Mimi was still in Riom; she said, 'I want to finish my baccalaureate and when I've got the 'bac' I'll come down to Spain because once I've passed the exam I can get a decent job, but without it nothing.' But once we were in Gijón I became aware that things were no longer the same between me and my brothers; there had been a kind of break and I wasn't a brother for the others like they were to each other because we had been separated too long. Brothers who stay apart like that are no longer brothers. And seeing that I didn't want the same thing to happen to Mallory and Mimi and I decided that it would be better to return to France so that the children could grow up together. Consuelo didn't want to return and she is still resentful about it. She says, 'At that time Mallory was young, he would have adapted to Spain.' And it's true, he would have got used to it. But we found a little house at Ballan-Mire, a small village just outside Tours where José lived. In the summer of 1974 we began to cart all our stuff back again in Jean-Paul's van.

But at Ballan things didn't get any better. Mimi started at the Gramont College to finish her 'bac' and one day she said, 'I want to give up my studies.' I said, 'Shit, that takes the biscuit. We've done all this for you, so that you can be together with Mallory again, and Mama who reproaches me because she didn't want to leave Gijón and, after all that, you want to quit school!' 'Yes, because I've realised there's no jobs to be found when I've finished. There's no point in me wearing my brains out for nothing. I'm going to start looking for a job now.' A few days later she went off to work in an hotel in the Isère and after a while she wrote to us saying, 'I'm coming home to introduce you to a boy whom I've met; we want to get married.' I thought, 'That's it, she's now well and truly hitched up.'

So she came home with Kermel and then left for Germany and not long after they got married in Berlin.

That left just the three of us in the house. Mallory was bored all the time; he said that apart from José we never saw anyone else in the family. José would come round every day but we rarely saw the others because they were in the Puy-de-Dôme or elsewhere. All the time Consuelo was saying, 'We should go back to Spain; I don't want to die in this slum.' 'But whether you die in one place or another it's all the same.' 'We've got to go; we've got to return to Spain.' Well I had to go to Spain quite often to make all the arrangements for a disabled soldier's pension I was to get from the Spanish government and sometimes I would be away a month at a time. When I returned to Ballan I'd find them both in a black despair and finally we saw that we had to come to a decision. We said to Mallory, 'What if we return to Spain?' He was glad so Consuelo returned to Gijón and rented an apartment and we hired a lorry and brought all our furniture and possessions down. That was in July 1978. Within a year we could see that that was not going to work out either and once again we made the long journey back to France, to live in a small house at Menetrol, a village just outside Riom. I think that we are totally uprooted; we can no longer find a way to settle down. We've moved around too much from place to place. We are not like those folk who have never been away from the place where they were born and raised and are very attached to the one spot so that they can't possibly live elsewhere.

Looking back it's not easy to explain in just a few words why I could not adjust to living in Spain. But first I need to explain how I came to get a disabled person's pension from the Spanish government. For years there had been discussion in the Spanish parliament that something needed to be done for those soldiers who had fallen wounded on the Republican side. Whenever something appeared in the newspapers in Spain my family would cut it out and send it to me and a friend of mine who lived in Madrid, Eusebio, also kept me informed so that always gave us some hope. Finally it was announced in the official government gazette that a law giving us a pension was passed, but it still took a year for it to become effective and for all the bureaucratic procedures to be cleared.

Some Republican exiles were opposed to me, or anyone else, claiming the pension, just as they had been years earlier to those who returned to Spain. I remember that I had to write to a fellow at Bordeaux in the League for the Disabled, to a man **called Guillaume**.

He wrote to me saying that to accept a pension like that from the Spanish government was a complete abdication; it showed a lack of dignity and meant bowing your head. Us disabled fighters of the Republic should never accept such charity. Perhaps that man, like some others, made a good enough living and could afford to refuse the pension, but he had never returned to Spain to see how the disabled had to live. I had seen a Republican in Gijón who had lost a leg and he would go all over the city with a little barrow on two wheels collecting waste cardboard, in the full heat of the summer. And the only way he could drag the handcart along was with one hand in his pocket like those do who have a leg amputated very short so they can pull their leg along. That's how he survived. And there were others who polished shoes in the street or had to eat in soup kitchens for the down-and-out. It was quite incredible that Guillaume should say what he did. The most reasonable thing to do was to accept the pension first and to continue to fight as we could.

Anyway, after the pension became law I had to go from Ballan to Asturias to get a whole lot of paperwork arranged; it was a really complex process. I had to provide proof that I really was disabled and that it was a consequence of being wounded in the Civil War. I went to see the doctor at Santullano to get a certificate – I knew him well enough – and with that I had to go to the town hall with two witnesses. There was my friend Corsino, who had fought with me, and another called Vicente. When we came into the town hall the official behind the desk knew very well who I was, what had happened to me during the war and everything because he was a Falangist. He looked at me blankly, pretending that he didn't know who I was. I said, 'There we are, I've come to do the papers for a disabled soldier's pension, wounded on the Republican side.' He said, 'All right, have you got some witnesses?' 'Yes, these two here are my witnesses.' And he knew perfectly well who Corcino and Vicente were; so there we were, three of the left and him of the right. The secretary asked, 'Right, give your name.' 'My name is David Granda Gonzalez.' He knew who the Granda family was for sure because his father and mine had been friends of a kind. And he went on pretending not to know who I was, not a word of recognition: it made him as sick as a dog to make out the papers but he had to do it because it was the law. He began tapping away with two fingers on a typewriter and then he asked Corcino, 'Right, and you, in what capacity do you know the man?' 'Bah! Do I know him! Why it was me who pulled him out when he fell wounded. I was on the spot. So I think you can say that I know him.' And just to rub in the point about the pretended ignorance of the Falangist, I recognised the other person working in the office as a nephew of Juan de Valle. I said, 'I know you don't I? You're the son of Constantina.' 'Yes, I've heard about you from my mother; she's often spoken to me about you.' 'How are things, OK?' And with that we left.

After that I got advice from a specialist who handled the affairs of pensioners, filled a lot more papers, and then returned to France to wait. One day my nephew Abilio sent me a telegram from Paladin to say that I had been called up to go before a medical tribunal on a certain day. I went straight away by train. The tribunal was made up of military and civilian doctors and it was rather strict because somebody might, for example, come to claim a pension who had received a bullet wound in the arm and be turned down on the grounds that it was not disabling. But for those of us who had lost a limb there was no problem. 'Down with your trousers. OK, that'll do.' And so back to France again for another wait. Then one fine day a letter came to say that we could collect the pension which, with all the back-dated arrears, came to a lump sum of 280 000 pesetas. I went with Consuelo to pick up the money in cash but we decided we couldn't walk about town with all that – it was quite a tidy sum – and went to open an account in the Bank of Bilbao. The cashier began to count the notes like lightning and Consuelo said, 'I know this man, he comes from Infiesto.' Since he worked in a bank I thought that I'd ask him about my old friend Benavides who had been in hospital with gangrene and helped me when I was in the French concentration camps. I asked, 'Have you ever heard of a bank employee from Oviedo called Benavides?' 'No, I've never heard the name: I don't know him. There are so many banks.' The cashier was too young to have known him perhaps. Later I went to ask in some other banks too and at the League for the Disabled, without success. Anyway, after we had put all our money in the bank, except for 25 000 pesetas, we went to have a big meal in a restaurant and we ordered all the best things. We really went on the town.

But it should be said about the pension for the wounded Republican soldiers that the law was phrased in denigrating terms. Ever since the Civil War those who fell on the Nationalist side received a fat pension and were called *Caballeros mutilados*, disabled heroes. But we who were given a pension on the Republican side eventually got only half as much money as the others and the law referred to us as, 'Those who cannot claim to be *Caballeros mutilados* and who were

"Citizens of honour of the Republic".'[1] They did that because they are a bunch of dirty bastards and they tried to make a big division between us soldiers who were on opposite sides. One of my best friends, Eusebio – we were at school together – was near Pravia staying with an uncle when the Civil War broke out and just because he was young and his uncle was right-wing he was shoved into the Falange and ended up fighting on the other side. He too lost a leg. Whether he was on one side or the other in the war changes nothing for me because he's a good bloke. And I think that he sees me in the same way. If we speak of those times we agree that it was a great tragedy; we never argue. And if I had not been on leave from the army when the war broke out but still in Burgos and had then lost my leg I would be a *Caballero mutilado*: but I'd still be the same person. So by the mere chance of being on leave I found myself on the Republican side, one of the defeated, a less-than-nothing, a 'Red'.[2]

My cousin, José Camacho Duarte, who later became a commander in the civil guard, but is now retired, was stationed at Soto del Barco in Asturias when the Civil War started. He was among the civil guards that Aranda managed to call into Oviedo and there he got a bullet in the kidneys during the siege. He was a big strapping fellow and very tall, but now his body is all twisted and he can hardly walk. Well of course, having been wounded as a sergeant in the civil guard he got the full fanfare, *Caballero mutilado*, a big pension, rapid promotion, the whole works. The first time I met him on my return to Spain he said, 'In all our family there's just us two who got wounded, you on one side and me on the other, and we're both the losers.' 'No', I replied, 'I'm the one who lost; you lost nothing.' He said, 'Blow me, do you think I won anything being like this? I can't even get into a car by myself.'

When the government gave us Republicans a lower pension I often discussed it with Eusebio and José, I said, 'Those bastards in the government. Is it that your leg is better than mine: do you think that it's worth more than mine?' They said, 'No, of course not, they shouldn't be doing things like that.' 'And those who are doing this call themselves the "Representatives of God's Justice on Earth", and you see how they are.' 'I don't agree with that and there's lots of people like me, David; don't think that us, the Nationalist disabled, are all in agreement with that because we aren't.' 'Yes, but people have to speak out because imagine for yourself that but for a few kilometres or a few yards you would have been on my side and me on yours.' They said, 'That's true; you are right.'

That makes me think of Benavides. When we were both recuperating from gangrene at Santander we would go out for some air and he once said, 'We are fucked, eh? We're the losers in the war. Today, us two, we're heroes: people say, "There go the Republican heroes", and everyone gives us special attention. But one day you will be the limping one-legged man of Paladin and me the one-armed man of another place. We'll be the wreckage.' I remember well that word he used, 'wreckage'. People would say to him in hospital, because he was wounded, 'Benavides, is it hurting?' He said, 'Yes.' 'Where is it hurting?' 'It's not my body which is hurting, it's my soul.' He was a good bloke. I don't know where he is now; he could be in Mexico or dead, I don't know.

The two times we moved to live in Spain, in 1973 and 1978, we went to Gijón, a big, working-class town. It's not like the other big city in Asturias, the capital Oviedo, because in the capital there's no industry, just the government administration and people have a superior air. They always go out with a collar and tie, the collar well pressed and stiff, and the folds of the trousers well ironed. It's a bourgeois place. But in Gijón things are different because with all the industry and the port it's more working-class, more popular, and the people are much more friendly and approachable. If you go into the street and talk with folk you'll find that four out of five don't come from Gijón originally; they are peasants who have given up their little scraps of land or they are from mining families. Gijón is a city of displaced persons and that's why we chose to go there, because we are migrants too. We would be treated the same as everyone else and not be looked down on.

But from the very beginning I was aware that there was something wrong; I was uprooted and felt almost like a stranger in my own country. When you look at life in Spain from a distance, without regard for the detail, it's fine; you would say that the people live well and that they are happy. But when I went out into the streets for a walk I would be making a comparison of everything with how things were in France and it was quite intolerable, I couldn't stand it. It was easy to strike up acquaintance with people in the street; you would take a seat in a square and immediately there was somebody ready to strike up a conversation. But they didn't think like me; they spoke about things which were quite empty and didn't interest me at all. It was just the same for Mallory; he didn't make good friends at school. He said, 'I have got friends but they always talk about the same thing, football; if Real Madrid has done that, Bilbao this . . . You can't talk with them about anything else.' I thought to myself, 'This is not possible, it can't be true; we are strangers here in our own country.'

Some things I found quite intolerable. For example, I had to go and see a doctor to get a medical certificate for Mallory to start school and the surgery was on the third floor. There was a queue of people waiting there right up the staircase from the first floor and I waited a whole afternoon just to get a piece of paper. And I saw friends waiting there who had to get up early in the morning to come and get a place in the queue and they would be given a ticket, say number 224 in the line, and they would go and kick their heels around in the park waiting until their number came up. And it might be midday before they got in. It's incredible how things are done there. Another time Consuelo and I went to the town hall to get inscribed on the electoral register and while we were waiting the official at a table talking to another lost his biro; perhaps it had fallen and rolled somewhere or got lost. But he began shouting, 'Get out! Get out! Someone has stolen my pen.' 'Listen', I said, 'if someone has taken your pen it's not us.' And there he was kicking up a terrible row. Well, Jesus Christ, when you see something like that you realise things haven't changed that much, that somebody like that could be employed in an office.

It was the same for the question of politics. For forty years everyone had been looking just after their own interests, nobody else counted. First me and to hell with everyone else. They didn't care a bugger about the future.[3] When Franco died there was euphoria, but not long after people were already fed up. They began to say, 'Things were better before.' There was no consistency to their politics. I am in agreement with those who say that Franco died too soon, because he kicked the bucket just at the moment when the Spanish economy began to go into a crisis. Franco should have lived on for one or two years more to see the house fall round his ears, because he thought that he'd set things up for a thousand years and he would have had to witness that the whole structure was rotten. In addition it would have been a good thing for the Spanish people because today there's over a million unemployed and they would have experienced that under Franco. But now there are those who are ignorant or people of little trust who say, 'If Franco was alive today this situation would never have arisen.' But if he was still alive things would be even worse and that's why I say that he died too soon. Well when I came across that kind of mentality I realised that after forty years of dictatorship people were simply not going to change overnight and it didn't help me to settle down in Spain to see that people were more narrow minded and selfish than they had been under the Republic and during the Civil War.

Another reason why we decided to return to France was that Mallory was not happy in Spain. That was particularly true the second time that we went to live in Gijón in 1978–9 because by then he was much older, fourteen years. Each day that he came back from school, from the '*Instituto*', he said, 'Bah, they are teaching us things that I already learned in France two years ago. It's no good, I can't study here.' He didn't make friends and you could tell there was something wrong. For my part I couldn't go on living in Gijón either and one day Consuelo said, 'All right, because of Mallory we'll go back to France.'

But what leaves the most bitter memory is the changes that have taken place between me and my brothers and relatives in Paladin. I thought that when we first moved back to Spain that with six brothers we would see each other a lot and have a good family life, but things didn't turn out like that. When I first went to France at the end of the Civil War I was still very young and so I lived for too long outside the family while my brothers continued to grow up without me. I was so long separated from them that now anything that happens to me doesn't affect them very much. I'm like a poor relative. If a child of one of my brothers falls ill all my other brothers will know immediately; it's just like a clan, because a clan hangs together to survive. Everyone shows concern, whether the illness is serious or not, but if for example my wife is ill in bed for a month nobody will come and visit her. They're not concerned as they are among themselves. One day my daughter Nadia was seriously ill in Spain on her way back to France after a holiday and she had to have an operation there and then. Later my relatives said, 'Is it true then that Nayou was ill when she left here after the holidays?' I said, 'So ill that they had to operate immediately on the spot and she managed to pull through.' And it didn't make any real impact on them because she was raised so far away. But on the other hand a son of my brother Jesús had the flu, or just a silly little thing like that, and all the time people were getting off the train to come and visit him. My sister Valentina said, 'Look, there's another one come to see how the son of Jesús is.'

Looking back on things I can see that I was the outsider even before I moved back to Gijón. When my daughters first came to Paladin with Consuelo they were still small and they were all well dressed because Consuelo made all their dresses herself, embroidered and very pretty. And it seems that my mother, looking at Ethelvina, at her pretty dress, said, 'Oh, that dress would go well on Paquita, just right; oh how beautiful Paquita would look in that dress.' Paquita is the daughter of my brother Mario; she lived only a hundred yards from her grandmother and was always with her. To my mother her other granddaughters were not the same. And the house where my parents lived, which was originally a barn, had been rebuilt with bricks that Enrique and I had bought from the brickmaker in exchange for coal that we had lifted from the Nalón when we were young. My mother said one day, pointing to the vine which grew up beside the door and made a thick shade. 'You planted that.' I didn't remember. She went on, 'But the bricks of the house, it's Enrique who paid for them with coal.' But I had given as much coal, if not more; but that's how things were and you couldn't change it.

One day I was at Paladin when the two children of Jesús, who live at Mieres, a girl of nine and his son aged twelve, arrived. There were several other of my brothers and me. The children said, 'Hello uncle' to one, 'Hello uncle' to another, greeting each in turn, but to me they said nothing at all. Later I said to the boy, 'Do you know who I am?' He said, 'Yes, you're the one who lives in France.' I said, 'I am your father's brother and so an uncle to you.' He said, 'Ah, yes.' 'All right, from now on if you meet me coming along the track from Valduno will you recognise me as an uncle?' He said, 'Yes.' But of course that couldn't change anything.

As my parents got older it was always worrying to me that they might get ill while I was so far away in France. In 1978 my father became seriously ill and the doctor came to see him every day. He must have known that he was dying and he clung on for ten or twelve days, yet my brothers didn't send me a telegram or anything. And all of them were present in Paladin. When my family sent word it was to say that he had died and I set off immediately to see if I could get there for his funeral. The journey was very difficult because of floods around Bordeaux and instead of getting to Hendaye at seven in the morning to catch the bus for Oviedo I got in at ten o'clock and missed the connection. There was no train for Oviedo that could get me there in time so I asked a taxi driver if he could catch up with the bus. He said yes because the bus went by the ordinary road along the valleys but if he went by the motorway he could guarantee to catch it in Bilbao, but it would cost me three thousand pesetas.

I agreed and I managed to get the bus, but when I reached Paladin it was all over, my father was buried. Yet my family knew that in Spain when somebody dies they have to be buried within twenty-four hours and they didn't contact me. When there is a death in Paladin a funeral bulletin goes up on the door of the bar so everyone knew that the funeral of Francisco Granda had taken place. And below they put a list of relatives in attendance, Enrique Granda, Luis Granda and so on, and against my name, David Granda, was marked '*Absente*'. If they had thought a bit they might have sent a telegram earlier and I would have come, I would have got there in time.

And for my mother who died in 1966 it was the same story. My mother was very will for some time before she died; she had a kind of diabetes and went into a coma. That time they didn't even send a telegram or let me know that she was ill or anything; I just got a letter saying she had died on 11 December and by the time it reached me she had been buried two weeks. Yes, that's how it was.

After my father's death I felt even more of a stranger in Paladin. While he was alive there was a bedroom which was called after me, it was my room. 'That', they said, 'that is David's room', and the younger people said, 'That's the room of the Frenchman.' In that bedroom there were two beds and one day my sister Valentina and her daughter-in-law Anna, who lives in the house, took out one of the beds and put it in the attic. They replaced it with a new cupboard and a new bed. Well my father got angry, 'I don't want you to touch this room; this room is David's and he must find it as it is when he comes.' But then he died and the relatives of Anna, four or five Andalusians, began to come to the house all the time.

Paladin is not the same; it's completely different. For example, Consuelo went recently on a visit at Easter and when she got off the train at Vega she met Anna who said, 'Oh, my relatives are in the house; I don't know where you are going to sleep.' Consuelo said, 'But I'm not staying overnight. I've come and I'm going.' She stayed only two hours.

I don't know if my father left a will. Before he died he would always say, 'It's all arranged, it's all arranged.' But after he died nobody heard a thing. Sometimes when I came to Paladin, Valentina took out all the title deeds and papers for all the property he had bought; there were fields and woods and houses. There was the house of Mario, which was my father's, and lots of land on the hillside opposite and woods. But none of my brothers said anything about the inheritance because they're all quite happy each of them with his own house. Mario has got the house which belonged to my father, and

Luis, Enrique, Jesús, Paco, they've all got their house. The only one who might be in need was me, but they never considered the question. When I was in France in the camps and they were all down there in Spain with work and everything, they must have thought, 'David has lost a leg, he must be in great difficulty.' But after, when I bought a car which was worth nothing and went to Paladin, they thought that I was much richer than them: I think that's what they thought. In the end everything in Paladin that belonged to my father was inherited by Mario and Valentina, just the two of them. Mario for example has a big house with the garden in front, a forest with chestnut trees opposite, a big piece of land near Valduno, and he can even rent out fields to others and draw a rent.

Well since my other brothers are quite comfortable they didn't do anything about the inheritance. It's not me who is going to start raking about in that business; they can keep everything because I will never say that the property must be divided, never. I say nothing. My father kept all his faculties right to the end and one day, talking to my brothers, I said, 'His mind did not fail him, euh? So if he didn't make any provision it's because he wanted it that way.' So it's not me who is going to stir up that affair. As to the house of my parents which I had lived in when young and helped pay for the bricks, I thought it was only right that Valentina should keep it because it was she who looked all the time after my mother and father in their old age. She should have got more than the others. But I never thought that when my father died the whole lot of them would smother the affair, be completely silent like that.

When my mother died, some eleven years before my father, she had some property too and they didn't do anything about dividing that up either. Normally the inheritance of the mother is shared out among the children equally. If her husband is still alive he looks after the property and can make use of it, but it does not belong to him but to the sons. So when my father died that property should have passed on too. Again my brothers said nothing. My mother didn't own much; I think there was a chestnut wood on the hillside and a meadow which was rented to a fellow for the hay and to pasture his cows. The only thing I have of my mother's is a little broken piece off her spectacles which I keep as a memento on a chain round my neck and one day Valentina said, 'What's that thing there?' I said, 'That's my inheritance from my mother, a piece of her glasses.' She went very red and didn't know what to say.

Well that's how it is; I am the son of my parents and I am my brothers' brother, but in the village I've nothing, nothing at all. And I don't want anything. If one day one of the others says, 'We should look into this matter', we will; but it's not me whose going to ask. There's a French proverb which says, 'Parting is to die a little'; I say to part is to die completely.

Now I live in France again in a small village outside Riom. There's not many of us Spanish Republicans left. There's Pastor, who I still go to see because he lives in the same village; there's another one called Huerta, then Tena, Fernandez Emiliano, and an Asturian woman called Belarmina who I saw the other day for the first time in years at a funeral, and perhaps a few others. Over the years a lot of Spanish exiles from Riom returned to live in Spain and, like us, they nearly all came back. Tena went with his wife to see what things were like in Barcelona, to settle down there, but he returned later. He said, 'I can't stay in Spain for more than a month, it's impossible for me to live there.' The same happened to Tena's friend and there's a lot like that. But there are others for whom things are different – I don't know – like Theodoro for example, who is much happier in Spain. Perhaps it's because he's got a good job and things appear rosy.

When you leave your home country like I did when still young you become completely rootless. I am Spanish by birth but I feel like a stranger there and I don't feel as if I'm French either because I'm not, I was born elsewhere. I don't mean to say that Spain means nothing to me, that if there was an earthquake and it disappeared from the face of the earth it would leave me cold. You can love the country of your birth and that country has given you something, because you owe something to your country and it in turn has a duty towards you. But in my case all I got from Spain was a kick up the backside. That's what it amounts to because up to the age of twenty I never had a job to earn my living; I had to work on the river with my father on a miserable task which paid almost nothing. We worked like slaves for nothing, our guts crying out for food. I lost my leg in Spain and all I get is a pension worth nothing, because even if they paid it to me for forty or fifty years it would add up to nothing at all. It's like I count for less than a dog.

And what can be more uprooting than to see that your own children are not Spanish? When Mallory moved to Gijón he learned to speak very good Spanish. But at school the children would say, 'Hey there Frenchy!' He would say, 'What do you mean, Frenchy? I am Spanish like you; my father is "Asturiano", my mother "Asturiana". I'm Spanish, no?' In France Mallory is Spanish and down there he's a foreigner, and it's the same for all the children. That must be a thing that all emigrants experience. When the older children were small their first language was Spanish, we spoke Spanish all the time at home and we went to Asturias every year. But if you ask, for example, Ethel if she would like to go and live in Spain she says, 'It's OK to go and spend a holiday, but to live there? No.' The children don't feel themselves to be Spanish and they don't want to be. It has to be recognised that they were born here in France, educated here. Yes, when you leave your country like I did you lose everything, everything, and there is no pension that is going to pay for that.

Once I wrote some poems while in the concentration camp. Perhaps I can tell them to you. They are the kind of poems that people make who haven't been to school; they say something to them perhaps, but for other folk ... I said in one poem, 'I have been banished from my sun; I have been driven away from my mother, my friend, my fountain, over there, beyond the mountains. I am an uprooted tree; I am a man with no soul.' That I made up in the concentration camp; already I saw everything so black because in reality we had been driven out. And then when we reached France we thought that it was a country of Fraternity, that Republican exiles would be welcomed like brothers, and immediately we were treated badly by them. I made another poem which said. 'I have not got the plague and yet they have sounded the warning bell; and they have cried out, "Beware, the mad dog", at Rome, at Lourdes and at Compostella.' That's all. Because in France they said we had eaten priests and they took great care to put us in camps so that we should not mix with the ordinary people. They were AFRAID! We were treated like carriers of the plague. That's why I made that poem.

When you think about it we not only lost the war, we lost everything else too. Everything.

Notes

INTRODUCTION

1. See P. Preston, 'War of Words: the Spanish Civil War and the Historians' in P. Preston (ed.), *Revolution and War in Spain 1931–1939* (London: Methuen, 1984).
2. Figures taken from P. Preston, 'The Anti-Francoist Opposition: The Long March to Unity, in P. Preston (ed.), *Spain in Crisis: The Evolution and Decline of the Franco Régime* (Hassocks: Harvester, 1976), p. 133. See also H. Thomas, *The Spanish Civil War* (Harmondsworth: Penguin, 1965), pp. 760–1.
3. See for example V. Cunningham (ed.), *Spanish Front: Writers on the Civil War* (Oxford: Oxford University Press, 1986) and B. Alexander, *British Volunteers for Liberty: Spain 1936–1939* (London: Lawrence & Wishart, 1982).
4. On the emergence of oral history as a discipline and for the methodological issues which it raises see P. Thompson, *The Voice of the Past. Oral History* (Oxford: Oxford University Press, 1978); T. Lummis, *Listening to History: The Authenticity of Oral Evidence* (London: Hutchinson, 1987).
5. Ian Gibson's delicate investigation after 1965 of the murder of Garcia Lorca also used the interview and was an early sign of a changing atmosphere inside Spain. I. Gibson, *The Assassination of Federico García Lorca* (London: W. H. Allen, 1979).
6. The following account is based on a series of tape-recorded interviews with David and Consuelo Granda which began in Gijón, Asturias, in July 1979 and was completed in Riom, France, in the summer of 1982. Inevitably there has been some editing of the material; repetitious or irrelevant information has been removed and the whole rearranged into a broadly chronological sequence and divided up into chapters. However, every attempt has been made to stay as true as possible to the original account.
7. P. Preston (ed.), *Revolution and War*, pp. 12, 159.
8. On *caciquismo* see R. Carr, *Spain 1808–1939* (Oxford: Oxford University Press, 1966), pp. 366–79.
9. See J. R. Mintz, *The Anarchists of Casas Viejas* (Chicago: University of Chicago Press, 1982).
10. A. Shubert, *The Road to Revolution: The Coal Miners of Asturias 1860–1934* (Urbana: University of Illinois Press, 1987), pp. 6–7.
11. *Historia General de Asturias*, vol. 7, 'Octubre de 1934' (Gijón, 1978), pp. 33–48.
12. P. Preston, *The Coming of the Spanish Civil War. Reform, Reaction and Revolution in the Second Republic 1931–1936* (London: Macmillan, 1978), p. 158.
13. R. Carr, *The Spanish Tragedy: The Civil War in Perspective* (London: Weidenfeld & Nicolson, 1977), pp. 76–7.

14. H. R. Southworth, *Guernica! Guernica! A Study of Journalism, Diplomacy, Propaganda and History* (Berkeley: University of California Press, 1977).
15. The history of the Spanish Republicans in France has been studied mainly by non-French scholars, notably L. Stein, *Beyond Death and Exile: The Spanish Republicans in France 1939–1955* (Cambridge, Mass.: Harvard University Press, 1979), and D. W. Pike, *Vae Victis: Los Repúblicanos Españoles Refugiados en Francia 1939–1944* (Paris, 1969). More recently R. Schor has studied anti-Spanish propaganda in, *L'Opinion Française et les Étrangers en France 1919–1939* (Paris: Publication de la Sorbonne, 1985), Part 4, Chapter 7.
16. L. Stein, *Beyond Death and Exile*, p. 173.
17. See B. Pollack, G. Hunter, *The Paradox of Spanish Foreign Policy: Spain's International Relations from Franco to Democracy* (London: Pinter, 1987), Chapters 1, 2.
18. S. Carrillo gives an account from the position of a leading member of the PCE in *Dialogue on Spain* (London: Lawrence & Wishart, 1976), pp. 14, 92–6, 101; see also P. Preston (ed.), *Spain in Crisis*, pp. 133–6.
19. Jorge Semprún, expelled along with Fernando Claudin from the PCE in 1964, has revealed the damaging impact of Stalinism in his autobiographical study, *Communism in Spain in the Franco Era: The Autobiography of Federico Sanchez* (Brighton: Harvester, 1980).
20. R. Carr, J. P. Fusi, *Spain: Dictatorship to Democracy* (London: Allen & Unwin, 1979), p. 94.

CHAPTER 1

1. On living conditions in Asturias at this time see A. Shubert, *The Road to Revolution*, Chapters 1, 3.
2. Chestnuts constituted one of the staples in the diet of many peasant societies in the mountain regions of Europe, like the Cevennes and Corsica, down to the nineteenth century. The survival of this as a staple in the Asturian diet during the inter-war period is one indicator of the archaic nature of the rural economy.
3. An unprecedented demand for coal and high prices during the First World War appears to have made the exploitation of the river coal economic. After 1919 Asturian coalmines were hit by a severe crisis, and mechanisation of the pits in the late twenties, including self-acting washers and sorters, cut the amount of coal lost. A. Shubert, *Road to Revolution*, pp. 56, 121–3.
4. In the years preceding the Civil War the political and social divisions in Spain were reflected in the bitter opposition between the extremely reactionary Catholic Church and the popular forces of the left. In Valduno, as was common in many parts of Europe, the women showed a much higher level of religious practice than the men. The anti-clericalism of the Republican and socialist movements appears to have penetrated the parish from the nearby mining and industrial centres and led to a widespread alienation of the men from the Church.
5. Primary education in Spain before the Second Republic was hopelessly

inadequate owing to the very low level of state funding and the efforts of the Church to maintain this as an underprivileged sector, while concentrating its own efforts in secondary education which was the preserve of the fee-paying middle and upper classes. As late as 1930 some 26 per cent of adults were totally illiterate.
6. There was a long tradition of emigration from Asturias as one solution to the extreme poverty and relative overpopulation of the region. By 1898 some half a million people of Asturian origin were living in the Americas, two thirds of the total population of the home province. See A. Shubert, *Road to Revolution*, pp. 33–4.

CHAPTER 2

1. Manuel Villar wrote in *El Anarquismo en la Insurrección de Asturias* (Barcelona, 1935), pp. 19–20, 'The workers and peasants attributed a mythical significance to the republican form of government. To it they attached their yearning for social justice, and they believed it to be the cornerstone of a new society based on new economic and social precepts.' Quoted by A. Shubert, *Road to Revolution*, p. 141.
2. The most controversial legislation introduced by the Constituent Cortes of the Republic concerned the separation of Church and State: the Church would no longer have a special status, the annual government grant to the Church was ended, thus cutting off funds for clerical schools and parish priests, while divorce and civil marriage were legalised and churchyards secularised.
3. On the depression in Asturias during the inter-war period see A. Shubert, *Road to Revolution*, Chapters 6, 7. The miner's leader, Ramón González Peña, who was born in David Granda's parish of Valduno (see n. 9 below), wrote in 1928, 'Both this year and last thousands have been swarming from place to place unsuccessfully looking for work, and many have had to become beggars as the only means to avoid dying of hunger.'
4. The penetration of socialism and trade unionism into the rural zone around Grado, in which Paladin is situated, has been explained by the proximity to the National Cannon Factory at Trubia, a major centre of socialist activity and where a large number of workers were drawn from the surrounding peasant villages: see B. Fernandez, J. Giron, 'Aproximacion al Sindicalismo Agrario en Asturias, 1906–1923' in *La Cuestion Agraria en la España Contemporanea* (Madrid, 1976), p. 192. On the close interrelationship between mine and peasant communities see D. Ruiz, *El Movimiento Obrero en Asturias* (Madrid: Júcar, 1979); A. Shubert, *Road to Revolution*, pp. 36–41, 127.
5. The Federación Nacional de Trabajadores de la Tierra, founded in April 1930, underwent a phenomenal growth, increasing its membership from 36 639 in June 1930 to 392 953 in June 1932. P. Preston, *Coming of Civil War*, pp. 19, 54.
6. One of Javier Bueno's first acts on becoming editor in July 1933 was to organise a dense network of local correspondents, including one at Trubia and another at Grado, close to Paladin. See *Historia General de*

Asturias, vol. 7. 'Octubre de 1934' (Gijón, 1978), pp. 33–48; also A. Shubert *Road to Revolution*, p. 151.
7. The general aims of Gil Robles' Confederación Española de Derechas Autónomas (CEDA), founded in February 1933, were 'the defence of the principles of Christian civilisation' and the destruction of Republican reforms. P. Preston, *Coming of Civil War*, p. 43.
8. On the *caciques*' use of corruption and intimidation in the 1933 election see, P. Preston, *Coming of Civil War*, p. 95.
9. The Socialist leader Prieto organised the secret purchase of arms which were shipped in to San Esteban de Pravia, at the mouth of the Nalón, on the night of 10 September 1934. The police captured part of the consignment, but 300 rifles and 80 cases of cartridges were hidden at Valduno. Among those who helped unload the *Turquesa* was Ramón González Peña, President of the Asturian Miners' Union (SMA), born at Valduno in 1888 into a family of poor peasants. In 1938 he became Minister of Justice in the Negrín government.
10. On the history of the October Revolution see M. Grossi Mier, *La Insurrección de Asturias* (Gijón: Júcar, 1978 edn.); N. Molíns i Fábrega, *UHP: La Insurrección Proletaria de Asturias* (Gijón: Júcar, 1977 edn.); A. Shubert, *Road to Revolution*, Introduction; Chapter 8.
11. On 11 October the Oviedo-based provincial committee which was in overall charge of the organisation of the insurrection fled in panic as the army closed in. On 12 October a second committee, dominated by Communists, tried to form a 'Red Army' based on the conscription of all workers aged eighteen to thirty-five, but this organisation lasted only one day. See A. Shubert, *Road to Revolution*, p. 8.
12. Franco's use of North African troops caused particular shock because nationalist ideology placed a strong emphasis on the centuries-long Reconquest of Spain from the barbarian Moors. Asturians placed great pride in being from the only region of Spain never occupied by the Muslims. See P. Preston, *Coming of Civil War*, p. 129.
13. Cornelio Fernandez was tortured on 26 November and revealed the hiding place of the largest single sum ever recovered, 1 325 000 pesetas. His brother, Constante, disclosed the whereabouts of another 112 400 pesetas. The bulk of the money was never recovered by the police and was used to buy new presses for *Avance*, after the existing ones were destroyed by the right in October, and to fund an escape network for revolutionaries and the Popular Front election campaign of February 1936: *Historia General de Asturias*, vol. 8, pp. 187–9.
14. On the activities of the Unión Militar Española, the anti-republican conspiracy of army officers, and the manoeuvres it organised in Asturias and elsewhere in preparation for the rebellion, see P. Preston, *Coming of Civil War*, p. 158.
15. Lieutenant José Castillo was assassinated by Falangist gunmen on 12 July 1936, one month after the killing of another Assault Guard officer, Captain Faraudo. The monarchist leader, José Calvo Sotelo was in turn assassinated in revenge by Assault Guards on 13 July. These killings took place against a background of increasing violence and lawlessness in the spring of 1936 which was exaggerated by the extreme right to undermine confidence in the Republic.

CHAPTER 3

1. At 5.15 a.m. on 18 July Franco broadcast from the Canary Islands his famous manifesto announcing the Nationalist Movement, before flying to Tetuán in Morocco. The Republican Government first gave news of the rising on the morning of 18 July when Madrid Radio announced that, 'no one, absolutely no one on the Spanish mainland, has taken part in this absurd plot.' However, rebels seized a number of centres, including Seville, the same day.
2. When the military rising began on 18 July rebel officers at La Coruña in Galicia shot the commander, General Salcedo, and quickly took control. From there on 29 July columns began to march towards Asturias along the coast road to Luarca and through the inland mountain passes.
3. One commentator has described this as the 'picaresque stage' of the Civil War: 'The first scene provided by the Civil War was one of a large number of disparate columns, fighting on their own, carving out their operational sectors, where they lived, got their food supplies, and sometimes developed along independent lines.' Jean-Richard Bloch quoted in P. Broué, E. Témime, *The Revolution and the Civil War in Spain* (London: Faber, 1970), p. 174.
4. Manuel Otero, leader of the Socialist Youth in Sama de Langreo, emerged as a gifted director of military operations during the October Revolution of 1934. *Historia General de Asturias*, vol. 7, p. 146.
5. There was widespread distrust of those officers who joined the Republican side during the early stages of the Civil War, and with good reason. Many who were caught in the Republican zone at the time of the rising on 18 July were sympathetic to the Nationalists and were waiting for an opportunity to cross the lines or, in some instances, operated as a Fifth Column.
6. One of the most remarkable features of the Civil War was the rapid and spontaneous appearance of thousands of local revolutionary committees. Overnight the Republican state apparatus became virtually defunct and was replaced by a myriad network of Spanish 'Soviets' which exercised complete legislative and executive power, maintained law and order, controlled prices, expropriated the property of the clergy and fascists, requisitioned food supplies and buildings, organised education, propaganda and welfare and established communal kitchens. This has been described as the 'greatest revolutionary upsurge' in Europe since the Russian Revolution. R. Fraser, *In Hiding, The Life of Manuel Cortes* (Harmondsworth: Penguin, 1972). p. 230.
7. Grado fell on 15 September and on 7 October a major offensive, spearheaded by North African troops, was launched up the Nalón valley to try and break through to the vital artillery works at Trubia. The Nationalists, after heavy fighting, reached Paladin on the evening of 7 October. *Historia General de Asturias*, vol. 9, p. 178.
8. In Asturias the Communists and the majority of the Anarchist CNT agreed on the necessity for militarisation and from late September onwards the militias were integrated into a regular army. However,

opposition to this process was symptomatic of a profound division, which was to weaken the Republicans throughout the war, between those, mainly Anarchists, who saw the struggle as a popular revolutionary process, and others, most significantly the Communists, who argued that the prime objective was the military defeat of fascism and that this required a unified and disciplined command structure.

9. On 19 October Aranda received a report that the *Christopher Columbus* had docked in Gijón with a consignment of Russian arms. In all, the Soviet Union was reported to have supplied to the North some 15 000 rifles, some 'dating back to the Crimean War'. In addition the Asturians received Czech arms sent from Mexico and a consignment of old French rifles on the steamship *Reina*. Broué, Témime, *The Revolution*, pp. 392, 411. The Communist, Manuel Sanchez, reported the arrival of 'ancient, single-loading Czech rifles', in October. R. Fraser, *The Blood of Spain: The Experience of Civil War, 1936–1939* (Harmondsworth: Penguin, 1981), p. 251.

10. On the traditional hatred of Galicians in the Asturian coalfields see A. Shubert, *Road to Revolution*, pp. 71–2. An account of the October Revolution by Alfonso Comín was dedicated, 'To José Garcia-Crespo, who loves Asturias free of moors, of the Legion, and of Galician troops.'

11. The Republican command assembled a force of 27 000 men for the offensive to cut the supply route into Oviedo; the Nationalists had about 30 000 soldiers.

12. The *España* was a battleship of 16 400 tons. During 1937, in spite of the application of a Non-Intervention Agreement of 19 April, there was considerable tension between Britain and the Axis powers as a result of the stopping and searching of British ships on the high seas and a number of 'pirate' attacks by unmarked planes and submarines on neutral shipping. The British destroyer *Foxhound* was attacked off the north coast of Spain on 4 August 1937. Broué, Témime, *The Revolution*, pp. 486–7. However, it seems unlikely that the Royal Navy was involved in the sinking of the *España*. Hugh Thomas, in the 1965 edition of his *The Spanish Civil War*, p. 540, reports incorrectly that the *España* was sunk on 30 April by a mine off Bilbao, perhaps inadvertently repeating Nationalist disinformation.

13. The destruction of Guernica, the ancient capital of the Basque provinces, on 26 April 1937 was one of the most infamous events of the Civil War. Today, in an age hardened to the repeated mass destruction of civilian populations through aerial bombardment (Dresden, Hiroshima, Hanoi), it is not easy to recognise the profound shock that this first Nazi trial-run in the art of blitzkreig had on contemporary opinion. For a minute examination of the event see H. R. Southworth, *Guernica! Guernica!*

14. The major offensive against Bilbao, in which Italian soldiers played a prominent part, began on 31 March. The decisive break through the 'Iron Ring' defences of the city came on 12 June and Bilbao was occupied on the 17th. A battalion at full strength normally had about 600 men.

15. Only two Republican destroyers, the *Ciscar* and the *José Luis Diez* protected communications with the outside world, but the presence of a much larger Nationalist blockade force meant that the Army of the North was virtually cut off, isolated in a coastal strip, and was being rolled back from the east. Backed by the German airforce the Nationalists advanced rapidly through Santander province between 17 and 27 August.

CHAPTER 4

1. When the insurrection began the four civil guards stationed in Infiesto managed to escape to the west to Nava where they were able to concentrate their forces. As a result there was no major fighting in the town. On 10 October a column of soldiers under Colonel Solchaga set out from Bilbao for eastern Asturias and on the 14th a large military force was built up in Infiesto in preparation for an advance on Oviedo. *Historia General de Asturias*, vol. 7, p. 164; vol. 8, p. 76.
2. In the small provincial town of Infiesto the bourgeoisie, mainly shopkeepers and professionals, were very right-wing. The peasantry of the region were too far away from the mining and industrial centres of Asturias to be influenced by Socialism to the same extent as in Valduno. During the period of tension before the October Revolution a bus taking twenty members of the Socialist Youth on an excursion was fired on as it passed through the town. *Historia General de Asturias*, vol. 7, p. 72.
3. An *hórreo* in Asturias is a granary raised high off the ground on four or more wooden legs.
4. During the first months of the Civil War women assumed many functions traditionally reserved for men, including fighting at the front. The relegation of women to the rear and to the tasks of nursing and cooking was part and parcel of the process of militarisation and the reintroduction of traditional hierarchies, roles and discipline.
5. The fear of falling under the scalpel of fascist doctors who had become trapped within the Republican zone at the start of the war caused widespread unease. David Jato, a clandestine leader of the Falange militia, claims that so many doctors joined his organisation, 'that Madrid's health services were virtually in our hands.' In Catalonia Professor Trueta, a loyal Republican surgeon, was accused by a leading Anarchist of killing his brother by means of an injection. R. Fraser, *Blood of Spain*, pp. 487, 148.

CHAPTER 5

1. By March 1937 the Nationalist forces were bogged down on the heavily fortified Madrid front. Franco decided to turn his full weight to the northern front and to capture the coastal zone before concentrating his forces in the centre and east. Bilbao fell on 19 June, Santander on 26 August and the 45 000 men of the Asturian army fought a desperate rearguard action against better-equipped Italian, German and

Nationalist forces in the jagged Picos de Europa.
2. At 2 a.m. on 20 October Colonel Pradas reported to a meeting of the Council of Asturias that defeat was now inevitable. The Council voted against Prime Minister Negrín's cabled order to fight to the end and decided to save as much of the army as possible by evacuation through the ports of Gijón, Aviles and Candas. President Belarmino Tomás and other Council members left on board the fishing boat *Abascal* at 8 a.m. the same day. R. Fraser, *Blood of Spain*, pp. 422–3.
3. On 20 October there was a revolt of right-wing forces. Colonel Franco, commander of the Trubia armaments factory, backed by civil guards, began to take control of Gijón. Key buildings were seized and some two hundred political prisoners were released. Franco, who negotiated the surrender of Gijón to the Nationalists, whom he welcomed with open arms, was shot within a week for his pains.

CHAPTER 6

1. Dr Carlos Martinez, former parliamentary deputy, recounts being on an escaping ship stopped by the *Almirante Cervera*. 'Passengers began tearing up party membership cards; revolvers and other arms were thrown overboard . . . In fear, a passenger leapt overboard.' R. Fraser, *Blood of Spain*, pp. 423–4. Most ships which were stopped by the Nationalists were forced to sail to Galicia where the refugees were put into concentration camps.
2. This was not the Red Cross but an aid association supported by the French Communist Party.

CHAPTER 7

1. In March 1938 the Nationalists armed with well-equipped, motorised divisions, broke through the Republican front south of the River Ebro and reached the Mediterranean thus cutting the Republican zone in half and isolating Valencia.
2. Other commentators returning from the battle areas remarked on the frivolous nature of Barcelona life. Even greyhound racing continued as a collectivised entertainment run by the Anarchists. R. Fraser, *Blood of Spain*, pp. 225, 453.
3. The slogan of the Alianza Obrera established in Asturias in March 1934 and which joined Socialists and Anarchists of the CNT in the most successful and united revolutionary movement in Spain. P. Preston, *Coming Civil War*, p. 120.
4. José Diaz, secretary-general of the Communist Party, stated, 'We wish to fight only for a democratic republic with a broad social content. There can be no question at present of a dictatorship of the proletariat or of Socialism, but only of the struggle of democracy against Fascism.' See Broué, Témime, *The Revolution*, p. 195.
5. A reference to the famous Communist Fifth Regiment, the 'Quinto'.
6. In Barcelona in May 1937 explosive tensions developed between a dissident Communist group, the Partido Obrero de Unificación Marx-

ista (POUM), backed by some Anarchists, and the Communist and Socialist Parties. This ended in bitter street-fighting in which some five hundred people died. The PCE seized the opportunity to launch a campaign against 'Trotskyist' and 'Fascist' elements and some of the more unpleasant features of Stalinist purge techniques crept into Spanish politics.
7. The first heavy bombing came in seventeen raids during 16 to 18 March carried out by Italian planes flying from Majorca. In all 1300 people were killed and 2000 wounded by penetrating explosive bombs, incendiaries and anti-personnel bombs. The German Ambassador in Salamanca, Stohrer, reported the effect as, 'terrible. All parts of the city were affected. There was no evidence of any attempt to hit military objectives.' H. Thomas, *The Spanish Civil War* (Harmondsworth: Penguin, 1964 edn.), p. 658; R. Fraser, *Blood of Spain*, p. 442.
8. At a meeting of the Cabinet on 16 March some ministers, including Prieto, barely concealed their defeatism and leaned towards a negotiated settlement of the war. A Communist-led demonstration protested outside. H. Thomas, *Civil War*, pp. 662–3.

CHAPTER 8

1. Prime Minister Negrín and his government abandoned Barcelona on 23 January and Nationalist troops entered, virtually unopposed, on the 25th. The roads to the north and the French border were jammed with soldiers and civilians fleeing in panic. Constancia de la Mora thought that a Fifth Column deliberately spread panic in the crowds. At Figueras she had seen an officer of the Carabiñeros in the main square shouting that the Nationalists were about to enter the town and that everyone should flee. At that moment there was no threat from the enemy. L. Stein, *Beyond Death and Exile*, p. 26.
2. According to L. Stein, *Beyond Death and Exile*, p. 27, the border was opened to women, children and the elderly on the night of 27–28 January.
3. Some 1500 wounded soldiers from the military hospital at Camprodón crossed into France. A nurse working in a hospital at Perpignan recalled, 'How can I begin to tell of what happened? They came walking, all the way from Argelès, some of them, with all kinds of terrible wounds . . . They had cut branches off the trees and improvised splints. Their plaster casts were black with mud. They tried to keep their filthy dressings from unravelling by tying rope around them because they thought that even a dirty dressing was better than nothing at all. Many of them were gangrenous, all of them were emaciated, hungry and exhausted.' L. Stein, *Beyond Death and Exile*, p. 31.

CHAPTER 9

1. The frontier was opened to women, children and the elderly on 28 January but not to able-bodied men. In France there was a widespread fear, whipped up by the right-wing press, that a huge army of

Anarchist and Marxist 'terrorists' would sweep into the south. The government moved a large military force up to the frontier and agonised at the prospect of a confused and bloody battle raging if the Republican army was left trapped between Franco's forces and French machine-guns. Finally the order to allow the Republican army to cross over was given on 5 and 6 February.
2. The Nationalists reached the frontier at Perthus on 8 February. The last Republican forces, left behind to fight a rearguard action, retreated in good order during 10 and 11 February.
3. Many Spanish soldiers, expecting a warm welcome and some solidarity in the sister Republic, were bitterly disillusioned when they were stripped of arms, searched and treated in a hostile or brutal fashion as if they were criminals or prisoners of war. See L. Stein, *Beyond Death and Exile*, p. 34.
4. The famous Anarchist Durruti Division, the Twenty-Sixth, along with Communist units under Juan Modesto and Enrique Lister, was chosen to make a last ditch defence against the advancing Nationalists so that the remainder of the Spanish Republican army could be evacuated across the border. The Durruti Division finally entered France on 10 February: one of its members, Antonio Herrero, relates that, 'as soon as we arrived reinforcements were sent for. We were considered the most dangerous of the refugees.' L. Stein, *Beyond Death and Exile*, p. 37.

CHAPTER 10

1. During the inter-war period France faced a major shortage of labour and this was compounded during the war itself by the imprisonment of about 1.8 million French soldiers. Although it was not openly acknowledged by the government, the influx of Spanish refugees provided a source of cheap and easily exploited labour and a major boost to the French economy.
2. 'Ils mangent notre pain' was an almost universal refrain during this period: see H. Schramm, B. Vormeier, *Vivre à Gurs: Un Camp de Concentration Français, 1940–1941* (Paris: Maspero, 1979), p. 210. Press and radio whipped up an unprecedented racist and xenophobic fear and hatred of Spanish Republicans; see L. Stein, *Beyond Death and Exile*, Chapter 3, and R. Schor, *L'Opinion Française et les Étrangers*, Part 4, Chapter 7.
3. The French authorities placed considerable pressure on the refugees to return to Spain even when this was dangerous for many. The journalist John Stevens reported that refugees were 'harried night and day by a barrage of Franco propaganda from loudspeaker automobiles. They are told of the joys of life in Franco Spain and urged to return there immediately . . . The French policy seems to be to make things so hard for them that they will be glad to go.' L. Stein, *Beyond Death and Exile*, p. 81.
4. In order to transfer from one region of France to another a refugee required the authorisation of the department to which he or she wished

to go. Generally the prefect refused or required a certificate guaranteeing a place of residence and sufficient funds to be self-supporting; or alternatively a French citizen had to act as a guarantor. For this reason many Spaniards were forced to stay in the concentration camps although they were technically 'free' to leave. Schramm and Vormeier, *Vivre à Gurs*, p. 41.
5. The '*Travailleurs Étrangers*' units comprised groups of 2000–5000 men placed under strict discipline. Pablo Casals described them, with reason, as a 'modern version of organized slavery'. L. Stein, *Beyond Death and Exile*, p. 130.

CHAPTER 11

1. During 1939 the French government constructed literally dozens of concentration camps at Gurs, Agde, Septfonds, Bram, Rivesaltes and other locations, mainly in the south. At their peak these contained about quarter of a million refugees.
2. Ybarnegaray, deputy for the Basses-Pyrenees, and a supporter of the fascist Croix de Fer, repeatedly vented his hatred of the Spanish Republicans in the Chamber of Deputies.
3. Some French military co-operated directly with Spanish Nationalists in the repatriation drive. General Solchaga, notorious for his brutality in the repression of Spanish Republicans, was even allowed to tour the camp at Gurs. L. Stein, *Beyond Death and Exile*, pp. 62, 81.
4. A curious feature of life in the camps was the way in which local inhabitants would be invited to attend theatrical and artistic performances. At Gurs villagers even paid a modest entrance fee to attend a cabaret in which professional German musicians, singers and actors performed. Schramm and Vormeier, *Vivre à Gurs*, p. 138.
5. Spanish Republicans and International Brigade members who were identified as Communist or Anarchist activists were sent to the special punishment centres at Collioure or Vernet where they suffered from appalling brutality and hardship. Internees were expressly excluded from the protective provisions of the Geneva Convention. L. Stein, *Beyond Death and Exile*, pp. 72–5; Schramm and Vormeier, *Vivre à Gurs*, pp. 251, 305–12.
6. By the German–Soviet treaty of 24 August 1939 the two states agreed to a Pact of Non-Aggression and, in a secret protocol, to the division of Eastern Europe into spheres of influence. This opened the way for the partition of Poland.
7. Eventually some 15 000 Spaniards saw action with the Foreign Legion. The enormous contribution of these experienced fighters to the Allied side during the Second World War has been well documented by Louis Stein.

CHAPTER 12

1. In the course of 1941 French doctors and relief organisations began to recognise the classic signs of severe malnutrition within the camps. The

money spent on food for each refugee was officially set at the same level as for a French soldier, 11.5 francs per day, but at Gurs refugees received food worth only one third of this. During 1940 the bread ration declined from 400 to 350 grammes per day but conditions deteriorated even further in 1941 and by the late summer rations were down to 500–600 calories per day. Dysentery was widespread and hundreds of internees, weak from malnutrition, died. Schramm and Vormeier, *Vivre à Gurs*, pp. 17, 56, 147, 278. On the health conditions see especially Joseph Weill, *Contribution à l'Histoire des Camps d'Internement dans l'Anti-France* (Paris: Editions du Centre, 1946).
2. Thousands of young Frenchmen were compelled to go and work in Germany by the Service du Travail Obligatoire; many chose the moment to join the Resistance in the *Maquis*.

CHAPTER 13

1. Jesús Ibanez was one of five CNT delegates to the founding conference of the Profintern, the Communist federation of trade unions, held in Moscow in 1921. He joined the PCE and lived for some time in Russia where he was secretary to Andrés Nin and an agent of the Comintern and helped organise an insurrection in Uruguay. He was imprisoned in the Soviet Union under Stalin, an experience that may account for his bitter anti-Communism. He played a leading role in the 1934 Revolution and the Civil War in Asturias and was a major Marxist theoretician.
2. A prime obsession of the Vichy police from 1940 onwards was the location of known Communists and Anarchists, including Spanish Republicans. From time to time extensive search operations were carried out, like the raid on Perpignan on 12 December 1942 which involved 298 police officers, 61 roadblocks and a house-to-house sweep of the city. See R. Kedward, 'The Maquis and the Culture of the Outlaw', in R. Kedward, R. Austin (ed.), *Vichy France and the Resistance: Culture and Ideology* (London: Croom Helm, 1985), pp. 238–9; L. Stein, *Beyond Death and Exile*, p. 127.
3. Previously most concentration camps had been holding centres for the temporary containment of refugees prior to dispersal. The *camps de répression* had a much more severe discipline, were heavily guarded and generally contained political 'subversives', Jews and gypsies.
4. The law of 4 October 1940 authorised prefects to intern foreign Jews and by the time of the first big round-up in the Occupied Zone at Paris in July 1942 there were already 20 000 Jews detained in the camps under the control of the Vichy government. In all some 65 000 Jews were deported from France and only 2800 survived the extermination camps. M. R. Marrus and R. O. Paxton, *Vichy France and the Jews* (New York: Basic Books, 1981).
5. Rivesaltes was the assembly point for Jews who were sent there from the other camps in the south of France prior to final deportation. Schramm and Vormeier, *Vivre à Gurs*, pp. 154–76. On the terrible conditions at Rivesaltes see Marrus and Paxton, *Vichy France*, pp. 173–4.

Notes

6. Gurs, built in 1939 to house Spanish refugees and the International Brigades, was perhaps the most famous of all the camps. The political philosopher Hannah Arendt was interned here in September 1939 as was the Levy family in Andre Schwartz-Bart's novel, *'The Last of the Just'*. On conditions here see Marrus and Paxton, *Vichy France*, pp. 172–3.
7. The first of several German commissions recruited in the main camps from 17 to 19 August 1942. Very few Spaniards volunteered in spite of German promises of better treatment and in reality workers in the Todt organisation lived in near slavery, were brutalised by guards and at risk from allied bombing raids. L. Stein, *Beyond Death and Exile*, pp. 136–7.

CHAPTER 14

1. The US 7th Army, under the command of General Alexander Patch (not Patton), landed on 15 August and advanced rapidly up the Rhône Valley after the 20th.
2. Forty-nine towns in France were liberated totally or in part by the Spanish *Maquis*. L. Stein, *Beyond Death and Exile*, p. 148.

CHAPTER 15

1. Jews who had the means, instead of being interned, could be sent by the police to 'assigned residence', usually hotels in rural areas. See Marrus and Paxton, *Vichy France*, p. 169.
2. Arthur Koestler, who was imprisoned at Vernet, reported that thirty internees who had been in Dachau, Oranienburg and Wolfsbuettel found the conditions worse in the former than in the Nazi camps. See Marrus and Paxton, *Vichy France*, pp. 174–6.
3. On the role of Spanish Republicans in the Resistance movement in the Puy-de-Dôme see J. F. Sweets, *Choices in Vichy France: the French Under Nazi Occupation* (New York: Oxford University Press, 1986) and L. Stein, *Beyond Death and Exile*, Chapter 9.
4. There was a half-hearted attempt to isolate Spain diplomatically through the United Nations resolutions which were debated in April to June 1946, but Britain, France and the United States refused to make any decisive move against the regime. By 1950 the USA was advancing economic aid and on 23 September 1953 a ten-year military and economic pact was signed.

CHAPTER 17

1. 'La Pasionaria', Dolores Ibarruri, achieved international renown for her fiery speeches during the Spanish Civil War. After the war she lived for many years in the Soviet Union and was a leading member of the central committee of the Spanish Communist Party.
2. *Nuestra Bandera*, was the monthly theoretical journal of the Spanish Communist Party. In a number of speeches and unsigned editorials in June 1945 and later, Santiago Carrillo warned against Francoist agents

and other 'enemies' infiltrating the party. Stalinist techniques of denunciation and suspicion were used to enforce submission within the ranks of the party. See J. Semprun, *Communism in Spain*, pp. 83–91.

CHAPTER 18

1. A common ritual of humiliation in vendetta and other killings in the Mediterranean countries was to cut off the testicles and to stick them in the mouth of the victim. A *'chorizo'* is a spiced sausage.
2. In January 1939 there were at least 800 guerrillas in the mountains of Asturias. Those who were unable to get out by boat were eventually reduced to a semi-bandit existence and were hunted down by civil guard operations. The right-wing newspaper *ABC* claimed that between 1943 and 1952, 5548 guerrillas were killed in the whole of Spain, 624 wounded, of whom 256 died of their injuries, while another 19 407 accomplices were arrested. See L. Stein, *Beyond Death and Exile*, p. 224; R. Fraser, *Blood of Spain*, p. 429.

CHAPTER 19

1. Manuel Cortes, the Socialist Mayor of Mijas in Malaga, states that during the post-war repression a few men held the village in their grip because to denounce somebody, 'It needed only three people, one to sign a "denuncia" and two witnesses. They could take it in turns, between them they could accuse one of any "crimes" they wanted ... There were always people in the villages ready to denounce – even those who had served in the Nationalist army might, on their return from the war, be denounced locally and sent to jail for three or four years.' R. Fraser, *In Hiding: The Life of Manuel Cortes* (London, 1972), p. 10.
2. In 1939 some 271 000 political prisoners were held. How many Republicans were summarily executed by official organisations or murdered by 'freelance' gangs of fascists will never be known, but the figure probably exceeded 200 000. See. H. Thomas, *Civil War*, pp. 760–1; P. Preston, *The Triumph of Democracy in Spain* (London, 1986), p. 4; R. Graham, *Spain: Change of a Nation* (London, 1984), pp. 24–5.
3. On the practice of arbitrarily shooting prisoners in small batches over a long period as a form of mental torture see I. Gibson, *Assassination of Lorca*, pp. 100–2.
4. Only official, government-controlled trade unions were legal after the Civil War.
5. The Law of Labour Contracts of 1944, the work of the Falangist Minister of Labour J. A. Giron de Valesco, made it difficult to sack a worker once employed and gave a substantial proportion of workers complete job security. See R. Carr and J. P. Fusi, *Dictatorship to Democracy*, p. 138.
6. The period immediately after the Civil War was a time of extreme hardship and near starvation: in the south the peasants were reported

Notes

to be eating thistles and weeds. R. Carr and J. P. Fusi, *Dictatorship to Democracy*, p. 95.

CHAPTER 21

1. As Raymond Carr points out the most important legacy of the Civil War was the division of Spanish society into two camps, the victors and the vanquished. The *vencedores* would rule and enjoy the fruits of power, the *vencidos* never. In 1968 when it was proposed that Republican ex-combatants should get pensions as did the Nationalists, Franco was outraged, 'You can't combine a glorious army with the scum of the Spanish population.' R. Carr and J. P. Fusi, *Dictatorship to Democracy*, p. 19.
2. During the first hours or days of the Civil War thousands found themselves caught on the 'wrong side', trapped in the Republican or rebel zone with which they had no sympathy. The experience of Paulino Aguirre, a Madrid philosophy student on holiday in July 1936 in an hotel near the River Ebro, was typical. 'Little did I realize the role geography was to play, how the chance of *where* one happened to be was going to define one's position for one I saw people leaving the hotel to join relatives in near-by towns. I didn't know that, in effect, they were crossing from one zone to another – and that it cost some of them their lives.... The zones lacked definite frontiers, front lines; everything was fluid, ambiguous; and yet – who can imagine it? – it was going to be years before the frontiers which were being invisibly created could again be crossed.' R. Fraser, *Blood of Spain*, p. 119.
3. The Franco regime survived on the basis of a mass depoliticisation. In the immediate post-war years famine, unemployment and repression cowed the working class and an atmosphere of fear, indifference and insecurity flourished. After the apathy of privation came, with the prosperity of the 1960s and 70s, the apathy of consumerism, and mediocre television was described as the 'Spanish vice'. The atmosphere was reflected in the words of the popular singer Conchita Piquer:

> I don't want to know
> Don't tell my neighbour
> I prefer to go on dreaming
> To knowing the truth.

See R. Carr and J. P. Fusi, *Dictatorship to Democracy*, pp. 47, 94–5, 102.

Index

Acelino, 70, 75
Aguera, 27, 90–1, 137
Albe Feuille la Garde, 147–8
Albericias airfield, 74
Alberto of Paladin, 27–8, 32
Alfonso XIII, King of Spain, 6–8, 40
Alianza Obrera, 10, 15, 236 Ch.7 n.3
Almirante Cervera, blockade of Asturias, 94, 236 Ch.5 n.1
Alphonso of Paladin, 32–3, 204
Alonso Alonso, José, army captain in Burgos, 55
Alvarez, Paulino, Asturian miners' leader in Septfonds, 134
Álvarez del Vayo, Julio, 166
Anarchists: and collectivisation, 102; attack on churches, 59–60; in Asturias, 5, 9–10, 45, 47; in exile at Riom, 186, 188–9; in Galicia, 68; in Septfonds camp, 132–3; lack of discipline, 66; *see also* Confederación Nacional de Trabajo (CNT)
Aniseto of Valduno, Republican soldier, 62–3
Antonio, leader of disabled soldiers at Vich, 112: director of disabled centre in France, 147–8
Antonio, uncle of Consuelo, 82: imprisoned by Nationalists, 122, 197; Consuelo's post-war visit to, 194–5
Aragon, anarchist collectivisation in, 102
Aran, Valley of, invasion, 23: participation of Riom Communists, 175–6
Aranda, Colonel Mata, ruse to seize Oviedo, 14, 57–8, 220
Argelès concentration camp, 20
army, under Second Spanish Republic: conditions in at Burgos, 53–5; preparation of July coup, 54–5

army, Republican, during Civil War and in France: disarmed by French, 113,238 Ch.9 n.3; Durruti division, 114–15, 238 Ch.9 n.4; February offensive in Asturias, 70–1, 75, 84–5; in Catalonia, 100–2; medical tribunals, 90; military training, 66; regularisation of militias, 66–7; retreat through the Pyrenees, 106–10,112–15, 237 n.3, 238 Ch.9 n.2; weaponry, 67, 234 n.9
Artir of Paladin, killed by Falange, 205
Aspres concentration camp: conditions in camp, 141–4; Consuelo imprisoned, 141; escape from, 146
assault guards: during seige of Oviedo, 58; on Asturian western front, 61; patrol Catalan frontier, 96
Asturian Center, New York, 135–6
Asturias: anarchism, 45, 47; battles on western front, 59–71; Communist Party, 47; economic and social conditions before Civil War, 5–12; fall of and evacuation, 17, 88–95, 236 Ch.4 n.2; outbreak of Civil War, 57–8; post-war Communist underground, 182; post-war repression, 196–8, 205–8; requisitioning by militias, 59, 64–5, 80–3; strong political unity, 101–2; unemployment and strikes, 9, 44–5, 68, 231 n.3
Aulnat airfield, 178
Avance, 11: influence in region of Paladin, 47, 49, 231 Ch.2 n.6; on fall of Asturias, 91; presses destroyed in October insurrection, 232 n.13
Aviles, 46, 66, 90
Azaña, battalion, 69

244

Index

Ballan-Mire, 216–17
Barcelona: and October insurrection, 49; bombing of, 103–4, 237 n.7; David's experience of during Civil War, 99–105 fall to Nationalists, 18, 237 n.1
Barcerès concentration camp, 20
Basque region, fall of, 76
Batallôn de Defensa, 92
Bayard Pass, 146, 161
Belarmina, Spanish exile in Riom, 182, 227
Belsen concentration camp, 167
Benavides, Republican soldier: David's attempt to locate after war, 219; wounded and contracts gangrene, 72–4; work with Quaker relief organisation, 149, 153, 159
Benjamin of Casuco, uncle of David, 65, 193, 204
Biedes, front at, 58–9, 67–9
Bilbao, Nationalist offensive against, 75, 84, 86, 234 n.14
Bordeaux, Asturian refugees arrive by sea, 93–5, 99
Bueno, Javier, editor of *Avance*, 11, 47, 149
Burgos, the army and the July conspiracy, 12–13, 53–7

caciques, power and electoral corruption in Asturias, 6–8, 12, 48, 65, 79–80
Calvo Sotelo, José, assassination of, 56, 232 n.15
Camarcho Duarte, José, David's cousin, civil guard commander, 220
Campradón, 18: anarchists in, 95; Asturian refugees in, 96; hospital of, 96, 106, 237 n.3
Cardes: Consuelo's post-war return, 194–6; repression by Falange in, 196–8; school, 78
Carola of Paladin, 34–5: son killed by Falange, 205
Carreno of Paladin, 33–4
Carrillo, Santiago, 241 Ch.17 n.2, 230 n.18

Casares Quiroga, Santiago, Minister of War, 57
Casas Viejas massacre, 9
Castillo, Lieutenant José, assassination of, 56, 232 n.15
Catalonia, 17–18: Consuelo's experience in (1937–9), 95–8; David's experience in (1937–9), 99–105
Catholic Church, 6, 231 n.2: anarchist threat to church of Trasmonte, 59; religious practice in Valduno, 36–9, 44–5, 230 n.4
Chapuis, Charles, French volunteer in Republican army, 67–9
Chateauneuf-les-Bains, hotel for refugees, 170: David escapes from 170–1; French Resistance threatens director, 173–4
Civil Guard: defence of Oviedo, 58, 220; during the October insurrection, 36, 50–2, 148; investigate David's Civil War record, 201; post-war repression of Asturian guerrillas, 24, 198; repressive functions, 6, 9
Clermont-Ferrand, 23
coalminers of Asturias: Asturian Miners Union (SMA), 10–11; crisis in mining industry, 10, 230 n.3; during the Civil War, 58–9; role in October insurrection, 48–9
Collioure concentration camp, 21, 239 Ch.11 n.5
Comarcal, secretary of Spanish Communist Party from St Eloy, 187
Combronde, 172
Communist Party, Spanish (PCE): in Catalonia, 101–5; in pre-war Asturias, 47; invasion of Aran Valley, 175; organisation of Riom cell, 24–5, 181–3, 186–9; oganisation in Septfonds, 132–3; Stalinism in, 102, 236 n.6, 186–8, 230 n.19
Companys, Lluis, execution, 135
comuña system, 6, 31, 65
concentration camps, 21–2, *see also*

concentration camps – *continued*
  under Argelès, Aspres, Barcerès, Belsen, Collioure, Gurs, Maidenak, Rivesaltes, Septfonds, Vernet
Confederación Española de Derechas Autonomas (CEDA), 9–10, 232 n.7
Confederación Nacional del Trabajo (CNT): in Asturias, 9–10, 47; in Catalonia, 18, 102; *see also* Anarchists
Confédération Générale du Travail (CGT), 126, 185
Contreras, Angelina (sister of Consuelo), 20, 77–8: Consuelo visits her after war, 194–5; lost in Pyrenees, 107, 111; repatriated as 'orphan' to Spain, 124
Contreras, Maria (mother of Consuelo): aid to prisoners in October insurrection, 79; emigrates to Mexico, 77; evacuated from Asturias, 88–9; fear of return to Spain, 120–3, 192, 211; lost in passage of Pyrenees, 107–8; work as nurse in Civil War, 80–6
Cornellana, 62–3
Corsino, Republican soldier, 59–60, 66, 218
Council of Asturias, 17, 236 Ch.4 n.2
Croix du Fer, 141
Czechoslovakia, arms supply to Republicans, 67

de Gaulle, Charles, 25, 176
Diaz, Juan, parish priest of Valduno, 38
disabled soldiers: flight over Pyrenees, 106–10, 237 n.3; in *Garcia Lorca* barracks at Vich, 104–5; League for Disabled in Barcelona, 103; League for Disabled in Montauban, 149; post-war pensions and Republican disabled, 217–21
Durruti, Buenaventura, controversy over his death, 188–9

Durruti division, arrival in France, 114–15, 238 Ch.9 n.4

Ebro, battle of, 17–18, 97
education in Spain: backwardness of school at Paladin, 39–43, 230 n.5; Consuelo's school at Cardes, 78; decline in education under Franco, 208
elections under the Second Republic: April 1931, 8; November 1933, 9, 48; February 1936, 8, 12, 79
El Fondon mine, strike at, 45
'El Hecho' prison, Mieres, 52
El Rapin, battalion, 68
emigration from Asturias to Americas, 4, 6, 32–3, 42, 52–3, 77, 321 Ch.1 n.6
Enriqueta (aunt of Consuelo), 82, 122, 124, 146, 179, 194
Escamplero, front at, 67, 103
España (Nationalist battleship), sinking at Santander, 74, 234 n.12
Esther, Asturian prisoner in Aspres, 143: role in Resistance, 162–3
exile, experience of: Consuelo, 211–12; David's inability to settle in post-war Spain, 217–28

Falange, the: active in Valladolid, 54; destruction of *Avance* press, 47; organisation of pro-government parades, 207–8; post-war repression in Asturias, 1, 15, 196–8, 205–8, 242 Ch.19 nn.1–3; trade unions, 206, 242 n.5
Federation of Land Workers (Federación Nacional de Trabajadores de la Tierra – FNTT), 11–12, 46–7, 231 n.5
Feliciano family of Paladin, 32, 52
Fernandez, Constante, killed by civil guard, 50
Fernandez, Cornelio, socialist leader of Valduno, 48–9: role in Civil War, 57–9; role in October insurrection, 48; tortured by civil guard, 50, 232 n.13

Index

Ferro of Paladin, 31, 204
Fifth Column: activities of fascist doctors in Republican Spain, 14, 71–2, 85–6, 235 n.5; during the retreat from Catalonia, 106, 237 Ch.8 n.1; fear of in Republican army, 233 n.5; operating during fall of Gijón, 91, 236 Ch.4 n.3
Force Française de l'Interieur (FFI), 175
foreign workers brigades (GTEs) in France, 22, 125, 140, 239 Ch.10 n.5: Manzat brigade, 160, 169–73; Mozac brigade, 171–2, 177–8
France: anti-Spanish sentiment and propaganda, 19, 120, 127–8, 228, 237 Ch.9 n.1, 238 Ch. 10 n.2; government response to Spanish refugees, 19; policing of Spanish frontier, 110, 112–15, 238 Ch.9 n.3; post-war hostility towards Spaniards, 180, 191, 211–12, 214; repatriation of Spanish refugees, 122–3, 238 Ch.10 n.3, 239 n.3; role of Spanish exiles in Liberation, 21n 166–7; Spanish soldiers in French army, 139–40, 239 n.7; war with Germany, 20, 139
Franco, General: attitude of Allies towards, 23, 25, 176–7, 241 n.4; death of, 26, 196; impact of his dictatorship on Spanish society, 222–3, 243 n.3; organisation of military revolt, 12–13, 233 n.1; role in repression of October insurrection, 50, 232 n.12
Fraser, Ronald, 2

Galachi, Lieutenant Julian, 51
Galicia: Asturian hostility towards Galicians, 67–8, 234 n.10; Nationalist advance from, 14, 59–64, 233 n.2
Gallego, Angel, Communist exile in Riom, 183
Gap, 161–2
Garcia, José, exile in France, 149, 170–1
Germany: and Resistance in the Puy-de-Dôme, 174; blocks Spanish refugee funds, 135, 147; bombardment of Guernica, 17, 75; occupies Rivesaltes camp, 156; operations in south of France, 162–5; treaty with Soviet Union, 133, 239 n.6; war with France, 20
Gijón: anarchism in, 45, 47; fall to Nationalists, 91–2, 236 Ch.4 n.3; Republican military academy, 66; Simancas barracks captured, 60; the Grandas' post-war life there, 215–17, 221–3
Gil Robles, José Maria, 9, 12
González Peña, Ramón: leader of the miner's union, 11; role in the October insurrection, 48, 232 n.9
Grado, 11, 59–61, 63–5
Granda, Enrique (elder brother of David), 46, 55: post-war imprisonment, 25, 205–6; role in Civil War, 57, 63–4, 193
Granda, Francisco (father of David): David misses his funeral, 224–5; Falangist post-war action against, 207–8; refugee during Civil War, 65–6, 90–1, 203; Republicanism, 44; secretary to the FNTT, 11–12, 46–7; secretary to the River Nalón coal workers co-operative, 30
Granda, Paco (brother of David): post-war imprisonment and blacking, 25, 205–6
Granda (David's uncle): in Cuba, 53; offer of aid to David in Septfonds, 136–7
Great Britain: and Non-Intervention Committee, 16–17, 104; patrol ships off northern Spain, 74, 94
Groupements de travailleurs étrangers (GTEs) see foreign worker brigades
Guernica, bombardment of, 17, 74–5, 139, 234 n.13
guerrilla fighters in post-war Spain, 17, 24, 175–6, 197–8, 205, 242 Ch.18 n.2
Gurs concentration camp, 156–60, 169, 241 n.6, 239 n.3, 239 n.4

Hendaye, 199, 202, 224
Hitler, Adolf, 9, 176–7

Ibanez Frias, Alfredo, 54–5
Ibanez, Jesús, 148–9, 240 n.1
Ibarruri, Dolores (La Passionaria), 187, 241 Ch.17 n.1
immigrant workers in post-war France, 186, 189–90
Infiesto: and the October insurrection, 12, 78–9, 235 n.1; Consuelo's first post-war return, 193–4; fascism in, 235 n.2; hospital, 15, 76, 80–2, 86–8
International Brigades, 18, 100, 158
Italy: bombardment of Barcelona, 18, 103–4, 237 n.7; role in Civil War, 234 n.14, 235 Ch.6 n.1

Jews: detention in Rivesaltes and deportation, 153, 155–6, 240 n.5; detention in Septfonds, 150; hiding in forest of St Eusebe, 164–5; internment by Vichy government, 240 n.4; refugees at Chateauneuf-les-Bains, 170, 241 Ch.15 n.1
Juventudes Libertaria, 147–8

La Espina, 60–1
La Felguera, 5, 47, 91
Largo Caballero, 135
Las Regueras, 45
La Tour de Carol, 113–15
Légion des Volontaires Français (LVF), 173–4
López de Ochoa, General, repression of October insurrection, 50
Lus-la-Croix-Haute, 118–25

Madrid: defence of, 16–17, 102; fall to Nationalists, 120; in October insurrection, 49
Maidanek concentration camp, 156
Manolo ('El Rubio'), killed by Falange, 198
Manzat: foreign worker brigade, 169–73; Resistance movement, 174

Maria Elena, ship used in Asturian evacuation, 91–3
Marseille, Spanish role in Resistance and Liberation of, 22–3, 162–3, 165–7
Maxim Gorky battalion: and Communist recruitment, 103; David joins, 16, 66–7; in February offensive, 70–1, 75
Menagère Aluminium (factory), 178, 185–6, 213–14
Mexico: arms supply to Republicans, 67, 234 n.9; emigration to, 32, 77; Republican exiles in, 24, 128
Mieres, 5, 11, 52
Milan, regiment, 57
militias, role in Asturias during the Civil War, 14–16, 60–7, 80–1, 233 n.3, 233 n.8
Mola Vidal, General Emilio, 13
Mollo, 95–6, 107
Montauban, Spanish exiles in, 148–9
Montseny, Federica, 166
Moroccan soldiers ('Moors'): in Asturias during the Civil War, 68, 75, 82, 203–4; repression of October insurrection, 50, 232 n.12
Mozac, 171–2, 174–5, 177
Mundo Obrero, journal of PCE, 188
Mussolini, Benito, 9, 176

Nalón River and coalmining from, 10, 29–30, 41, 46, 224, 230 n.3
Nationalist forces: advance from Galicia into Asturias, 59–64, 233 n.2; advance on Valencia, 100, 236 Ch.7 n.1; blockade of Asturias, 17, 92, 94, 235 n.15; bombardment of Guernica, 234 n.13 and Barcelona, 18; capture of Gijón, 91–2; July rebellion, 57–8, 233 n.1; post-war repression of Republicans, 1, 19, 25
NATO, 25
Negrín, Juan, Prime Minister, departure from Barcelona, 18, 237 Ch.8 n.1
Novara, Spanish Resistance leader in Puy-de-Dôme, 173

Nuestra Bandera, Spanish Communist journal, 188, 241 Ch.17 n.2
Nueva España, Asturian newspaper, 47

October insurrection, Asturias, 5, 9–11: events in Infiesto, 78–9; events in Paladin region, 12, 48–52; repression of, 36, 50–2, 78–9, 148, 232 n.13; *see also Turquesa* oral history, 1–4, 229 n.4
Ordás, Republican exile: escape from Septfonds, 138–9; role in Resistance, 139
Otero, Manuel, militia leader, 62–3, 233 n.4
Oviedo: capture by Nationalists, 14, 58; pre-war strikes in, 45; seige of, 57–60, 70, 82–4

Pablo, Republican exile: aid to Consuelo in Aspres camp and St Eusebe, 146, 162; capture by Germans and experience of concentration camp, 167–8
Paladin, 4–6, 11–12: capture by Nationalists, 203–4, 233 n.7; Consuelo's first post-war visit, 192–3; David's post-war return, 199–200, 202–10; inter-war politics, 47–8, 231 n.4; return of Granda family, 204–5; social and economic conditions during inter-war period, 27–39, 44–6; village school, 39–43
POUM (Partido Obrero de Unificación Marxista), conflict in Barcelona, 102, 236 n.6
Pétain, Marshal Henri, 20
Pico del Arca, battle at, 70–1
Piñón, militia leader, 61–2
Pola de Lena, 91, 134
Prats-de-Mollo, arrival of Republican refugees, 109–11
Prieto, Indalecio, 58, 103–4, 166, 232 n.9, 237 n.8
Primo de Rivera, Miguel, dictatorship of, 6–8

Puigcerda, 95, 112
Pyrenees: clandestine crossing of Communists from Spain, 182; guerrilla incursion through Aran Valley, 23, 175–6; Jews escape across into Spain, 155; Spanish refugees crossing of, 18–19, 106–15, 237 Ch.8 nn.1–3; Ch.9 n.1

Quakers, relief work among Spanish refugees, 149, 152–3, 159–60

Ramón, Republican exile, activities as Communist guerrilla and arrest, 175–6
Red Cross, aid to Spanish refugees, 121–2, 124, 129, 136, 160
Republic, Spanish Second (1931–9): coming of, 8, 44, 78, 231 n.1; economic and political crisis under, 8–13
Resistance in France: in Puy-de-Dôme, 172–5, 241 Ch.15 n.3; in south of France, 162–3, 167, 241 Ch.14 n.2; role of Spanish exiles in, 22, 139, 240 Ch.13 n.2
Riom: Grandas' post-war life in, 178–91; Spanish Communist cell in, 24–5, 181–3, 186–9
Rivesaltes concentration camp, 152–6, 240 n.5
Royal Oak, the, at Santander, 74
Rueda, Juan: anarchist leader in post-war Riom, 188–9; Spanish Resistance member in Puy-de-Dôme, 173

St Cyprien concentration camp, 20
St Eusebe, Consuelo's escape to, 146, 161–4
St Georges-de-Mons, Resistance group in, 173
St Hypolite, Resistance in, 173–4
Sama de Langreo, mining centre, 5, 45, 58, 82, 89
San Esteban de Pravia, port of, 30, 48, 220
Sangre de Octubre, battalion, 69

Santander: capture by Nationalists, 76, 86, 88–9, 92; David's convalescence in, 73–6, 221; sinking of the *España*, 74, 234 n.12
Sarraut, Albert, French Minister of Interior, 19–20
Secours Populaire Français, aid to Spanish refugees, 158–60
Secours Rouge Français, aid to refugees, 95, 99
Septfonds concentration camp, 20, 115, 126–40, 150–2: clandestine politics, 131–4; disease and malnutrition, 135, 151–2; repatriation propaganda, 128–9
Service de Travail Obligatoire (STO), 145, 163–4, 167, 240 n.2
Socialist Party, Spanish (PSOE), 8–12, 15–16, 46–50, 102–3, 132–3
Soviet Union: German-Soviet treaty, 133, 239 n.6; military aid to Republicans, 17, 102–3; Republican exiles in, 24, 128, 187
Stalingrad, battle of, 23

Teruel, battle of, 182
Todt organisation, 159–60, 241 n.7
Tomás, commander of Maxim Gorky battalion, 67
Toulouse, tribunal for repression of Republican exiles, 150
Trasmonte, church of, threatened by Anarchists, 15, 59
Trubia: armaments and engineering works in, 35, 45, 57; centre of pre-war socialism, 6, 11, 231 n.4; battle for, 70; hospital in, 83–4
Turquesa, the, arms smuggled aboard for October insurrection, 12, 48, 51, 232 n.9

Unión de Hermanos Proletarias (UHP), 101–2

Unión Militar Espanōla, military conspiracy, 12–13, 54–5, 232 n.14
United States of America: army landing in Provence, 23, 165, 241 Ch.14 n.1; post-war recognition of Franco, 25, 176–7

Valduno: civil guard repression of October insurrection, 50–2; religious practice in, 36–9; River Nalón coal co-operative, 30; socialism in, 11; *Turquesa*, arms cache in, 12, 48
Valence, Republican refugees in, 111, 116–18
Valencia, Nationalist offensive, 100
Valle, 5, 26, 77–8, 80, 82
Valle, Juan de, of Paladin, 65, 207
Velasco, the, Republican destroyer, 74
Vernet concentration camp, 170, 239 n.5, 241 Ch.15 n.2
Vich, centre for disabled Republican soldiers, 97, 104–5, 112
Vichy government, 20, 22
Vigile, commander of foreign worker brigade in Manzat, 160, 172–3
Villaviciosa, 89–91, 127–8, 173
Volgues, 33, 39, 42, 205

war committees during Civil War, 14–15, 233 n.6: in Infiesto, 80–1; in Valduno, 64–5
women, role in Civil War, 16, 66, 84, 235 n.4

Yague, General Juan, 18, 50
Ybarnegaray (French deputy), anti-Republican propaganda, 127, 239 n.2

Zapatero of Paladin, 34, 203–4